Visualizing Beauty

Visualizing Beauty

Gender and Ideology in Modern East Asia

Edited by
Aida Yuen Wong

香港大學出版社
HONG KONG UNIVERSITY PRESS

Hong Kong University Press
14/F Hing Wai Centre
7 Tin Wan Praya Road
Aberdeen
Hong Kong
www.hkupress.org

ISBN 978-988-8083-89-3 *(Hardback)*
ISBN 978-988-8083-90-9 *(Paperback)*

British Library Cataloguing-in-Publication Data
A catalogue record for this book is available from the British Library.

10   9   8   7   6   5   4   3   2   1

Printed and bound by Liang Yu Printing Factory Ltd. in Hong Kong, China

Contents

Contributors

Yeon Shim Chung (Ph.D., Institute of Fine Arts, New York University) is Assistant Professor in the Department of Art History & Theory at Hongik University in Seoul, Korea. Her dissertation "Ultra-sauvage, Ultra-moderne: Paul Gauguin's Ceramics and Sculpture" studies the intersections between colonialism, feminism, nationalism, and design theory. Chung's research interests encompass both modern and contemporary Western and East Asian art. She worked as a researcher at the Guggenheim Museum for the retrospective exhibition "The World of Nam June Paik" in 1999, and as coordinator and curator for "Special Effects: Media Arts" in Korea in 2002. In 2005, Chung was one of the international exhibition commissioners for "Digital Paradise, Media Art Exhibition: FAST," while concurrently curating "The Moving Drawing of Jheon Soocheon: The Line that Crosses America." Her recent book project deals with installation and media art.

Lisa Claypool (Ph.D., Stanford University) is Associate Professor of Art History and the Mactaggart Art Collection Curator at the University of Alberta. She publishes widely on exhibition culture, Shanghai's visual culture, and has published essays and interviews about contemporary art. Her most recent publications include "Ways of Seeing the Nation: Chinese Painting in the *National Essence Journal* (1905–1911) and Exhibition Culture," "Sites of Visual Modernity: Perceptions of Japanese Exhibitions in Late Qing China," and she is completing a monograph on art practice as part of the nineteenth-century urban imagination entitled "Figuring the Social Body: Painting Manuals in Late Imperial China." She is now working on three projects: a book about the mediation of science through visual arts in Republican-era Shanghai; an essay on the transformation of calligraphic script forms into "State avatars" at the 2010 Shanghai World Expo; and a collaborative curatorial project titled "China's Imperial Modern," focusing on "modern" technologies of vision produced and circulated during the last dynasty.

Francesca Dal Lago (Ph.D., Institute of Fine Arts) is an independent scholar. Her research interests focus on the history of twentieth-century Chinese visual culture, representations of gender, and the connection of art, politics, and museum practices. Her current work deals with the transfer of art technical knowledge from the French academic system to China during the first part of the twentieth century. She has published numerous articles and reviews on contemporary Chinese art. Her current projects include an edited volume, *China on Display: Past and Present Practices of Selecting, Displaying and Viewing Chinese Visual and Material Culture* and a manuscript exploring the transfer of artistic education between China and Europe and the experience of Chinese artists in France.

Karen M. Fraser (Ph.D., Stanford University) is Assistant Professor in the Department of Art and Art History at Santa Clara University. Her research focuses on modern Japanese photography, with particular interests in the role of photography in creating cultural identity, intersections between photography and other visual media, and the uses of photography as a conduit for international exchange ca. 1860–1960. Her recent publications include the thematic survey *Photography and Japan* (London: Reaktion Books, 2011), and she is currently working on the history of nineteenth-century commercial photography in Japan.

Hung-yok Ip (Ph.D., University of California, Davis) is Associate Professor of History at Oregon State University. She is the author of *Intellectuals in Revolutionary China 1921–1949: Leaders, Heroes and Sophisticates* (Routledge, 2009). In addition, she co-edited/edited two volumes, respectively entitled *Beyond the May Fourth Paradigm: In Search of Chinese Modernity* (Rowman and Littlefield, 2008), and *Buddhist Activism and Chinese Modernity* (Journal of Global Buddhism, 2009). She is now finishing a book manuscript on Mozi.

Kaoru Kojima (M.A., Tokyo University, Ph.D., Chelsea College of Art & Design) is Professor in the Department of Aesthetics and Art History at Jissen Women's University. Her research focuses on modern Japanese painting. She is particularly interested in the issues of gender, national identities, and *bijinga* (paintings of beautiful women) 1880s–1945. Her works include *Fujishima Takeji* (Shinchōsha, 1998), "Kimono no josei-zō ni mire kindai nihon no aidenttiti keisei" (Images of Women in Modern Kimono and Their Representation of Japanese Identity) in *Bijutsu to jendā: Kosa sure manazashi* (Art and Gender 2: Intersecting Visions) (Brücke, 2005), and "The Changing Representation of Women in Modern Japanese Paintings" in *Refracted Modernity: Visual Culture and Identity in Colonial Taiwan* (University of Hawai'i Press, 2007).

Yisoon Kim (M.A., Hongik University and the State University of New York at Buffalo, Ph.D., Hongik University) is Associate Professor of Art History at Hongik University. She is the author of *Hanguk geunhyeondae misul* (Modern and Contemporary Art in Korea) (Chohyong Gyoyuk, 2007), *Hyeondae jogak ui saeroun jipyeong* (The New Horizon of Contemporary Sculpture) (Hae-an, 2005), and a number of articles on Korean sculptures in journals such as *Hanguk geundae misul yeongu* (Research on Modern Korean Art), *Misulsa yeongu* (Journal of Art History), *Jeongsin munhwa yeongu* (Korean Studies Quarterly), and *Misulsahak yeongu* (Journal of Art History).

Sarah Teasley (Ph.D., University of Tokyo) is Tutor in History of Design and Critical and Historical Studies at the Royal College of Art, London. Her research focuses on design and architecture in modern Japan, with particular attention to the agency of media technologies in shaping design concepts and practice. Her publications include *Global Design History* (Routledge, 2011) and *20th Century Design History* (Petit Grand Publishing, 2005) as well as articles in *The Journal of Design History, Design Issues*, and *Japanstudien*. Current projects address technical drawing education in Meiji Japan, furniture design during the American Occupation, and the impact of geopolitics on the wooden furniture industry in Tohoku, 1890–1960.

Aida Yuen Wong (Ph.D., Columbia University) is Associate Professor in the Department of Fine Arts and Chair of East Asian Studies at Brandeis University. Her primary scholarship focuses on twentieth-century Asia, especially China and Japan, their interconnections and shared historical conditions. Her book, *Parting the Mists: Discovering Japan and the Rise of National-Style Painting in Modern China*, was published in 2006 by the University of Hawai'i Press. She also contributed essays to several volumes, such as *Writing Modern Chinese Art: Historiographical Explorations* (Seattle: Seattle Art Museum, 2009), *Shadows of the Past: Okakura Tenshin and Pan-Asianism* (Kent: Global Oriental, 2007), *Crossing the Yellow Sea: Sino-Japanese Cultural Contacts, 1600–1950* (Connecticut: EastBridge, 2007), and *Japanese Cultural Nationalism: At Home and in the Asia Pacific* (Kent: Global Oriental, 2004). Other recent projects include Kishida Ryūsei and the Mingei Movement, Japanese-style painting in Taiwan, modern Sino-Japanese calligraphy history, and the aesthetic theory of Kang Youwei.

Note on Language

Chinese, Japanese, and Korean personal names in general are rendered surnames first. Exceptions are citations from sources in which given names come before surnames.

The Romanization systems used here are Pinyin for Chinese, the Revised Hepburn System for Japanese, and the Revised Romanization System for Korean approved by the South Korean government in 2000 as the official replacement for the McCune-Reischauer System.

Acknowledgements

This volume was made possible in part by a Brandeis University subvention and the Theodore and Jane Norman Fund for Faculty Research and Creative Projects. The editor would like to thank Dean Adam Jaffe and Senior Associate Dean Elaine Wong for their support. Special thanks go to Pamela Allara for her careful reading of the first draft. Gannit Ankori, Jennifer Stern, and Alfred Wong provided valuable comments on the introduction. Suggestions from two anonymous reviewers helped sharpen the volume's focus considerably. The excellent technical assistance from Colleen O'Shea and John Axon at the Visual Resources Center at Brandeis University made the preparation of the manuscript a smooth task. It was a pleasure working with Michael Duckworth, Clara Ho, Jessica Wang, and their team at Hong Kong University Press who oversaw the production of the book with professionalism. Most of all, the editor would like to thank all the contributing authors for their insightful and ground-breaking scholarship.

Introduction

Aida Yuen Wong

In early twentieth-century East Asia, two female types dominated the visual media: the Modern Woman and the Traditional Woman. The Modern Woman was depicted in the latest fashions and enjoying a lifestyle of the urban West; the Traditional Woman, in contrast, was the embodiment of the Confucian "good wife and wise mother." The way in which these two constructs reinforced nationalism, colonialism, and consumerism is the subject of this collection of essays. By examining photography, painting, painting manuals, newspaper cartoons, exhibitions, women's magazines, and calendar posters, these eight essays present a kaleidoscope of imaginations about women in China, Japan, and colonial Korea roughly between 1900 and the 1940s. The authors elucidate the conditions that shaped local perspectives on womanhood, beauty, and feminine prerogative; taken together, they bring into focus both the shared ideological orientations and the conflicts across East Asia.

Gender discourses in East Asia have historically coalesced around Confucian ethics, which teaches that the family is the microcosm of "all under Heaven." Centuries of didactic texts and images preached female subordination to husbands and parents-in-law, in addition to thriftiness and chastity. These values were easily transformed into the modern ideologies of nationalism, colonialism, and socialism, with an emphasis on sacrifice to the collective good. Symptomatic of this phenomenon were the recurrent appropriations of the Confucian ethical paradigm to glorify "womanly" attainments. Even the Modern Woman who rejected domesticity and patriarchal subordination had to be understood under the shadow of Confucian influences.

The Modern Woman stood for free will and personal liberty. She was proud of her sexual and professional autonomy and defied age-old conventions of female propriety. Besides donning Western high heels and cutting her hair, the Modern Woman publicly asserted her artistic ability, intelligence, and political views. Her individualism challenged social stability but also countered what many local reformers accepted as internal weaknesses of the East. To reconcile these two aspects, East Asian governments and intellectuals drew up protocols that nurtured and celebrated female achievements (through educational, professional, and creative opportunities) but

in such a way that reaffirmed the primacy of the State and the national ideologies that reinforced patriarchy. Therefore, although the Modern Woman
no doubt became a popular icon in the twentieth century, the trope of the
"good wife, wise mother" frequently resisted it so as to emphasize a woman's
special ability to strengthen the moral fabric of her country.

The intimate relationship between gender and ideology can be gleaned
from an examination of official actions and policies. In Japan, the Meiji
government provided a basic education to ninety percent of Japanese
boys and girls,[1] but besides fulfilling the State's vision of a civilized society
that could stand on a par with the most advanced Western nations, the
system wanted to engineer gender norms. To prepare girls to be effective
housewives under the emperor and to preserve a male-centered bureauc-
racy, girls' education stressed art, feminine etiquette, and home economics
rather than math and science.[2]

Gender control pervaded Chinese politics. Yuan Shikai, the first president of the Chinese Republic, who briefly made himself emperor (in office,
1912–16), endorsed a chastity cult that exalted Confucian paragons of
female virtue such as the *zhennü,* a woman who remains a virgin for life
even after the death of her fiancé. Some historians interpret Yuan government's blatant suppression of modern womanhood as a symbolic reasser-
tion of Han culture after the removal of the "barbaric" Manchus in 1911.[3]
The Chinese Communist Party (CCP) in the 1920s and 1930s, despite its
professed support of gender equality, was reluctant to make women's rights
a dominant issue in the villages, for fear of antagonizing male peasants.[4]

In Japan-occupied Korea (1910–45), women's emancipation also did
not find much success, as Korean men "obsessively disciplined and regulated women's bodies as metaphors for their uncontaminated, uninterrupted
homonational (or homosocial) identity,"[5] perhaps a hypermasculinist reaction to national emasculation. Added to this condition was the Socialist
vitriol against colonial, capitalist exploitation in which the Westernized
(bourgeois) Modern Woman was conveniently complicit. During Japan's
wars with China and the Allies from 1931 to 1945, the colonialists exhorted
Korean women to procreate and be good mothers, so their children would
grow up to be eugenically fit imperial subjects.[6] A reflection of this policy
was the proliferation of paintings and sculptures depicting virtuous wives
and breast-feeding mothers.

Of course, most rear-guard models of womanhood in East Asia created
a certain tension with women's emancipation, which originated in the West
and, especially in the United States, where the fight for female suffrage
reached its peak in the 1910s. Even then, Western proponents of the "New
Woman" had to tread carefully. To make a New Woman look *normal*—
instead of appearing strident, mannish, and selfish—publications like the
Ladies' Home Journal emphasized beauty and domestic talents.[7] One might
say that America's passage of women's suffrage in 1920 owed much to these
moderate depictions.

The culture of women's magazines then spread to East Asia. In China and Japan, the *found* iconography of the home-loving Modern Woman might also have had normalizing effects, although women's suffrage in East Asia would be slower to bear fruit. It was not until 1936 that the Chinese Nationalist Party (GMD) generally granted women the right to vote in regions under its control, but only because the party was "not going to let the CCP have complete control of the 'social issues' agenda. Rather than a sign of sweeping cultural reform, allowing women's suffrage activists into the political class presented no particular threat to the GMD's continued hold on power because these active women were primarily elite or middle-class urbanites whose outlook clearly mirrored that of the men in the political class."[8]

In Japan, where they were unable to overturn the government's legal prohibitions on female membership in political parties, suffragists redirected their attention to issues such as wage equality, better working conditions, efficiency in housekeeping, and the need for government support for stay-at-home mothers.[9] In Japan-controlled Korea, it was even more futile to demand female suffrage, as Korean men themselves had limited election rights on the local level and none on the State level. Without a suffrage movement, Korean women's groups—in a spirit similar to that of their Japanese counterparts—devoted their energy to expanding educational opportunities, protesting labor abuse and sexual harassment, and reforming dress codes—issues that affected their daily lives.[10] Both Japanese and Korean women had to wait until after World War II to win the right to vote.

Although the women's rights movements in East Asia did not lead to immediate success, they captured the mood of the interwar period (1910s–30s), when a large segment of the region was seeing change and clamoring for more. The year 1919 was a landmark: both China's May Fourth Movement and Korea's March First Independence Movement occurred. The former event, which began as a student-led protest against the transfer of Chinese territories to Japan at the Paris Peace Conference, evolved into an intellectual revolution. The latter was a mass demonstration that compelled colonialists in Korea to abandon their brutally repressive governing style for, at least on the surface, a more "cultural" alternative (*bunka seiji*, 1919–31). During this period, mechanisms were put in place to reward the talents and raise the social status of Korean (presumably male) subjects. As one scholar puts it, the "Cultural Rule" was a clever tactic "to reintegrate [the Korean] souls with the spirit of the Japanese nation,"[11] or to use a Japanese expression, *shinpuku* ("submission out of loyalty").

China's May Fourth Movement overlapped with the New Culture Movement (mid-1910s–20s) and the New Literature Movement that promoted foreign-influenced theories, subjects, and techniques in modern Chinese creative work. In 1918, Hu Shi, a forerunner of New Literature, paid tribute in a special issue of the influential magazine *Xin Qingnian* (New Youth) to the Norwegian playwright Henrik Ibsen. Thereafter, "Ibsenism" and especially Ibsen's feminist play *A Doll's House* became icons among

Chinese liberals. The central character, Nora, who leaves her husband and her "doll" life in order to find herself as "a human being," resonated with an entire generation of Chinese men and women who desired intellectual and social emancipation from feudal ways.[12] The same play had caused a sensation in Japan in 1911, under the direction of the theater critic and littérateur Tsubouchi Shōyō, an Ibsen admirer. His cast included female actors, breaking a centuries-old ban that the Tokugawa shogunate had imposed to stem moral corruption in the theater.[13] Ibsen and Nora went hand in hand with new culture, new morality, and new opportunities. Nora became a model for many East Asian writers and artists.

One of the greatest watersheds in East Asia during the second decade of the twentieth century was the death of Emperor Meiji (r. 1868–1912). He had been the first emperor of Japan's constitutional monarchy, and his portrait used to hang in every school. During his reign, "elite politicians from the two powerful fiefs of Nagato and Satsuma…pushed Japan toward industrialization and Westernization for fear of being colonized by the West. Their leadership was strongly supported by the Neo-Confucian ethic which promoted compassion by the ruling classes and obedience by the subjects."[14] However, since Japan's stunning but costly military victory over Russia in 1905, the masses had grown fatigued of the sacrifices the state demanded of them in the form of higher taxes and other hardships.[15] Popular discontent erupted into strikes, calls for reform, and riots that lasted through the 1920s.[16] Although Confucian ethics would remain inviolable in the imperial ideology, the people came to see its injunctions as no longer adequate to encompass the changing social morality. Important demographic shifts were taking place both in the cities and in the countryside. Thousands of farmers and their families were leaving the fields to work in hospitals, factories, and department stores, which hired both men and women. As more women earned income outside the home, even living away from their husbands or not marrying,[17] the old Confucian tenet that "women should obey their husbands" lost some of its practical meaning.

A blanket term frequently invoked to describe Japan's experience between 1910 and 1930 is "Taishō Democracy" (coinciding roughly with the reign of Emperor Taishō, 1912–26), when the state "lost its monopoly over gender [and other social] constructions."[18] People were speaking out on many issues from many positions. The period featured such distinguished women as Yosano Akiko, whose literary career spanned four decades, from 1901 to 1939. She wrote tens of thousands of poems, published and lectured regularly, and provided for a large family (eleven children and a literary husband whom she married for love). In her writings, she discussed such themes as the importance of female financial independence, "mutual submission" between husband and wife, the nobility of childbirth, and the honest expression of women's perspectives over masculinist fantasies.[19] Yosano held that "any human being should be allowed to take on as many roles as she or he can manage,"[20] a point of view that some of her female contemporaries criticized as too grandiose. In her essay, "My Views on

Chastity," she rejected enforced chastity at the expense of a woman's physical and emotional freedom. Yosano lamented having been habitually kept indoors by her overly strict parents while she was growing up, so that no man could "defile her chastity."[21] In 1918, a Chinese translation of this essay was published in *Xin Qingnian* by the Japan-educated "new literature" proponent Zhou Zuoren (1885–1967), who needed a corroborating voice in his own denunciation of the Early Republican government's chastity cult.[22]

Yet, the majority of male intellectuals in the three principal East Asian entities argued for women's rights in academic terms only; in their own households, patriarchal domination prevailed. For example, the giant of Chinese left-wing liberalism, Lu Xun (1881–1936) (also Zhou Zuoren's brother), insisted that his "modern" lover Xu Guangping, who had literary aspirations, put his domestic (and secretarial) needs over her desire to develop a writing career.[23] Analyzing the "patriarchal recidivism" of Lu Xun's kind, Wang Zhen writes:

> [The modern male] himself dreamed of being an independent person with individual freedom. Moreover his fundamental crisis was generated by a painful realization of his peripheral and subaltern position in China's semicolonialization by the West. The comforting, centuries-old sense of superiority enjoyed by Chinese male literati was forcefully undermined by the powerful, "superior" West. Taking a leading role in identifying an "oppressed" and "inferior" social group—women—the modern intellectual reaffirmed his own superiority ... The professed purposes included overthrowing of feudalism, advancing the nation toward modernity, overcoming imperialism, and later, saving the nation ... The altruistic nature of Chinese women's emancipation eventually made some women feel more used than liberated [....][24]

In other words, the incomplete translation of the rhetoric of women's rights into real-life practice betrayed more than a personal failure of Early Republican intellectuals. The very discursive logic of gender equality in East Asia was frequently muddled by sets of competing dialectic: East and West, self-fulfillment and the greater good, national preservation and modernity. Perceptions of womanhood were the joint products of politics, education, literature, and visual culture circulated and transmitted through translation, the commodity market, and the mass media. Although it is not the purpose of this volume to account for all their means and manifestations, visual uses of gendered ideology will be tied to a network of other cultural and political apparatuses.

Since the works of Marsha Weidner, Patricia Fister, and Fumiko Yamamoto two decades ago,[25] surprisingly few scholars have published volumes on East Asian women in the visual field (with the exception of film).[26] Two notable contributions are *Gender and Power in the Japanese Visual Field* (2003) and *Performing "Nation": Gender Politics in Literature, Theater, and the Visual Arts of Japan and China, 1880–1940* (2008).[27] The former covers Japanese topics from the premodern to the contemporary period, including an essay on Korea. The latter focuses on China and Japan from an interdisciplinary perspective. Like these recent works, the present volume is a response to the burgeoning interest in gender research that goes beyond the White, Euroamerican zone, and in addition tries to understand East Asian phenomena cross-culturally.

Visualizing Beauty builds on previous studies by discussing China, Japan, and colonial Korea more inclusively. It also concentrates on visual artifacts over a confined period of several decades, when the motif of the Modern Woman was widely circulated. Despite the Modern Woman's evocation of feminist freedom, this volume draws attention to the concurrent assertions of Confucian patriarchy in the region. This "conservative" strand of cultural production is relatively overlooked in discussions of women in the twentieth century, due to epistemological assumptions that the "modern age" must be about radical change. This volume demonstrates that the Modern Woman and the Traditional Woman were equally present in modern East Asia. Understanding how they were represented, diffused, and consumed brings out some of the most powerful ideological forces that shaped the region's politics and societies.

Chapters in the Book

Karen Fraser's essay analyzes the first open-admission beauty contest in Japan. In 1907, young women from across the country submitted their photographs to compete for the title of "the most beautiful woman in Japan." The event was organized by the *Jiji shimpō* newspaper in response to a call by the *Chicago Tribune* to look for attractive women with international appeal. *Jiji shimpō* specifically requested that the contestants be "ordinary" young women, that is, women from proper middle-class families. Public display of feminine beauty had been limited to the circle of geisha and entertainers, and photographic reproduction in newspapers had just been made possible by the North American invention of the half-tone process, and later, photogravure. With the aid of new technologies the contest, which was a startling, public subversion of norms of feminine behavior, acquired an aura of modernity that made it more acceptable than it otherwise would have been. Fraser tells us that photographs of the emperor and deceased soldiers were also being disseminated in newspapers to foster national pride at that time. Hence, this beauty contest, which placed Japanese women (whose photographs were often "submitted without the sitter[s'] consent or even [their] awareness") in competition with other women around the world, represents one of the earliest extensions of the propaganda machine to middle-class females. Occurring on the heels of Japan's military victory over Russia in 1905, the event could not have been more timely. Of course, we might be reminded of the ideological precursor of Japan's participation in the world's expositions since the 1870s, when indigenous arts and crafts were deployed to bolster national pride and international prestige.

Gendered discourses depended vitally on print culture for their dissemination. It helped to circulate and contest new concepts of womanhood in a commercial context, while also raising questions about the ethical implications. Lisa Claypool tackles some Chinese painting manuals that distilled body parts (such as eyes, noses, and hands) from old master paintings in traditional styles. She positions this visual corpus, which served as a guide for both professional and amateur painters, in the polysemous culture of Shanghai in the late Imperial and early Republican era. While it is tempting to stop at the conservative typology that these painting manuals extol—a dreamscape of beautiful women, all of whom are vaguely alike—Claypool adroitly reads the images of "gentlewomen" in these painting manuals as a backlash against the iconographic overkill of the Modern Woman: "For the editor Ye Jiuru, a key part of his project was importing *shinü* paintings into the domain of a particular language and keeping them there, divorced from a different language calling for female equality of the May Fourth Movement (1919) and earlier. The genre, defined internally between the manual covers, aimed to 'speak' of a one-dimensional femininity that was deliberately conceived to be out of touch with contemporary progressive discourse on women's roles and lives, and was made distinct from modern representations of 'new bodies.'" Even though the painting manuals promote a kind of homogeneity in feminine portrayal and are starkly traditional in style, the timing of its publication as well as its meshing of certain female types (good wives and virtuous women) with nationalist ethos put the work squarely in the gendered ideological debates of the time.

The painting manuals analyzed by Claypool provide a useful counterpoint to Francesca dal Lago's essay "How 'Modern' was the Modern Woman? Crossed Legs and Modernity in 1930s Shanghai Calendar Posters, Pictorial Magazines, and Cartoons." The essay offers insights into the quintessential Modern Girl with reference to a specific body language. The eroticized "crossed-legged" posture was widely used in advertisements and posters produced by manufacturers of modern novelties such as cigarettes and light bulbs. "Conceived as an amalgam of local and foreign expressions, which made it one of the most original products in twentieth-century Chinese visual culture," the calendar posters "developed a distinct representational method to achieve heightened realism in color and anatomical definition." Dal Lago demonstrates that the sexualized female body as a recurrent trope in Shanghai commercialism was entwined with the visual representations of city life as well as with the literary and filmic conceptions of the urban spectacle. She goes on to trace leg-crossing to other erotic bodily signifiers in older Chinese imagery, underscoring a shift to a standard Western body type for beautiful women as part of semicolonial Shanghai's embrace of free-market capitalism.

Dress codes and body language are potent expressions of gender politics. However, they are not always stable signifiers, as Hung-yok Ip demonstrates. She explores the visual celebration of feminine beauty and fashion in an unlikely context: China's Communist Revolution. Scholars have generally assumed that Communist female iconography from the pre-Cultural Revolution era was already dominated by austerity, androgyny, or both. However, an interest in female beauty was fully present during the revolutionary process. Women revolutionaries represented another kind of Modern Woman who used beauty politically, to win converts by demonstrating cosmopolitanism and refinement, "temporarily act[ing] out alternative social roles" to that of the militant proletariat. Interaction among Communists themselves also seemed to reinforce the perception that female beauty was rewarding. Ip's essay conveys the variety of aesthetic practices that women activists adopted in service of the Communist cause.

Activism took on a more personal form in the life of the painter-writer Na Hye-seok (1896–1948). A "Korean Nora" who refused to be constrained by the discourse of patriarchal femininity, Na pursued free love, got divorced, and vehemently defended her self-reliant lifestyle. Eschewing simple biographical interpretations, however, Yeon Shim Chung meticulously presents Na as a case study of the Modern Girl in colonial Korea. The quintessential Modern Girls are "shopping girls [who] challenged traditional gender roles and centuries of Confucian morality by accumulating products that enhanced female beauty and sexuality." The homonationalists would cast these material girls as byproducts of unbridled capitalism and insensitive to the plight of their village sisters. As a woman allied with the urban, bourgeois camp, Na came in for her share of social censure. Yet she unstintingly pursued modern womanhood through her art and became the first significant female painter in colonial Korea. Surprisingly little has been written about this important artist. This essay is a rare analysis of Na's works that takes into consideration the larger contexts of gender and colonial politics.

Elaborating on the patriarchal gender discourse in colonial Korea, Yisoon Kim presents a group of artworks produced for the Joseon Art Exhibitions (1922–45) by male Korean artists. Launched during the period of Cultural Rule, these were government-sponsored, annual juried events (modeled after Japan's official Bunten and Teiten) at which Koreans competed with resident Japanese for de facto recognition as leaders of the colonial art world.[28] The paintings and sculptures Kim focuses on celebrated virtuous women, nursing mothers, and devoted housewives—opposites of what Na Hye-seok stood for. These images were not merely updated versions of exemplary women from the Confucian tradition. Notably, the recurrent portrayals of the chaste but tortured heroine Chunhyang perpetuated a gendered politics in which both the Japanese colonizers and Korean nationalists called for women to sacrifice their own interests and desires for the betterment of society. So represented, women existed only as a political idea inscribed in the patriarchal symbolic order. As Julia Kristeva tells us, whereas production of a child secures for the woman a place in the patriarchal order, childbirth indicates her bodily difference, her distinction from the male—a state that Kristeva calls "m/other."[29] Those Korean males who exhibited maternal imagery seemed comfortable with their hegemonic gender position and wittingly or otherwise acted as mouthpieces for Japan's imperialist ideology.

By comparison, the Korean females featured in the works by Japanese painters of the same period appear much less narrowly defined although equally stereotyped. Kaoru Kojima considers the works by Fujishima Takeji (1867–1943), Tsuchida Bakusen (1887–1936), and Hayami Gyoshū (1894–1935). The three painters' attraction to the Western figural tradition reflected their cosmopolitan education and travel experiences: "'*Gisaeng* (Korean geisha) Tourism' was a main entertainment for Japanese travelers, and postcards with photographs of *gisaeng* were widely circulated… [The *gisaeng* in one Bakusen painting] seemed to be largely an amalgamation of popular imagery and stylization." At the same time, these peculiar Japanese depictions created a fantasized femininity with latent assertions of Japanese nationalism and colonial superiority over the Koreans. These works naturally invite comparisons with European Orientalist representations of African and Middle Eastern women popular during the nineteenth century.[30] In the 1920s and 1930s, paintings that took the colonized female bodies as their theme could be found in both traditional-style brush paintings and Western-style oil paintings in Japan. Doubling as *fūzokuga* (genre pictures), these images epitomized the urban Japanese male gaze in the age of rapid industrialization.[31]

In the final essay, Sarah Teasley discusses a more specifically disciplinary manifestation of gender divisions. She probes the opposition between architecture and interior decorating in Japan, the former conceived as a male practice, the latter female. Unlike architectural texts that taught men to design structure and rational form, interior decoration guides for women stressed the creation of beautiful domestic environments as part of bourgeois women's responsibilities. Teasley explains these female responsibilities as outcomes of Japan's holistic molding of its national subjects: "the refined sensibility produced by aesthetic education would make the creation of beautiful interiors almost automatic, the application of the general principles of beauty of heart and form that the user—the housewife—had learned through moral education, physical education, academic study, and practice." To support these women's mission, new art and interior decoration sections of department stores supplied household furnishings appropriate for a variety of seasons, room functions, and social ranks. Investigations of these materials simultaneously raise the important issue of class in determining attitudes towards the relationship of beauty to the ideal housewife.

The encoding of gender was a highly elaborate and varied enterprise. The positions staked out in this book remind us of how integral women's bodies, visual attributes, and lifestyles were to the modern imagination in all three cultures studied here. Although the influential works of Said and others have debunked notions of sameness among the non-West,[32] before discarding all categorical thinking, we might ask if there were *specific* contexts and *certain* circumstances in which an intentionally encompassing view of a region could in fact be useful. This volume makes the case that, in the early decades of the twentieth century, China, Japan, and Korea possessed a proximate set of *mentalités* with respect to their gendered ideologies. Instead of a mere coincidence, the phenomenon can be vividly illustrated as an extension of specific "East Asian" biases as well as an expression of a common ambivalence towards modernization and Westernization during one of the most creative, materially diverse, and sociopolitically intricate periods in the region's history.

Beauty Battle
Politics and Portraiture in Late Meiji Japan*

Karen M. Fraser

In the fall of 1907, the newspaper *Jiji shimpō* (Current Events or The Times) sponsored Japan's first open-call beauty contest. Selection was of the most "beautiful woman" (*bijin*) in the country, and judging was based on photographic portraits, which the newspaper printed to boost its circulation. While ranking women had long been a customary practice in the pleasure quarters, this contest required that the entrants be "ordinary" females from good families, stipulating that geisha and actresses need not apply. This was a foreign idea, a response to the *Chicago Daily Tribune*'s call for newspapers around the world to recruit beauties for an international competition. Occurring shortly after Japan's military victory over Russia in 1905, the *Jiji shimpō* contest became more than a frivolous commercial event. This gentrified beauty competition bespoke a shifting regime of aesthetics in Japan, deploying female beauty as a symbol of Japan's new confidence on the world stage.

Genesis and Development of Meiji Beauty Contests

The beauty contest was a direct response to a telegram from the *Chicago Daily Tribune* in early autumn 1907, inviting Japan, especially the *Jiji shimpō* (a leading daily), to participate in what would culminate in an international competition to find the "most beautiful woman in the world." As the telegram revealed, an American girl, Miss Marguerite Frey, from Denver, Colorado, had already been named the winner of a nationwide contest in the United States on July 7, 1907. Newspaper-sponsored beauty contests had become commonplace in America by the end of the nineteenth century.[1] The *Tribune* contest and others like it judged the entrants on the basis of photographs, often printing pictures of the winners. Publishing photographs of young beauties garnered a bit of fame for the top contestants and

* Research for this article was conducted while I was a Robert and Lisa Sainsbury Fellow based at the School of Oriental and Asian Studies, University of London. I would like to thank the Sainsbury Institute for the Study of Japanese Arts and Cultures for their generous support. Special thanks to John Carpenter, Naoko Gunji, and Akira Hirano, all of whom provided essential assistance. In addition, I am especially grateful to Aida Yuen Wong for her invaluable suggestions.

increased circulation for the newspaper. Such contests often involved an element of local or regional competition as well. The *Tribune* contest was started by a bet in December 1906 between two men about whether women from the Chicago area were as beautiful as those from New York.[2] The bet soon turned national, with other areas of the United States wanting to join in, resulting in more than 100,000 entries.[3] National pride quickly superseded regional pride, with the *Tribune* claiming that Frey was "the most beautiful woman in America, and therefore in the world."[4]

While similar beauty contests for the general public had not yet developed within Japan, there was a precedent of evaluating attractive young women. The Japanese were no strangers to the concept of ranking beauties: Printed manuals rating popular courtesans had been published since the Edo period (1603–1868), for instance. However, such rankings were limited to women who were part of the floating demimonde. The 1907 event explicitly banned professional beauties from entering. The older rankings had other key differences from the *Jiji shimpō* contest. They were not based on printed or painted images but on other aspects such as the women's skills and reputations and lacked formal organization and sponsorship. They were also not determined by a committee, as the 1907 contest would be.

In the second half of the Meiji period, the concept of official beauty competitions started to take root, intricately connected to the development of the news media and the spread of photography. Inoue Shōichi has traced the history of early beauty competitions, dating them to the 1880s. In 1883, the *Tokyo nichi nichi shimbun* (Tokyo Daily News) ran an article on March 29 promoting a *bijin kyōshinkai* (competitive beauty competition). It indicated that there was to be a competition held the following year of photographs of beauties that would be put on display in "an exhibition." The intention was to rank them via a voting process. Inoue notes that, as the first government-sponsored national art exhibit, the *Naikoku kaiga kyōshinkai* (Domestic Painting Competitive Exhibition), was held in 1882, the 1883 exhibition was probably a reference to this.[5] Inoue was unable to recover further documents regarding the beauty contest, so whether it in fact took place cannot be ascertained. If it did, the occasion would very likely be the first public beauty contest-cum-exhibition.

Another female beauty competition based on a display of photographs was held at the *Ryounkaku*, or Asakusa Twelve Stories building, in Tokyo in 1891. Widely celebrated as Japan's first skyscraper, the *Ryounkaku* had been completed the previous year. It soared to a height of sixty-seven meters (220 feet) and featured Japan's first elevator. For the exhibit, Ogawa Kazumasa, one of Tokyo's best-known photographers, took pictures of 100 beauties, all professional geisha. Visitors to the *Ryounkaku* were invited to climb the tower in order to view the images on display. They would then vote for their favorite, the woman who received the most votes being named the winner. But the contest was essentially a savvy marketing ploy. The much-vaunted elevator, the main attraction of the building, had to be removed because of safety issues. The beauty contest opened shortly afterwards as a means of attracting spectators to the building and enticing them to ascend to the top.[6]

A decade later, the first known contest involving photographs published in the news media took place. In May 1901, the *Hinode shimbun* (Rising Sun News) advertised a contest for the "Five Beauties of Tokyo-Yokohama." This contest listed five categories of professional women: geisha, apprentice geisha, prostitutes, waitresses (that is, women in the serving industry, such as teahouse waitresses), and female *gidayū* players (a form of chanted narration accompanied by the shamisen). Voting was conducted by submitting a special form printed in the paper. Readers had to cut out the form, write in their choices for each category, and send it in. This contest again served as a marketing ruse: Since the form was only available in the paper, it was necessary to buy a copy in order to vote.[7]

These early examples demonstrate that beauty contests were gradually becoming more common and broader in scope, although they were still restricted to geisha and other entertainers. They relied on Meiji-era new media—photographs and/or newspapers—to achieve their aims. And they were becoming increasingly public in nature, moving from posting individual photographs in a building to circulating photographs in a newspaper. They also clearly advanced the commercial interests of both the sponsoring entities and the participants, all of whom were professionals. The 1907 contest would take the public display of beauty in an unprecedented direction, and it too would rely on the new photographic media. It was no doubt intended to help sell newspapers as well, but the timing and context of the event ultimately imbued it with far more significance than a mere commercial enterprise.

Upon receiving the *Tribune* telegram, the *Jiji shimpō* published a notice on September 15, informing readers of the event and stipulating the contest regulations.[8] The rules were as follows: Photographs of those who made a living based on their looks, such as actresses and geisha, would not be accepted. Photos were to be publishable. On the back of submitted photographs, each contestant was instructed to write her name, address, age, whether or not she was employed, and her parents' occupation or social status. Contestants were also encouraged to include their height, bust, and hip measurements. Several photos showing different poses could be submitted. The photos were to be entered via mail and sent to a newspaper designated for each region. The deadline for receipt of entries was November 10. The final regulation spelled out the judging process: The first round would be judged by appointed committee members at each newspaper, and first through fifth places would receive a prize. There would be no public vote.[9] The photos of the top five winners were then forwarded to the *Jiji shimpō* for a second-round contest, again judged by a specially appointed committee.[10] For this round, the committee narrowed the field to forty-three, choosing the top candidate from each district, and in the third and final round they selected the winner.[11] The *Jiji shimpō* notice also announced that it would award the first-place winner in the national contest an 18-karat diamond ring worth 300 yen, while participating newspapers would receive an 18-karat gold ruby and pearl ring valued at 30 yen.[12] The contest ultimately attracted thousands of entries, the vast majority half-length portraits of young women in Japanese dress.[13] Miss Suehiro Hiroko, a sixteen-year-old student, won the title of Japan's top *bijin*.

Recruiting nationally for photographs of "ordinary girls" was the first noteworthy aspect of the contest. Perhaps Japan was on the verge of developing such a contest already, but the *Tribune* certainly spurred the initiative. The competition Marguerite Frey had entered stated that: "no artist's models, actresses, or women whose pictures have ever been published need apply."[14] As Inoue Shōichi explains, this requirement determined *Jiji shimpō*'s rules, including how the contest came to specify that actresses, in particular, were singled out for exclusion. In 1907, female actresses were a rarity within Japan, so it was a bit strange that they were explicitly prohibited from participating. Not only that, but they were first on the list of those excluded, before geisha. However, actresses were far more prevalent in the West, and the Chicago contest had prohibited them, so the Japanese version followed suit, directly citing the original American conditions.[15] By excluding "those who made a living based on their looks" but inviting everyone else to enter, the contest provided an unprecedented opportunity for a broad demographic to step into the public realm. The lack of geographic restrictions further encouraged participation. Edo period beauty rankings tended to be based on various local entertainment districts, such as the Yoshiwara or Shimabara, while early Meiji contests such as the one organized by *Hinode shimbun* limited their scope to a single region. In searching for the country's number one beauty, the *Jiji shimpō* event transcended both these geographic boundaries.

Published Photographic Portraits as a New Visual Genre

Open to any girl, from anywhere in the country, the *Jiji shimpō* competition was truly progressive. Inviting such broad participation seems especially meaningful given the timing. The contest coincided with the emergence of a new middle class, which grew significantly in the years immediately following the Russo-Japanese War (1904–05). It offered this newly expanded social group the opportunity to share a novel experience. Although in theory the contest was open to anyone, in practice it seems likely that the daughters of families with greater social prestige may have had more success. The top-ranked Suehiro Hiroko and second-place winner Kaneda Kenko were both "good daughters from good families," their fathers having distinguished careers (Suehiro's father was a mayor, and Kaneda's father was the head of a prefectural office). As the rules required contestants to reveal their families' occupation and social status, it is not hard to imagine that judgment might have been biased towards certain women based on this information, the daughter of a mayor being viewed as a more appropriate representative of the nation than the daughter of a laborer, for example.

The reliance on visual media, namely, photographs, formed the next groundbreaking aspect of the contest. As mentioned, prior beauty contests had already made use of photographic portraits, but the *Jiji shimpō* case marked a new standard in the circulation and usage of this genre. The spread of photography throughout the Meiji period had served to popularize portraiture, making it possible by the late 1880s for virtually anyone to have her likeness reproduced. Whereas pre-Meiji *bijin* images were restricted to the well-known beauties of the floating world, photography permitted any young woman to capture her beauty. However, for most of the Meiji period, portrait photographs had been meant for private consumption. They circulated primarily among family and close friends, carefully kept in family albums or treasured keepsake boxes.[16]

By the end of the 1880s, photographs of ordinary young women had gained a slightly wider circulation outside the immediate family, as they started to be used in introductions for *miai* (arranged marriage) via the mail, but this was still essentially for private viewing.[17] Only photographs of geisha and courtesans found a wider audience, as they were sold or given as souvenirs to admirers. But even these did not circulate freely in print, since print technologies were not advanced enough to publish photographs in newspapers or magazines until the 1890s. Around the time of the First Sino-Japanese War (1894–95), photographs were first published as special supplements, and by 1904, newspapers had developed the ability to print photographs as part of the regular edition.[18]

There was another important factor affecting the publication of portrait images: the question of propriety. Since the women who did have portrait photographs freely circulated were those connected to the sex trade, photographs of *any* women published in the media were easily interpreted as depicting women with dubious virtue. In 1895, for example, the new literary journal *Bungei kurabu* (Literary Arts Club) began to publish photo spreads of *bijin*, featuring geisha from the licensed entertainment quarters. In an unprecedented move, the December 1895 issue published photographs of women writers, laid out in a manner similar to the page design used for the photographs of beauties. Reaction to the issue was mixed and included strong criticism directed towards the women for allowing their portraits to be published. Moreover, the journal seemed to encourage an eroticized interpretation of the writers by presenting them in a visual manner identical to that of the *bijin*. As Rebecca Copeland has written, the photo spread strongly suggested "that a woman who sells her fiction is little more than a woman for sale."[19] During a period in which the public role of women was being severely restricted by the Meiji government, any kind of public action, including allowing one's photograph to be reproduced, was easily criticized as transgressive behavior. The notable exception to this was the Meiji Empress, whose likeness was widely available as *kaika-e* (civilization prints), which depicted her modeling appropriate modern behaviors.

Additionally, portrait photographs of both the emperor and the empress started to circulate in the 1890s. Distributed to help foster a sense of national pride, his was sent to schools and local government offices, while hers was sent to girls' schools. For ordinary women, however, drawing public attention to a portrait image would be anathema.

New developments in print technology helped to shift social norms, and by the early 1900s, the appearance of portraits in print had started to become more commonplace, losing the stigma of just a few years prior. Women's magazines of the late Meiji and Taishō (1912–26) eras began to include photographs of the imperial family, nobility, and wives of important men. According to Satō Sakuma Rika, the activities and images of the upper ranks of society were introduced to the public in magazines from the latter half of the Meiji 30s (1902–07), a period spanning the Russo-Japanese War. In addition, magazines printed portraits of potential brides, serving as a kind of catalog of marriage candidates. Because there were few mixed-gender social events to provide a means of meeting potential mates, these publications provided a method for young women of marriageable age to market themselves to potential husbands.

By the Meiji 40s (1908–12), women's magazines began to request photographs from readers and printed special sections of readers' portraits.[20] The 1907 competition coincided with this period when the publication of photographs in newspapers and magazines rapidly started to become more widespread—and in particular photographs of women who were neither well known nor part of the floating world. Both the increase in the frequency of published portraits and the contest itself marked a significant shift in the usage of the visual medium of portrait photography from private to public. Even so, when a book featuring portraits of the 215 *bijin* who had passed the first round of judging in the contest was published in 1908 (*Nihon bijinchō* or *Book of Japanese Beauties*), the foreword stated explicitly that they were "women of good family."[21] Care had to be taken to reassure the public that their beauty was pure and had not previously been for sale.

This newly public function of *bijin* portraits resonated with a similar development in one significant category of male portrait photographs. As Kinoshita Naoyuki has demonstrated, the decade spanning the First Sino-Japanese War and the Russo-Japanese War saw important shifts in the commemorative and public uses of photography for soldiers. During the Sino-Japanese War, periodicals began to publish special supplements of portrait photographs of the war dead, first of officers and, later, those of ordinary soldiers. The journal *Nisshin sensō jikki* (Record of the Sino-Japanese War), for example, featured six portraits of deceased soldiers in each of the first eight issues and increased the number of portraits reproduced until it reached sixty-six in the last issue. The decision to print portraits was likely tied to sales: Conscription only became truly widespread in the 1890s, and the families of conscripted soldiers would probably have read these magazines. Such publications helped to expand the role of portrait photography, transforming portraits of the war dead from private mementos to public images.[22] Kinoshita further discusses how official commemoration ceremonies developed over the next decade as well. Prior to the Russo-Japanese War, the practice of officially collecting portraits of the war dead was not yet institutionalized, but as these ceremonies became more commonplace they produced three important effects: They helped to establish the genre of war dead photography, they made photography into the standard medium for memorial portraiture, and they transformed the role of the portrait photograph from a private possession of the bereaved to a public symbol of the war.[23] As commemorative images of the war, portraits represented Japanese military success as much as they represented individual loss. Although the implications of a new public role for *bijin* portraits of teenage girls were perhaps not as profound, they represented a parallel development in co-opting private images to serve as symbols of national pride.

Reluctant Beauties

So what did the photographs submitted to the *Jiji shimpō* contest look like? Compared to the images published in the *Tribune* of contestants from the United States and other countries, the Japanese photographs tended to be remarkably conservative and formulaic. The portraits of the winner, Suehiro Hiroko, are representative.[24] The first photograph of her to be published in the newspaper (on December 8, 1907, and then again on February 4, 1908) is a soft-focus image of a shy-looking girl with two large bows in her hair, wearing a kimono and holding roses (Figure 1.1). On March 5, she was declared the winner, the accompanying photo depicting her in a considerably more coquettish fashion. Here Suehiro appears in a half-length view with her elbows on a table. She holds a fan with both hands in front of her chin, tilting her head to gaze up to the right of the camera in a flirtatious manner (Figure 1.2). Photo spreads of the top three winners on April 3 and 4 featured additional photos of Suehiro, including several full-length photographs showing her in a lavish kimono and elaborate *obi* (sash) with a traditional hairstyle (Figure 1.3). While analyzing the standards of beauty used to judge the contestants is beyond the scope of this essay, there is no doubt that Suehiro Hiroko was a very appealing young *bijin*.

Despite the publication of portraits becoming more commonplace, there was some significant resistance to the

Figure 1.1 *Jiji shimpō* Beauty Contest Winner Suehiro Hiroko, ca.1907. Published in *Jiji shimpō*, December 8, 1907 and February 4, 1908.

Figure 1.2 Suehiro Hiroko, *ca.*1908. This portrait was used to announce Suehiro as the country's number one beauty on March 5, 1908.

Figure 1.3   Suehiro Hiroko. Published in
Jiji shimpō, April 3–4, 1908, and later in
Nihon bijinchō, 1908.

idea of the contest among a crucial faction: the potential contestants themselves. For young Japanese ladies of the early twentieth century, diffidence and modesty were both encouraged and expected. The very idea of being so bold as to declare oneself a beauty, and then to take the even more audacious step of entering a beauty contest, pushed the limits of decorum. To promote the contest and assuage socio-moral anxieties, *Jiji shimpō* and other participating regional newspapers appointed special recruiters, one newspaper president even visiting girls' schools himself. Articles about the contest appearing in the various newspapers encouraged family members and friends to submit photographs of *bijin*. Indeed, many photographs were submitted without the sitter's consent or even her awareness. Both Suehiro Hiroko and Kaneda Kenko, it seems, were entered without their prior knowledge.[25]

Despite the fact that it had become more acceptable for the portrait of a young woman to be published, the outcome of the contest did result in some controversy. Suehiro faced significant personal distress as a result of her top finish. The sixteen-year-old daughter of the mayor of Kokura City in Fukuoka Prefecture, Suehiro was living in Tokyo with her brother-in-law in order to attend the Peeresses' School at Gakushū-in. He submitted her portrait without obtaining her consent. When she found out, she had a premonition that the contest would result in trouble. As she moved through the various stages of the competition, her portrait was published three times: once each following the first and second rounds, and then again after she was declared the winner. General Nogi Maresuke, the highly decorated war hero, was the director of Gakushū-in at the time, and he ran the school in a strict fashion. When Suehiro was declared the winner, the officials at Gakushū-in expelled her.

The school issued a denunciation, stating that the kind of girl who would participate in such a contest was unsuited to the upstanding atmosphere of the institution, citing bad influences on her classmates. Interestingly, there was no negative fallout after the first two times her photo was published, and none of her classmates was expelled, despite the fact that some of them had entered the contest as well. Since the reason given for her expulsion was that her victory caused a disruptive atmosphere at school, a burst of jealousy or excitement among her classmates might have compelled the school to penalize her. The *Jiji shimpō* and other newspapers wrote articles criticizing the school's actions. Their consensus was that, since Suehiro did not even participate of her own volition, it was wholly inappropriate to blame her for winning, let alone punish her with such an extreme action.[26] Her crime was being a celebrity.

Ultimately the contest seemed not to have harmed the prospects of the top candidates. A notice published in the *Jiji shimpō* by the father of the second-place winner, Kaneda Kenko, indicated that she had received more than 200 marriage proposals as a result of her photo appearing in the paper.[27] And even Suehiro ended up benefiting, having an advantageous arranged matrimony brokered by General Nogi himself, who perhaps felt bad about the severe punishment. Suehiro married the son of another war hero, Nozu Michitsura, whose family had been appointed to the Japanese nobility (or peerage) as a result of his contributions in the Russo-Japanese War.[28]

Bijin Nationalism

While the reliance on amateur beauties and the expanded public usage of portrait photographs were significant, perhaps the most noteworthy aspect of the contest was its political nature. The competition coincided with an increasing emphasis on the potential of beautiful women serving the nation.[29] From the 1890s on, the term *bijin* appeared in increasingly politicized terms in a variety of cultural references, reflecting a modern fascination with the concept of beauty that was very much tied to Japanese nationalism. Journals such as *Bijin gahō* (Beauty Pictorial) promoted the cultivation of the *bijin* as a cultural asset, marking the female body as a politicized site and a symbol for nationhood. Japan strategically used the *bijin* to disguise its ascendant image as military aggressor. It consistently promoted itself by sending beautiful women to international expositions and world fairs, for example. One writer advocated that, in addition to the official government policy supporting various kinds of industrial exhibitions, Japan should promote exhibitions of beauties and beauty contests.[30] The *Jiji shimpō* contest was fully congruent with these new ideas, marrying the publication of *bijin* portrait photographs to a patriotic display and use of beauty.

The notice introducing the contest that was published together with the rules in the September 15 edition revealed how the *Jiji shimpō* framed the event. The *Chicago Daily Tribune* certainly employed a nationalistic tone in claiming that their American beauty was the most beautiful in the world. But while their correspondence merely suggested a friendly rivalry, the *Jiji shimpō,* on behalf of Japan, imbued the affair with a sense of dramatic conflict. The language used in the notice is striking, issuing in strongly militaristic terms a call to arms urging the nation's beauties to take on the United States and the rest of the world for a battle:

> Searching for photographs of Japan's top beauty: We have received from the USA a written challenge claiming that they have extremely beautiful women. If there is anyone among the troops of virtuous girls of victorious Japan who wishes to volunteer to engage in this battle, quickly name yourself ... Now, when we are tired of war with weapons, a war with women's beauty is a novel and very interesting

idea, and our company, on behalf of millions of beauties all over the nation, accepted the declaration of war.[31]

The notion of "victorious Japan" referred, of course, to the recent triumph of Japan in the Russo-Japanese War. "Volunteers for battle," "declarations of war"—the words chosen played on and played up Japan's recent military successes. But here the action was extended to new battlefields, enabling upstanding young women to fight for their nation's pride by parading their physical beauty in the visual realm. The tone of the challenge was significantly different from the contest Marguerite Frey had entered, which called for "a clean, sweet, fresh hearted, courageous, frank, unaffected American girl, the finest creature ever created."[32]

The contest extended the ability to participate in a battle to fight for Japan's status on the world stage to a new demographic—namely, young women. Although the contest regulations did not stipulate age, most of the contestants were approximately fifteen to twenty years old. As Vera Mackie has noted, during the Russo-Japanese War, women had several means available to support the war efforts: charitable activities, mourning their deceased husbands and sons, or working as nurses at the front, an occupation that had only recently developed in tandem with the development of the modern military.[33] Mackie also notes that a number of books were published emphasizing women's roles in supporting the state and its military activities. These included *Sensō to fujin* (War and Women), and two books with the title *Gunkoku no fujin* (Women of Militarism).[34] Another book went as far as drawing parallels between beauty and war: *Sensō bi to fujin bi* (The Beauty of War and the Beauty of Women).[35] The writer of this last text clearly drew inspiration from the West, arguing that in the West beauty was thought of as a public virtue, while in Japan *bijin* were kept for private pleasure. He advocated using *bijin* for the public good.[36] The demographic represented in the contest would have been too young to be nurses, mothers, or wives during the Russo-Japanese War. And although a beauty contest was considerably more lighthearted than a military confrontation, the opportunity to represent Japan in this "battle" provided young women with a chance to compete in order to defend their country's honor, just as young male soldiers had done only a few years earlier.

The *Chicago Daily Tribune* responded to the militaristic tone of the Japanese contest, publishing a feature on November 17, 1907, entitled "Japan Aroused by Beauty War with America." Stating that it thought a beauty contest "might be too audacious and western to please the Japanese, with their conservative ideas about womankind," the *Tribune* was happy to report that was not the case: "Japan at once proved itself to be one of the most progressive nations in the world [by immediately taking up the challenge]." Indeed, "little Japan [came] forward as the most energetic searcher." The *Tribune* reported that the *Jiji shimpō* had dubbed the contest a war but reassured American readers that "Japan has no intention of declaring war militant, either on land or sea, against the United States…Japan's war against America is a friendly one—a war not of battleships or big guns, but a war of beauty. The newspapers of Japan, in fact, have declared war upon Marguerite Frey." The article continued with the military analogy by describing Japan's battle plan in detail:

> With Japanese thoroughness the *Jiji* laid out its beauty campaign like a good general makes his plans for a real war ... the *Jiji* divided Japan into twenty-two districts or prefectures outside of Tokio and selected the leading newspaper in each district to conduct its beauty quest ... [a] selection of five of the most beautiful women will be made in each district of Japan, and among all of these, "able judges will select the three most beautiful." These three most beautiful women of Japan will be entered in the international beauty quest, one of them a claimant for the honor of being the most beautiful woman in the world.

The story concluded by commenting on the Japanese sense of national pride: "The men and women of Japan are intensely patriotic. They believe that nothing anywhere surpasses the bravery and honor of their men and the beauty of their women, and the whole kingdom at once became interested in the beauty quest."[37]

No doubt the Japanese felt that, if the bravery and honor of their young men could defeat the Russians, then surely the beauty of their young women could triumph over the rest of the world. By appealing to patriotism and opening the competition both geographically and socially, the contest was a masterful commercial maneuver. While earlier examples like the *Ryounkaku* geisha exhibit and the *Hinode shimbun* Five Beauties of Tokyo-Yokohama contests had provided a participatory element for the audience by encouraging the public to vote, a panel of judges determined the outcomes of the *Jiji shimpō* contest. Nevertheless, despite the public being uninvolved in the voting process, the competition served to attract readers. Were any of their friends or acquaintances participating, and if so, what were their results? Who would be named the most beautiful woman in the nation? And how would the Japanese *bijin* measure up against the American beauty Frey and other winners? Inquiring minds wanted to know.

How did Suehiro Hiroko fare on the international stage? Unfortunately, the final results have proven very difficult to determine. Japanese sources have claimed that she ultimately won sixth place, though this author has not been able to confirm this.[38] Her photograph was published in the *Chicago Daily Tribune* on May 17, 1908, in an article that described the Japanese competition and included photographs of the top three winners (Figure 1.4).[39] Short features on the winners from other countries are scattered

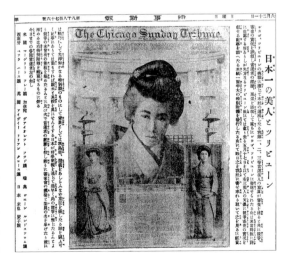

Figure 1.4 *Most Beautiful Women of Japan.* Published in the *Chicago Daily Tribune*, May 17, 1908. This page was also used as an illustration in the *Jiji shimpō* on June 21, 1908.

throughout 1908 and into 1909, and a brief article published on November 28, 1909, states that the *Tribune* had just recently received five late entries from Central America. Unfortunately, this last article does not mention whether a winner had already been chosen or would be any time soon. A thorough search of the archives of the *Chicago Tribune* has not yielded any final announcements about the winner of the international search for the world's most beautiful woman. The contest unfolded over a very long time: Nearly three years had passed between the initial wager that prompted the American competition and the late arrival of the Latin American photographs. Perhaps interest had dissipated and no ultimate winner was announced. Or perhaps the *Tribune* had never really intended to announce a winner, preferring instead to exploit interest in the contest by publishing feature articles and pictures of pretty girls from around the world as long as it sold newspapers.

Conclusion

The *Jiji shimpō* contest offered a heady blend of commerce and politics. Ordinary women shared in the limelight of the newly victorious Japan and helped to advance national pride. With beauty as their weapon, these women were perceived as warriors fighting for Japan's prestige abroad. The country's number one *bijin* may not have conquered the world. Her creation nevertheless symbolized a competitive spirit in a country that saw itself increasingly as a contender for international leadership. Granted that the contestants were not always active agents and sometimes had to endure reproach, they showed how it was possible for women of their background to attain social celebrity. Photography played a critical role in this. As an artistic medium with mass appeal, printed photographs in newspapers made private portraiture public, transporting feminine beauty to the platform for discussing politics and international affairs. The *Jiji shimpō* contest demonstrated how Meiji-era new media acted as conduits for women's entry into the public sphere, both as symbols and as individuals.

Painting Manuals and Gendered Modernity in Republican-era Shanghai

Lisa Claypool

In a color lithographic poster printed in Shanghai in the early 1930s, a cheerfully smiling woman lifts her head as though we have just interrupted her from her book (see Plate 1). The woman's warm prettiness, with her Marlene Dietrich brows, points away from Shanghai and towards Hollywood—but also points to a long-lived Chinese literary tradition, in which the flower is a poetic trope for woman, here suggesting she is just one more object of visual pleasure in this garden scene. Like the woman, the advertisement itself (for cigarettes) is a visually pleasing object: The reds and oranges of the floral pattern on the woman's dress are picked up in the colors of the art deco frame, emphasizing that this *is* a picture, after all, a color-coordinated composition by a named artist, Hang Zhiying.[1] Yet in the skies, planes appear through the clouds, and the book in the woman's hand, to which her finger delicately but insistently points, is an aeronautic engineering manual. Her gesture is tantamount to a knowing wink, a hint that she could, in fact, be that pilot, breaking free of the picture frame, guiding viewers of the poster and fellow travelers of modern China into the wild blue yonder of the future.

This poster and other print advertisements have been closely studied within the rubric of defining the Modern Woman. It is not surprising that we comply with the demands they make on us to think about gender and modernity. After all, they are glossy and candy-colored, the pictures evoke Hollywood glamor, they operate the way all advertisements do—through a set of signs that lend themselves easily to interpretation (woman as flower, for instance). They sell us happiness, as Ellen Johnston Laing aptly puts it.[2] Critically, they show us women as objects *and* as agents of their own futures. They are important pictures in writing a social history of women within a consumer society. But what I propose to do in this essay is to look elsewhere—to look at the strangely overlooked genre of *shinü hua* "gentlewoman painting," which nonetheless, in spite of its ghostly presence in art histories today, "retained [its] popularity with painters and audiences throughout the Republican era," as Yeh Wen-hsin has observed.[3] These pictures, ink paintings in styles dating from deep within the imperial past, served as a primary visual medium through which modern female gender was represented and transformed, and arguably were *the* primary medium of such negotiations.

And that was precisely because, in 1920s Shanghai, the relationship between *shinü* pictures and gender was never straightforward. It was contested and questioned, celebrated and mourned. As part of my exploration into this overlooked genre, I will consider the key issue consistently troubling its painters: What is the relationship between the genre and female gender? I will analyze the debate about representation and gender through study of *shinü* paintings and texts about them in figure painting manuals. The manuals are "how to" books about lifting the brush to make pictures with it, published in Shanghai from the turn of the twentieth century through the mid-1920s.[4] At the core of the study are the *Hall of Three Rarities* (Sanxitang) volumes published in 1924–25, which I will index to three editions of the *Mustard Seed Garden* painting manuals (1897, 1916, 1922), and the manual entitled *Compendium of New-Style Art, Classified Pictures* (Xinpai tuhua fenlei daquan, 1922).

Yet this is not strictly a social history through pictures.[5] This chapter is about the relationship of figure painting manuals to a melancholic imagination within the new politics of Shanghai society. Here, melancholy is considered an effect of the vertiginous space of urban Shanghai, a space that, by the 1920s, seems to have become dedicated solely to spectacle and entertainment (the theater, cinematograph shows, horse races, billboards on long streets of shop fronts, public gardens). Spectacle entranced the eye, incorporating the person on the street into a kaleidoscope of color and light; melancholy belonged to a different register of vision, what I describe below and flesh out as the "legible imagination," a long-lived mode of seeing and interacting with the world that was being displaced, or, at least, disrupted. In short, I propose to reconsider the making of figural pictures and its hold upon the emergent imagined modern social body, by mapping historical attempts to control the *shinü* gentlewomen-painting genre, and by extension, to control the imaginative looking that was engendered by such pictures and their relationship to the woman in the cigarette poster who dreamed of flying.

Genre is derived from the same root term as *gender*. It suggests taxonomies, classes, distributions of things that have some rational and thoughtful basis, concrete and real distinctions that all can agree upon, as do the Chinese terms used by the *Sanxitang* manual editor: *men* (class), *lei* (category), and *wenti* (body of texts). To put something into a familial group in which things are categorized on the basis of "likeness" means to build a structure around it, just like an architectural domain for a family. In this vein, one relevant cognate meaning of the Chinese term *men* or "class" is "gateway," denoting the entrance to the home, that, within Confucian thinking about gender, was the place for women. So it is important to acknowledge that genre does imply, somewhat darkly, hierarchies and dominance of one over another. Precisely because of that classifying impulse through which authorial power is performed (in China and elsewhere), genre has become decidedly old-fashioned in our transnational supermodern culture of appropriation, fragmentation, or rhetoric of social and cultural equality, and embrace of difference over search for shared traits.

But genre, like gender, also asks for interpretations. It thus possesses an emotional and less easily quantifiable and urgent import. Making a picture based on the lessons in the manuals especially complicates genre because, in the process of putting ink and pigment on paper or silk, a painter makes interpretive decisions about how to copy. Moreover, visual art can exceed neat and tidy classification and be appreciated not just for how it fits easily into a genre but how it does not. It is partly for these reasons that Jacques Derrida argues for the need for—and futility of—genre distinction. He points out that any generic classification system is untenable because "individual texts although participating in it cannot belong to it. Individual texts resist classification because they are interpretively indeterminate."[6] Still, he asks: "Can one identify a work of art, of whatever sort, but especially a work of discursive art, if it does not bear the mark of a genre, if it does not signal or mention it or make it remarkable in any way?"[7] For Derrida, genre is actual and potential, rational and imaginative, historic and poetic, at the same time. To elucidate genre is to communicate something socially, politically, and aesthetically meaningful, even while recognizing that the rational schematics of genre and genre formation might fail as individual works of art are seen to trouble the meanings assigned to them. Genre largely exists at the interstices between the text or object under social scrutiny and the peculiar response to its ambiguities and indeterminacy by an individual reader or observer. It is there and serves as a filter that determines the "essence" of things, yet repeatedly (and for Derrida, inevitably, and happily), it fades from view within the inefficient and unstable contingencies surrounding real-world readers and beholders as they engage, imaginatively, with the messy aesthetic object at hand.

Derrida's insights serve to make us aware of nuances and complexities of the discourse about gender and genre within the context of early twentieth-century Shanghai painting manuals. If control of a painting genre was thought to be tantamount to control of gender, as I am arguing, then Derrida's complications of it alert us to the ways in which genre and gender (what Derrida calls a "human genre") may both have imaginatively resisted ordering and the rhetoric used to contain it—even as they required that ordering to be socially meaningful. Indeed, part of my argument about the constitution and significance of "gentlewoman painting" as a genre is that Ye Jiuru, the editor of the *Sanxitang* painting manual, was acutely aware of the ways genre operated. He did not conceive of paintings in a reductive sense as simple objects to be manipulated, although he attempted to do just that by forming a genre out of them. He found them to be spaces for deeply personal engagement as well, what I call a "legible imagination," spaces of pictorial engagement long linked to shared imaginative worlds of the educated elite. The failure of the genre to become a part of art history today may lie precisely in the relevance of such a dialectic (between social articulation and individual imagination) to the historical moment that produced it; once that moment was over, Ye's delineation of the genre emerged in new forms, even including the poster calendar of the woman consulting her aeronautic engineering manual. Our project, then, will be to adopt Derrida's lens on the tensions marking genre within the early twentieth-century Shanghai context of artists' debates about the experiential relevance of *shinü* painting to modern women and modern life.

A Genre Crisis

To begin our investigation, we must identify cultural problems surrounding the formation of the "gentlewoman painting" genre in the 1920s. The focal painting manuals of our study were published as part of the multivolume *Sanxitang* set of painting manuals, edited by the Shanghai book publisher and editor Ye Jiuru (b. c.1871) in the mid-1920s.[8] Creating the *Sanxitang* series of manuals was an ambitious undertaking. Eighteen painting subjects are represented in ten manuals—forty-two volumes—from rocks and plum blossoms to insects and birds. Each is addressed in a preface by a noted luminary and introduced briefly with histories and observations on legitimate models for imitation. Prominent painters and calligraphers contributed titular inscriptions. Altogether there are roughly some 2,080 pictures and 1,090 diagrams or motifs for study. Most of the pictures date to the late Qing (1850–1911) and early Republican era (1911–30) by artists active in Shanghai, although paintings produced in mid-Qing Yangzhou and late-Ming (1500–1644) Suzhou are conspicuously present. The actual contents of the manuals (relatively accessible images, frequently reproduced in print, and easily acquired in catalogs of pictures on the market) do not precisely match up with the way the editor generally frames them as treasures of an emergent national patrimony. (The title—*Hall of Three Rarities*—was the name of Emperor Qianlong's study, tying the contents of the manual to the imperial collection.) As the preface to the volumes on figure painting (*renwu hua*) puts it,

> All of the Qing court's collected (and authenticated) paintings by Wu Daozi, and so on, all of the authentic traces of various painters from the Tang and Song, have been collected in the manual, as well as paintings by the Ming–Qing era artists Hua Yan [1682–1756] and Ren Xiong [1823–57], and so on, many of which have not been seen outside the court. The difference between these masterworks and the figure paintings available on the market today is like that between heaven and earth.[9]

The volume of *shinü* paintings in the manual is a hodgepodge of pictures, which nonetheless uneasily cohere, thanks to Ye Jiuru's editorial strategies, taken up below. His sensibility about genre clearly is formed and informed by a recognition that it is not immutable but changes over time—even if he believes it should not. Genres, to his mind, possess genealogies. Ye's essay "Origins and History of Painting *Shinü*" provides a starting point for investigation into his perception of the evolution of the *shinü* genre in the decades directly preceding the *Sanxitang* manuals:

> Liu Xiang wrote the *Biographies of Women*. Later people illustrated it with pictures. This was how *shinü* began to become part of painted biographies. When considering the method of painting *shinü*, it basically belongs to the genre (*men*) of figural imagery. Although there are a stream of ancient paintings well respected in the grove of paintings such as the portraits of Ehuang and Nüying [daughters of the legendary emperor Yao, who married his successor, Shun], Jin-dynasty Dai Kui's painting of exemplary women who demonstrated benevolence and wisdom (serving as the illustrations for the chapter of benevolence and wisdom in Liu Xiang's *Lienü zhuan*),[10] [Six Dynasties] Song dynasty's Yuan Qian's *Concubine Ding Playing the Crooked-neck Pipa*,[11] and Tang-dynasty Zhou Fang's *Yang Guifei*, with such a long time and many generations passing by, authentic traces of these paintings [literally, their visages] have failed to be fully transmitted.
>
> For the painting method to be correct and orthodox, you need to take Wu Daozi as a model. The court style of the Southern Song, although extremely meticulous and delicate, lacks Wu's brush power. Nevertheless, its coloring is very sophisticated: a little more dense, the painting would appear vulgar; a little lighter, then the composition would be too flimsy. Entering the Ming dynasty, painters such as Qiu Ying and Tang Yin only followed Wu Daozi as their model and later Chen Zhanghou [Chen Hongshou] emerged. His application of color exhibits clear influence of Wu Daozi's style. Along with Qiu and Tang, each of the three had his own strengths. Since they are not so distant from us in time, if students can concentrate their minds and efforts studying their marvelous works with tireless scrutiny, then they shall be able to surmount the Song and glimpse into the Tang era, getting to the bottom of it. However, from the middle Qing and later, those who paint *shinü* tend to excel in expressing feminine beauty and tender charm, deviating from the established norm of antique simplicity. Such a development parallels the process by which literary styles evolved from Han to Six Dynasties as a result of new fashions and trends. As long as the spirit of the brush does not turn away from the ancients, then the tradition [of *shinü* painting] still remains as one.[12]

To Ye's mind, the earliest iterations of what he understands to be a class of figure painting are lost to time. What pulls these dimly imagined images together as a group is that they function as illustrations to the lives of female paragons. His account then shifts from the virtuous or immoral action such pictures might be emblematic of or engender, to issues of style, arguing that, through the work of noted Ming Dynasty artists, the past can be recuperated. Style is not decorative color or strength of brush alone, he writes; it is a mode of communication. But by the later Qing Dynasty, the dialog between present and past has transformed, and the genre has been emptied of serious substance, frivolous "feminine beauty and tender charm" remaining behind in its place. Qing Dynasty portrayals of *shinü* pull away from discourse about virtue that originally sustained the genre and thus only tenuously embrace the "one" authentic and timeless tradition of *shinü* painting. Artists "turn away from the ancients." Evidently, Ye is distinguishing between depictions of women who are beautiful (perhaps obliquely referring to "beautiful women painting," *meiren hua;* Japanese, *bijinga*) yet not also exemplary, and what he would call *shinü* paintings. Moreover, he is correlating virtue with an expressive style of brushwork, rather than the costive brushwork and colorful paintings of the late Qing.

Since Ye's manual features many late Qing paintings of beautiful women, the question arises: How can Ye lament the lack in something that is so prominent in his own publication?

Answers may be revealed in part through analysis of three earlier *Mustard Seed Garden* figural painting manuals that stylistically, at least, do not depart too far from the *Sanxitang* volumes. Indeed, what Ye Jiuru identifies as *shinü* paintings by two of the editors of these earlier manuals, Chao Xun (1852–1917)[13] and Wang Kun (1877–1946), appear in the *Sanxitang* volumes. These manuals act as signposts from 1897 to 1916 to 1922 for shifting formations of the genre in the city of Shanghai. To place them in a genealogy respects their shared title and marketed purpose as "how to" books, their location in the same urban visual culture, and relatively close dates of publication.

The 1897 manual, the "fourth edition" (*siji*), features many then-contemporary paintings reproduced twenty-eight years later in Ye's volumes.[14] The last two volumes of the 1897 manual are reproductions of paintings by artists who were or had been active in Shanghai in the nineteenth century. The third ends with a series of paintings of beautiful women, bodhisattvas, and Daoist immortals by Feng Ji, for instance, along with pictures by other painters. Pictures in the fourth volume by painters now obscure intermingle with work by celebrities such as Ren Bonian (1840–96), whose work was regularly advertised in the newspaper *Shenbao*, and Qian Hui'an (1833–1911), who gained prominence not only for his paintings but also for the print designs he produced for the Yangliuqing publishing house. Painting subjects fall on the boundary of "type" figures that might be read about in the genre of "social fiction" (*shehui xiaoshuo*) of the day: languid women under peach trees, girls playing zithers, a young man poring over a book, a smattering of historical figures, and so on.

The paintings in the 1897 fourth edition could point towards a Shanghai identity or the artist's hand, or to the identity of the manual editor who collected, organized, and copied them. They could stand allegorically for the male painters who were at that time rethinking the nature of painting practice more generally as it fit into the public persona of an educated male elite. Such expansiveness of meaning suggests that images of women indeed acted, as art historian Wu Hung has argued, as "signifiers without a focus of signification" or "empty vessels" to carry meaning.[15] Openness of interpretation gently pushed *shinü* painting outside the discursive realm of Liu Xiang's paragons so admired by Ye Jiuru.

The apparently inchoate nature of painting pictures of women also seems to have pushed the editor of the 1916 fifth edition (*wuji*) of the *Mustard Seed Garden Painting Manual* (*Jieziyuan huazhuan*) in another direction: toward stricter regulation of it. In the fifth edition, categories of images have been realigned and reasserted. The volumes have titles: The first volume is entitled "Lofty Scholars and Beautiful Women" (*gaoshi meiren*); the second, "Vegetables, Melons and Fruit" (*yuanshu guaguo*); the third and fourth "Flowers, Birds, Grasses and Insects" (*huaniao caochong*). Each of the images, unlike those in the fourth edition, is by the same artist, Huang Jun (sobriquet Keming, from Hangzhou). Huang's preface to the manual announces that:

> Although painting is a small way, still, if you cannot transmit delicacy and power it cannot be successful. Painting has catalogues just as characters have rubbings. Their regulations are based on their structure. Regulate it, nurture it, practice it, and you will become proficient in it. Then you can proceed to imitate the traces of the ancients, internalize their way and make it your own. There is a difference between a painting that has origins and splashing ink around so that it looks like a black crow on a sheet of white paper. Recently there is a school of painting that greatly favors the fad of *xieyi* or "drawing the idea." In society it has become popular and trendy at the moment. People who are able to do *xieyi* from the beginning work at it and hence become excellent at it. It is not at all the case that a person can casually pick up the brush without thinking it through, and ignore all of the rules (*fa*). Hence beginners ought to start from painting manuals to train their hand.

Huang Jun launches a plea for study of the manual as a structured cultural experience. Through long and disciplined copying practice, a student of painting can internalize a delicacy and power of the brush as it is represented in the manual. Huang wants to preserve ancient methods. He observes that the rough scribbling of *xieyi* style is especially suspect, because it looks so easy but in fact requires disciplined adherence to method. The preface suggests, in fact, that more people are painting in 1916, and painting poorly. The manual is a corrective to poor brushwork; the paintings are uniformly alike, as they are all painted by Huang, and hence the practice of copying leads to development of one particular style. Paintings of beautiful women are essential to regulated practice of painting, in other words, but their meaning within the structured morphology of the manual is shifted only slightly from that of the 1897 fourth edition. Assertion of the old pairing of lofty scholar with beautiful women includes famous historical women such as Cai Wenji and Wang Zhaojun, an editorial decision that we might imagine Ye Jiuru would approve of, as typically they are identified not just as beautiful women but as exemplary. This period was one in which a "moderate" view of women, as companion if not equal to men, prevailed.[16]

Six years later, in the 1922 sixth edition (printed, like the fifth edition, at the Jiangdong shuju publishing house in Shanghai, though with a different editor by the name of Wang Kun), the *shinü* disappears.[17] The manual is organized into four volumes that are denoted by terms borrowed from the *Book of Changes* rather than by category of painting.[18] They display a mish-mash of images that lack even the minimal chronological underpinnings of the fourth edition. Most of the pictures, as Wang notes in his preface, are copies: "Since I was a child I was really good at handling brush and ink. Every time I saw a trace of a masterwork from the past or present, I immediately had the idea to copy it, its inscriptions, and even traced the seals. But I simply appropriated its appearance (*xi qi mao*), and was not able to capture its spirit. Over the past twenty-odd years, I have collected alto-gether 240 pages." Of the 240 images, only four depict *shinü*.[19]

A response was not long in coming, and dates to a period character-ized as one of conservative reaction to women's new social and profes-sional roles, which flourished just as the "genre" was becoming a ghostly one in 1922.[20] It was a moment when women were redefining performance of their social roles, debating the nature of female public comportment, political activity, educational opportunity and what they might study, and so on. We return now to Ye Jiuru's compendia of painting manuals and the four *Sanxitang* volumes devoted to the painting of gentlewomen. His short essay, "On Painting *Shinü*," notes that it is the appeal of actual women, and specifically non-elite women in the entertainment districts, that contrib-utes to the crisis in representation:

> Painters today earnestly seek [to paint] new bodies (*xinti*) such as those gracefully flexible with changeable demeanors as if "performers of the Pear garden" in theaters, those who appear on stage and act in operas, and singsong girls and concubines, and that is it. They don't know how the ancients made *shinü* pictures. Most *shinü* paintings either tell stories about palace women or noble women or depicted upright women and exemplary women. Their intention is serious. Therefore dignity and weighty seriousness are principles they aspire to.

To Ye's way of thinking, the pictures as a genre were mainly didactic: look and learn. That was not a new idea. At the same time, it's important to note that he was not simply rehearsing an argument about an estab-lished *shinü* genre. He found himself in a historical moment when he had to redefine it. The genre of *shinü* painting, in short, was what he said it was. And Ye's definition of the genre, as he puts it, was tantamount to control of gender representation—contending with one of the most public iterations of female gender performed in the theater and on the public stage, the kind of spectacular performance of gender glimpsed in print advertisements. How was the genre defined and such control manifested?

Genre in the *Hall of Three Rarities*: Boundaries and Containment

To read the painted figures of *shinü* in the *Sanxitang* manuals as true to their distant origins required a particular self-conscious elucidation of the genre that its immediate, troubled history demanded. For Ye, as we shall see, the genre was worked out in the manual pages so that any potential interference with a certain rhetorical position on gender was smoothed over in a number of complex, flexible, and often apparently contradictory moves: valorization of a particular kind of "ancient" painting, in spite of its general absence in the manual; attention to the material picture's "real" environment juxtaposed against the *shinü*'s represented one; manipulation of the pictorial surface—largely through a working out of text in seal form or inscription—on the pictures. Such visual strategies together bolstered a genre that, in spite of its made-up quality, did conform, as Ye repeatedly observes, to a virtuous and elite male vision of a virtuous and elite woman.

In Ye's presentation of the genre in the manual, for instance, he refers to it as biographical in its origins (*renzhuan*) and as a class or gateway of painting (*men*), markedly like a literary genre (*wenti*). There is something scholarly and textual about the pictures, from his perspective. Such fusion of text with image is supported in the title page of each of the four volumes featuring *shinü*: The leftist revolutionary Zhou Zhenlin (1875–1964), from Changsha, Hunan,[21] inscribed the title of the *shinü* compendium, as well as the first inner subtitle page, with a phrase from the drama *The Western Wing*; for the second volume, the painter Zhu Jiangcun borrowed a phrase from an early *fu* prose poem, "Adorned with Precious Jade" (*huanzi weitai*);[22] the professional calligrapher Yi Lixun (d.1940) selected the quotidian line "Treasures of Painting" (*huihua zhi bao*); and Yu Jiashen listed categories by which painting was appreciated: "Spiritual, Competent, Marvelous, and Untrammeled" (*shen neng miao yi*).

Subtitles of the first two volumes are tropes from literature about beautiful women abandoned and longing for their lovers;[23] subtitles of the last two refer to paintings valued for the way they look. Literature and painting here are connected by an aesthetic of beauty, and it is indeed this strange place between word and image, between textual meaning and visual appearance, neither entirely one nor the other, that brings the *shinü* into the realms of legibility, or what I call "scholarly vision." By that I mean vision is plugged into textuality, and vice versa.[24]

This is a kind of appeal that situates the eye within long-lived educated elite cultural practices of seeing. To "read" a picture might reveal a longing for a past dominated by a particular Confucian learning and social structure, a connection that takes on weight when we see that the first painting in the manual is from that distant past (and remarkably, it is the only one from that past). It shows a woman bathing a child in a tub, set within palatial walls, an image of maternal care and concern. It features a "painter in attendance" (*Xuanhe daizhao*) rank seal which would have been used by the twelfth-century court painter Su Hanchen, to whom Ye attributes the painting (Figure 2.1).

The painting in the manual, however, is not what it seems to be. And here we begin to more fully uncover Ye's editorial strategies and his use of the manual to position and reposition pictures of women socially and

Figure 2.1   *Woman Bathing Child.* Attributed to Su Hanchen (act. ca.1130–60). Lithographic print. Published in Ye Jiuru, ed., *Sanxitang huapu daguan* (Shanghai: Dahua Shuju, 1925) 13 (*juan* 1): 10a.

Figure 2.2   *Woman Bathing Child.* Attributed to Su Hanchen (act. ca.1130–60). Woodblock print. Published in Gu Bing, *Gushi huapu* (1606; reprint Beijing: Wensu Chubanshe, 1983), n.p.

culturally and to put them into a "conversation" with the ancient past. For the picture is not a copy of a Song Dynasty painting but a modified copy of a print published in the 1603 *Master Gu's Painting Manual* (Figure 2.2), to which Ye Jiuru added the twelfth-century seal.[25]

The biography accompanying the picture in Gu Bing's 1603 manual describes Su Hanchen as a painter whose strength lay in figural depictions and painting children, whose application of color was fresh and depiction of the body "as though alive" (*tidu rusheng*). That this is what it was important to know about Su's style points to a preoccupation with the status of the represented body; the way the brush lines on the page tease memory, perhaps invoking childhood memories and the nurturing care of a mother, sister, or nanny. And yet, although memory may possess a physical dimension—such as the memory of sneezing into a caregiver's hand—it also is essential to the abstractions of rhetoric. In the picture, memory is also evoked by reading the body as a symbol of comfort, a symbol pointing toward seamless identification of anonymous child with anonymous female caregiver. That is to say, the depicted scene complies with a universal visual grammar of mother-child relationships; it is this aspect of the painting that also opens it up to interpretation of the *shinü* here as exemplary/good mother (*liangmu*), embodying Confucian philosophical and moral teaching about social roles. The corporeal and sensual status of the body competes with but seems to be absorbed into the social; the body "reads" as a maternal figure.

Indeed, John Hay has argued of early imperial-era representations of the female body that pictorial bodies of elite women are kept legible by somewhat paradoxically seeming to become invisible, disguised beneath—or, more accurately, embodied in—the social surfaces of clothing and robes.[26] Fashion, along with an ornamental language of metaphor and object-hood, and the very materiality of the calligraphic brushstroke rendering the body (that gesture harkening back to the writing brush) keep the body inscribed within a grammar of beauty and decorum. For Hay, the calligraphic stroke in effect makes the bodies material, present, and "real" in profoundly cultural and yet abstract and historically transcendent ways. In that vein, the 1917 reprint of the 1906 preface to *Gujin baimei tuyong* (Pictorial Songs to 100 Beauties) indicates that the *shinü* paintings within it originally were thought to reveal how the transformative nature of painting correlates to the transformative power of the cosmos. In Foucauldian terms of subject, body, and power, on the other hand, we might consider more cynically that the figures were circumscribed within a discourse—in this case, a Confucian discourse—on good wives, mothers, and exemplary women. This is a discourse that, Ye reminds his readers, dates to the publication of imperial biographer Liu Xiang's (79–8 BCE) *Biographies of Women*, warning the emperor of the potentially corrupting influence of women at court on politics in 34 BCE.

Unlike Master Gu's print, in addition to the faked Song Dynasty seal, two faked eighteenth-century Qing Dynasty seals have been impressed onto the painting's surface.[27] Craig Clunas has argued that the pristine images in Master Gu's manual, without seals and inscriptions, may once have invited personal possession.[28] His idea is that you would look at the picture and put your own stamp on it, as though you and only you had owned it. But in the 1920s picture, the opportunity for the viewer to pretend that he or she is the very first to gaze upon the image is circumscribed by history. The history of the picture, its biography, purportedly from the moment it was made, is literally imprinted onto the surface of the painting. The faked seals of the artist and of Emperor Qianlong impress a "Chinese" past onto this picture of maternal devotion. The editor draws a connection, moreover, between that Chinese past and the nation. As the manual's preface puts it, "Recently fashionable beauties fill workshops and people learning to paint are beginning to tire [of them] and want to return to the original *shinü* of our nation." *Shinü* painting is thus freighted with meaning for the nation (*you yi yu wu guo*).

The seals also work to draw attention to the fact that Emperor Qianlong supposedly looked at this painting and found it authentic and worthy of collecting. The seals remind the viewer that *shinü* paintings have been collected as part of an imperial collection—a collection that was just then being transformed into a national patrimony, with the opening of the Palace Museum display gallery in 1914 and the establishment of the museum in 1925.[29] The seemingly inchoate organization of paintings may, in fact, replicate the disorder of the imperial collection at the time, though inclusion in museal space alone does not qualify pictures as a genre. Rather than acting as illustrations of types within a rationally structured domain, the paintings act "as emblems [rather] than as examples in the modern sense: they exist as objects, jumbled together in the memorial space of a *wunderkabinett* or treasure house."[30]

If the genre that Ye Jiuru was attempting to create, then, is one that is literary and is deeply connected to imperial-era elite male ways of seeing, it is political as well, referring to the palace as a protected and symbolic locus of China. There also seems to be a connection between the pictures as (1) a corrective to wayward gender performance through representation and (2) as objects to be contained that required protective walls. That connection points towards another critical way in which Ye Jiuru believed these pictures of gentlewomen revealed deep traces of the past.

Ye discusses the ways that architectural boundaries were said to allow the *shinü* to express genuine emotion (*qing*).[31] Once secluded from the male gaze, a woman's attitude revealed true depth of feeling. Educated readers might also recall that in 1320, the critic Tang Hou likewise emphasized the importance of architectural space in painting *shinü*, observing:

> The art of representing Palace ladies lies in catching the deportments of the inner chambers. Zhou Fang and Zhang Xuan of the Tang dynasty, Du Xiao and Zhou Wenju of the Five Dynasties, and more recently, Su Hanchen of later times grasped the secret of this. It does not reside in applying rouge and face powder, nor in depicting gold ornaments and jade trinkets—mere decoration mistaken for art. I have seen a picture of a Palace lady by Zhou Wenju. She has thrust her jade flute into her girdle and stands staring vacantly, her fingers clenched. Her feelings are held back; we know that she is filled with longing.

Feminine space was permeated with longing (a sentiment that itself is connected to a number of discourses about state and family), which, if contained, supported and informed ethical and normative behaviors. If uncontained, it degenerated into desire (*yu*).

In the manual, to create that visual sense of seclusion and contained emotion, architectural depiction had to have the right look, such as the look of ancient imperial palaces. Hence, the diagrammatic section of the first volume in the pages before Su Hanchen's painting begins by laying out palatial environments: ruled-line depictions of palatial terraces, ceremonial halls, pavilions, gateways and balustrades, stairways and bridges. It serves doubly as a reminder that the pictures themselves are in need of protective tending. This is a clever solution to drawing boundaries around the *shinü*, protecting it from the dangers of a shifting society in which *qing* was coming to mean different things, such as romantic attachment (*renqing*) and modern emotions (*ganqing*).[32]

The picture of woman and child attributed to Su Hanchen, however, is one of only eighteen pictures showing a woman in a familial role within a palace space. The spaces in which the other roughly 228 *shinü* are pictured are limited in range, mainly to gardens, abbreviated landscapes, or skiffs among lotus blossoms. A number show a single woman gazing forlornly over willows from inside a pavilion or in the company of a second female figure. The majority frame women within only a few architectural elements. For instance, a picture by Jiang Xun (1764–1821) (Figure 2.3) might be compared with Lu Ziwan's (1833–1911) (Figure 2.4). Jiang shows a woman peering out from behind heavy curtains hung at a moon window. The window floats abstractly in the center of the pictorial surface of the right-hand page as though a portrait picture within a picture; off to the left is a grove of bamboo. Lu tightens the composition by bringing the elements more closely together and shifts the scale so that window and figure appear closer to the picture plane. The brushstrokes articulating the drapery, in particular, are less discretely anonymous, more strongly hooked at the ends, while those articulating the face are more feathery. Style differs;

Figure 2.3 *Shinü at Moon Window.* Jiang Xun. Lithographic print. Published in Ye Jiuru, ed., *Sanxitang huapu daguan* (Shanghai: Dahua Shuju, 1925) 13 (*juan* 1): 32b–33a.

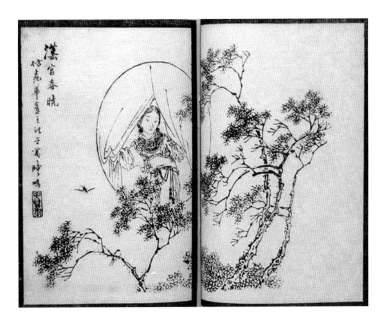

Figure 2.4 *Shinü at Moon Window.* Lu Ziwan. Lithographic print. Published in Ye Jiuru, ed., *Sanxitang huapu daguan* (Shanghai: Dahua Shuju, 1925) 16 (*juan* 4): 13b–14a.

compositional elements and their general arrangement, even the suggestion that the space of the page participates in creating a boundary between *shinü* and viewer do not. The *shinü* remain contained because the pictorial surface itself becomes a kind of playful artistic conceit, even in spite of—or precisely because of—spatial ambiguity.

In sum: The *Sanxitang* volumes reveal certain structured renderings of the *shinü* genre that are rhetorical in nature. The poetic tropes and delicate beauty of the *shinü* acknowledged in the title pages perhaps suggest a configuration of *shinü* that enfolds them within overlapping literary and aesthetic realms and, to push the interpretation, to an expressive representation in which the *shinü* stand in for the poet or painter, or serve as extensions of the individual poet's or artist's mind. Historically, the "genre" did do cultural work in that way, as evidenced in this study by Chao Xun's 1897 manual especially, in which representations of women became unmoored from specific meanings and were flourishing just as educated men were scrambling to recreate their own image, and the court itself was in an extended state of decline. And Ye's drive to make a genre out of disparate images pulls them into a similar project. His manual highlights the ways in which text—addressing female gender—is caught up and entwined with pictures within the genre of the *shinü*. He praises the "ancient" past, in spite of a general absence of ancient paintings in the manuals; he creates a history for the objects that is as made from whole cloth as the creation of an uncontested space for the *shinü* themselves; he privileges, in short, a particular educated elite male view of women just as he promotes a particular literary style of seeing and painting them.

Within the manual, then, the textual threads pulling through and around the images bind them to a discourse of gender that is conservative: It straightforwardly composes women by status and social roles as maternal, pure, chaste, untouchable. Gender was embodied on pictorial surfaces and produced and reproduced when the paintings were published, circulated, and one-to-one copies were made of them. For the editor Ye Jiuru, a key part of his project was importing *shinü* paintings into the domain of a particular language and keeping them there, divorced from a different discourse calling for female equality of the May Fourth Movement (1919) and earlier. The genre, defined internally between the manual covers, aimed to "speak" of a one-dimensional femininity that was deliberately conceived to be out of touch with contemporary progressive discourse on women's roles and lives and was made distinct from modern representations of "new bodies."

A Modern Genre

But was it really so out of touch? The relationship between the pictures and real life deserves more attention. By focusing on how the genre impinged on the visual culture surrounding women during this moment of gender reinvention (rather than its isolation from it), we might begin to more fully comprehend its relevance to modern women. Such consideration returns us squarely to the problem of genre definition: the schematic operations of genre in relation to imaginative interpretation. While the straightforward didactic content of the pictures makes them easy to categorize (and to talk about, or potentially to dismiss), the beholder's response to them brings them into the realm of the personal, "legible imagination."

For on the one hand, just as they provide a comforting image of familiarity, multiples of "beautiful women" in the manuals who were alike also challenged and complicated the emotional demands that pictures made on the viewer. That is, their alikeness created about them a mood of comfortable familiarity into which a viewer might relax, much like the toddler under the care of a palace woman within secure imperial walls, on the first page of pictures in the manual. And yet, on the other hand, the emotional and social appeals of such "likeness" left the genre vulnerable to a sometimes wayward imaginative response that might in fact have prevented individual pictures from neatly fitting within genre classification in the first place. We've already seen points at which figuration of *shinü* might trouble the discursive legibility of the pictures, from tiny disruptions of the rhetoric by the slightly ambiguous body of the caregiver in the painting attributed to Su Hanchen, to ambiguities of the space in which the *shinü* resides, and even the notion of painting as connected to the timeless cosmos becomes slightly problematic when cast against the time-bound problems surrounding the real imperial collection of which it was a part.

But to backtrack for a moment: As for the "likeness" between pictures within the manual's covers, it seems it is precisely the case that finding sameness of form and style is encouraged in the manual and that this would be part of Ye's process of containing the *shinü* within the realms of legibility described above—by keeping them uniformly alike and distinctive, bound inside a particular visual history. Similar to the figure painting volumes (*renwu hua*) in the *Sanxitang* set which begin with a taxonomy of facial features (borrowed from physiognomic manuals and published in the nineteenth-century figural editions of the *Mustard Seed Garden* painting manuals), the *shinü* volumes include their own compendium of eyes and noses at the beginning of the manual. It contributes to and participates in codification of figure and face. In the first preface to the manual, the painter Wang Xiangyan's comments on the relationship of *shinü* painting to figural painting help to clarify the function of the facial motifs:

> Although the genre of *shinü* painting emerges from figural painting, it still is more difficult than figural painting. There are twice as many who seek to create resemblance to beautiful women (*meiren*) but they don't want them to look like truly real beautiful women of their own time. They seek not to be vulgar and for transcendence. At the same time they do not turn their backs on ancient method. Of these three things, always if you satisfy one then you miss another.

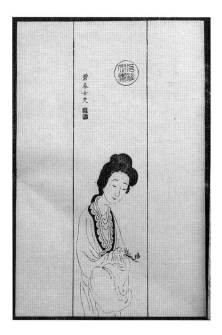

Figure 2.5   *Tang Jiaming*. Lithographic print. Published in Ye Jiuru, ed., *Sanxitang huapu daguan* (Shanghai: Dahua Shuju, 1925) 14 (*juan* 2): 5a.

Figure 2.6   *Model of Full Body*. Published in Ye Jiuru, ed., *Sanxitang huapu daguan* (Shanghai: Dahua Shuju, 1925) 13 (*juan* 1): 9a.

Wang's emphasis on transcendent imagery would seem to point to a purely semiotic understanding of the brushstrokes creating the female body, unconnected to the "vulgarity" of real life except through the material, calligraphic gesture of the artist's brush. Noses, hands, eyes participate in a grammar of the human form. In practice, however, by the nineteenth century if not earlier, the motifs were used in painting portraits. There are records of portraitists studying with specialists in *shinü* painting[33] as well as records of portraitists such as Xu Dong who, for instance, lived in the Little Qinhuai courtesan district of Yangzhou and specialized in making portraits of the courtesans there,[34] and most revealingly, famous portraitists such as Xu's teacher Ding Yicheng (fl. 1794–1823), who painted generically beautiful women for commissioned real-life portraits. One story relates that one of Ding's patrons in Yangzhou commissioned him to paint a portrait of his beloved concubine who was seriously ill; he revised it six or seven times and still the concubine felt that the image was not a good likeness, much to Ding Yicheng's disbelief. Eventually, the story goes, he made a picture of a generic *meiren,* or beautiful woman, and only at that point was she satisfied and proclaimed that the painting looked like her.[35]

There are approximately thirteen paintings in the *Sanxitang* manual that could be considered portraits, featuring one figure, typically in a studied three-quarter pose against a blank ground, gazing with an equally blank expression out of the pictorial space. The portrait of Tang Jiaming (Bichun nushi, n.d.), daughter of the painter Tang Yifen (1778–1853) and his prominent wife, Dong Wanzhen (1776–1849), is composed as a portrait (Figure 2.5).[36] The image, in vertical hanging scroll format, is impressed with one of Emperor Qianlong's seals (*Shiqu dingjian*), revealing Tang to be the focus of a connoisseurial eye. However, what Tang looks like is difficult to say, since her appearance matches that of other *shinü* in the manual; more precisely, she is the mirror in face and clothing of the full body model at the beginning of the manual (Figure 2.6).

It is critical to note, however, that although compositional elements tend to be similar throughout the manual, and styles can resonate, styles quite clearly also diverged. Some styles are immediately and easily identifiable as coming from the hand of contemporary well-known artists. A good example is a selection of prints from the series *Gujin baimei tu* (One Hundred Beautiful Women from Past and Present) by the late Qing Shanghai print artist and painter Wu Jiayou (Youru, d.1893), which are prominent in the third volume of the set. Originally the lithographic images were published as part of his painting treasury, *Wu Youru huabao*, in 1908.[37] The style of the image is mass-produced and easily recognizable; the aura of the original, if an aura exists, is attached to a printed object, not necessarily to the painted one from which the prints were drawn. Wu's professional connection to the illustrated newspaper *Dianshizhai huabao* (Studio for Touching the Stone Illustrated News) and *Feiyingge* (Fleeting Shadow Pavilion) compilation of pictures further renders these images "newsworthy," and outside the connoisseurial search for an authentic original. That is to say, the capsule biographies on the images highlight the function of the image to pass along information much as a newspaper illustration might do, or, at least, to raise questions about whether the text preceded the image, so that the picture would have been illustration, primarily, to a story. Moreover, the distinctive style of Wu's painting has absorbed some of its immediate context, becoming identified with a certain type of journalistic realism.[38]

The "real" is expressed through the reproduction of Wu's pictures in the manual, in other words, but it was to be suppressed as well. To counter the flow of *shinü* into the "real" in the manual, inscriptions of biographical information on the paintings are removed. Here, increasing the illegibility of the overall image, in a matter of speaking, by literally removing words from it, increases the legibility of the *shinü* figure. Wu's portrait of Ban Jieyu (b. 48 BCE), for instance, shows a woman leaning over her studio table, paintbrush and fan in hand (Figure 2.7). Ban is known for

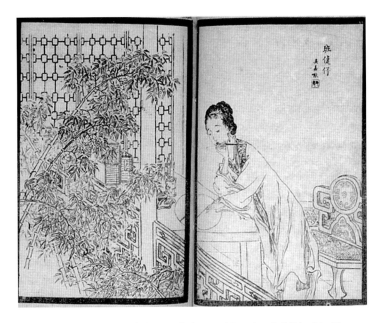

Figure 2.7 *Ban Jieyu*. Wu Jiayou. Lithographic print. Published in Ye Jiuru, ed., *Sanxitang huapu daguan* (Shanghai: Dahua Shuju, 1925) 15 (*juan* 3): 15b–16a.

her strict observance of social etiquette to the point that her official court title, "Jieyu," supplanted her real name; the meticulous attention Ban paid to status and rank is strangely echoed in the manual, where not only her name, lost to time, but also her story has been deleted, leaving behind only an iconic image. The meaning of the image resides symbolically in her surface appearance; she becomes the incarnation of feminine circumspection once again, distanced, if not too far, from her life as an illustration in mass media. Her mass existence is downplayed in favor of a unique one; her biography is downplayed in favor of iconicity.

In short, if the genre, then, was determined by an internal "likeness," it did so not only through pictures that looked the same but also on their own terms were connected with everyday life. But what I want to argue is that in both cases—the intersection with portraiture and newspaper print culture—what seems to be threatening is not that connection to the real, per se, but their threat to what I call the "legible imagination."

By "legible imagination," I mean the imagination that depended on the interplay between text and picture to exist, and seemed to bracket out "the real." For Ye Jiuru recognized—surprisingly, perhaps, in light of his rhetorical positioning described above—an imaginative dimension of the pictures in the manual, and even encouraged it. He saw engagement with such pictures not simply as a moment for learning about proper gender roles but in more profoundly personal terms and identified it with a kind of long-lived elite imaginary. For Ye Jiuru, as we have seen, before painting a *shinü*, it was important to understand the aesthetic mood and boundaries of the world that she inhabits. These boundaries permitted the viewer to understand that the depicted woman was giving way to genuine expression of otherwise discrete emotion. But significantly, he also says that the painter and viewer could pass through those boundaries. Collapsing representation and real space together, Ye writes that only the old-style depictions of architecture, many lost to time, were so fine and precise that looking at them was like entering into them, bodily. That crossing of boundaries (i.e., that boundary between illusion and reality) is what the aspiring painter should aim for. This was an imaginative process, in the end, a private interior one, but still one that depended on collapsing a particular style of painting with a shared elite literary past (including an appreciation for Liu Xiang's texts on virtuous women).

In this light, Ye's argument that contemporary painters of women—such as Hang Zhiying, the painter of the woman in the cigarette advertisement—fail because they look only to new embodied styles peopling Shanghai (*xinti*) and not to ancient bodies (*guti*)—takes on deeper significance. These "new bodies," after all, populate the spaces of a new kind of imagination: the theater and entertainment districts. Unlike the legible "old bodies" of the *shinü* in Ye's manuals, including full-body and half-body compositions (*quanshen* and *banshen*) diagrams, for Ye, a "new body" denoted paintings of bodies modeled after prostitutes and actresses. These are women who belong within the most commercially fabricated and "vulgar" public space of the day. Commerce is a visual arena in which, as Francesca dal Lago points out in Chapter 3, indexicality and symbolic value dominated as a mode of interpretation. It required a certain superficial interpretation, as all spectacles ultimately do. The connection of imagination not to intimate spaces of contemplation that were highly personal and individual but to commercial mercantile structures—and beyond that, to a nameless crowd—would seem, for Ye, to have some dire cultural consequences.

And yet, it turns out, these new representations are not all that different from the *shinü* paintings. After all, pictorial representation of these "new bodies," too, were subject to framing in painting manuals and subject to certain rhetorical pressures emerging from the same histories and figural typologies as did the *shinü* genre in the *Sanxitang* manuals. For instance, lessons from a painting manual advertised as modern (*xinpai*) aimed primarily to teach artists something about painting the human body (*renti*) and programmatically address difficulties of learning how to render "new bodies." The *Compendium of New-style Art, Classified Pictures*, published in 1922, includes in its six volumes one dedicated to figural painting. The manual uses the more scientific term of "category" (*lei*) to organize its pictures, in contrast to the literary terms used by Ye. An explanatory introduction describes the basic "how tos" of making figural pictures, from lips, eyes, ears to facial shapes, methods of painting hands and feet, half-body depiction, and whole-body depiction, as does Ye's manual. Of the body it notes,

> first [roughly] model the body with shading in order to create the correct shape and attitude. Next, go over the body with a heavier brush, and following that make distinctions about fashion. Regardless of whether you're a student painting entertainers, the ancients or foreigners, and even common men and women, in all cases you must start with the simple and enter into the complex, and only afterwards fill in the environment.[39]

Modeling with dark and light is the technical foundation for figural imagery, in other words. Paint the body first, the dress second, and the place in which the figure is located third. This mode of rendering form would to Ye's mind no doubt be what he calls "European" in essence and may be one shorthand way of defining corporeality in artful representation of the "new body." The *Compendium* further aligns its lessons with international painting practice by offering taxonomies of body parts that are drawn from model books published by the Jesuits at the Tushanwan painting studio in their mission on the outskirts of Shanghai, though, as Ellen Johnston Laing points out, the models are much simplified.[40]

Mimesis would seem to supplant aesthetics in the *Compendium*. It is still the case however, that the problem of depicting demeanor or attitude is not divorced from corporeality. Learning to paint is learning to aim for a kind of aesthetic expressivity of painted subject achieved through fully capturing the fleshy body in paint. Corporeality bound to this world is more complex than simply getting the body "right" by painting in an illusionistic style. A painter must "advance from the superficial to the profound in a marvelous way," as the *Compendium* editor puts it; he or she must make a visual argument, and, likewise, Ye underscores the same process by describing the body as a site for what ought to be deeply reserved emotion rather than fleeting smiles. Ye sums up:

> If you want to express emotion but stop at propriety, and to convey [women who are] chaste, demure and remote, then you ought to be indebted to the ancient school. There are those who still stick to the ancient methods. However, those who ignore such instructions imitate European-style painting, dress women in a contemporary manner and work on coquettish smiles and glances that are extremely seductive. By looking at [the work of] Gai Qi [1774–1829] and Fei Danxu you can compare for yourself and you will see who is elegant and who is vulgar.

The formal echo between representations of propriety in demeanor in *shinü* painting and advertising images gave rise to some interesting reactions: "China has lots of women who are healthy and strong," Lu Xun writes, "but calendar painters only draw sickly ladies so weak they could be knocked down by a gust of wind. This kind of sickness does not come from society. It comes from painters."[41] Writing in the 1918 radical journal *New Youth* (*Xin qingnian*), Lü Cheng observes that it was the inaccuracy of anatomical depiction that was "really lamentable. All beauty of art is lost and meaningful thoughts that great works of art show is lost."[42] That is, painted representations of women don't look "real" enough to function as high-order images that elicit complex response.

And further examination of "new bodies" and "old bodies" in the manuals reveals another significant similarity: depiction of social roles. That is, unlike the largely quiet, calm figures in moments of stasis and immobility in the *Sanxitang* volumes, in the *Compendium,* the connection between corporeality and demeanor is only articulated in fully worked-out pictures—of men, women, children, foreigners—all of whom are engaged in different projects and activities related to modern life. Women are depicted at different stages of their lives, doing things like playing badminton, or quietly sitting with knees drawn to chest, relaxing. *Compendium* readers can see women mature, marry, and turn into mothers. And yet, the absorption of the mother as she sits on a bench in an undefined place reading her newspaper, while her little boy sits at her feet equally involved in his own, is a somewhat surprisingly direct pendant image for the painting attributed to Su Hanchen in the 1925 *Sanxitang* manual (Figure 2.8).

Conclusions

Concluding this survey of painting manuals through time, it is useful to rehearse basic shifts in the genre that align with discursive if not actual changes in the place of women in society. In 1897, the genre signified practically anything, just as debate about the place of women in society was intensifying and possibilities for women to reinvent themselves expanding. Even the 1906 preface to the purportedly modernist album of images connects *shinü* not just to the state, or to the artist, or to social status and taste, but sweepingly, to the cosmos. By 1916, the genre was refocused and brought back to the purview of serious painters, through regulation. *Shinü* matched lofty scholars, just as the "moderate" position on women centered on polite discussion of equality between men and women. By 1922, following the passionate debates of the May Fourth Movement, old-style *shinü* were entirely eclipsed by new representations of modern corporeal "new bodies." And in 1925, a backlash against the corporeal body finds force in Ye Jiuru's manuals, which feature *shinü* as legible models of exemplary behavior, articulating a notion of gender that concerns itself with discursive social roles, in the main, but also deals with the spaces of femininity and habitual demeanor.

Figure 2.8 *Reading Newspapers.* Lithographic print. Published in *Xinhai tuhua fenlei daquan* (Shanghai: Xin Xin Meishushe, 1922) 3: 62.

The emergent language of the *shinü* genre in the late Qing and Republican era, in short, responds to and participates in shaping the personal subjectivity of women. The genre follows a rhetorical trajectory through the earliest to the latest painting manuals that does not sustain distance, as rhetoric might, from lived experience of women. And if formalism and rules that make Ye Jiuru's new formulation of the genre result in a reductionist articulation of gender possibly too simple to be relevant to contemporary readers, still, at the same time, Ye's genre construction is complicated by the fact that *shinü* paintings are powerful images. In the *Sanxitang* manual, the genre practically becomes the mimetic stuff of reality itself. Its legibility is always messy and complicated by demands placed on the eye by the paintings to see things differently; hence, or partly hence, the incarnation of the *shinü* in the manual causes them to spill quite literally into their immediate social setting (and to require protective boundaries and walls). It is this resistance to control, perhaps, that gives the project of defining gender through the act of painting it such urgency.

Can *shinü* painting become modern? I have characterized Ye Jiuru's articulation of it as deeply *retardaire*, and it would be an easy matter to position it against the modernity of the *Compendia*'s corporeal (and European) bodies. It is the body as a site of potential excess of meaning that in the end seems to have eclipsed the old-style *shinü* genre, shadowing its disappearance in the *Mustard Seed Garden Painting Manual* in 1922, and its disappearance, as well, from pictorial histories of the "modern" woman. But is it only in contraposition to the corporeal bodies that the legible bodies of the *Sanxitang* volumes fail to be "modern?" From our vantage point, it would seem that the fleshy bodies of the "fashionable beauties" carried the day. They embodied newness, however complex that newness might be. But paradoxically, pictures of women that are informed by European painting traditions and new gender performances do important cultural work in the same rhetorical fashion as the genre does in Ye's articulation of it. Discourse informing pictures of women has shifted, though perhaps not dramatically. The changes to representations of women as their own social surround changed may seem natural and evolutionary, in other words, though they deliberately contravene one thing—the legible imagination— leaving roughly everything else intact.

It is the aesthetics of unattainable beauty and exemplary character preoccupying painters of *shinü* that opened up the act of painting pictures of women to a particular legible imagination and made it not just an aesthetic practice but also a social one. It was the painting student's own competence that allowed the artist to enter into that imaginary space; associations of *shinü* with a familial "type" of pictures, in the end, generated an appreciation for a kind of cultural dream-work. Modernity was not simply available through the superficiality of consumer society; for certain educated members of society who were able to make associative connections, it asked for a deeper, more contemplative and imaginative response. For that reason, the schematic operations of genre were essential, and the imagination was not a substitute for "the real;" it was a return to the real, particularly if we recall Ye's insistence that *shinü* possessed "meaning for our China." Painting *shinü* was deeply connected to a fundamental aspect of everyday life; the manual prefaces reveal it was critical to debate about representation and its place in the construction of a gendered female subject. It is this adaptation of the *shinü* to the demands of the modern era that makes the genre so potent, and in the end, so new.

3

How "Modern" was the Modern Woman?
Crossed Legs and Modernity in 1930s Shanghai Calendar Posters, Pictorial Magazines, and Cartoons*

Francesca Dal Lago

Yuefenpai (calendar posters) portraying beautiful pinups in modern garb produced in Shanghai, Canton, and Hong Kong during the first part of the twentieth century have come to public attention as highly collectible items in the Chinese antiques market. Replicas grace the walls of restaurants, and their nostalgic styles have inspired designer clothing and accessories by Vivienne Tam, Alan Chan, and others.[1] Retro-chic is at the heart of a mass cultural and academic relapse into the legend of prewar Shanghai, a city much romanticized as a unique site of Chinese modernity.[2]

The commercial aesthetic of *yuefenpai* combining, as it does, elements of folk art, product advertising, and Chinese and Western graphic design,[3] makes these calendar posters an exemplar of what Heinrich Früehauf describes as "urban exoticism," in which the hybrid cluster of visual and cultural associations constituted an Other reality with broad appeal. As Früehauf writes:

> In an Oriental context, exoticism always bears the double-features of "popular" and "elite" aesthetics: at one end the term was associated with avant-garde trends… and at the other end its connotations are firmly rooted in the realm of popular culture.[4]

Designed to market new Chinese and Western commodities to an emergent urban middle class, calendar posters were capitalizing on the experience of the "exotic," provided to consumers through their formal values and the up-to-date nature of the products they advertised. The posters did not claim a high artistic status and were only produced for the mass audience, flourishing in a space largely unfettered by the ideologies of representation associated with the cultural elite.[5]

There is another feature that renders the posters particularly interesting: their different, often contrasting, layers of significance that provide an entrée into the complex system of gender representation of the Republican

---

* This essay, here modified, first appeared in *East Asian History* 19 (June 2000): 103–44.

period, when "woman" occupied an unprecedented importance in public cultural discourses.

Women were almost the sole subjects of the advertising campaigns for an extremely large variety of items, from cigarettes to liquor, from cosmetics to pesticides. This essay concentrates on images of women posing singly, both for their prominence within the genre and for the specific theoretical possibilities offered by this type of representation, deliberately excluding images of women in pairs, women with children, and women portrayed as historical and mythical characters, which were nevertheless very popular. Finally, I have chosen the period of the late 1920s to mid-1930s, since it is during this time that calendar posters attained their most mature and distinctive artistic character, before their painterly flavor was replaced by photography.

Within this selection of single portraits, the discussion turns especially to women seated with crossed legs, a specific bodily posture that, in China as in the West, can possibly be read both as a signifier of modernity and of sexual availability. As suggested by a 1930s article in the magazine *Jindai funü* (The Modern Woman) entitled, "Do You Know How to Sit, Stand and Walk?" a correct bodily posture could in fact constitute an important element in the image of a modern lady. The article provides specific suggestions on what could be defined as a kind of "modern postural etiquette," that is, how to sit, walk, and stand in the many social occasions offered to women in contemporary life that were previously open only to men.

> The contemporary woman has to mix with crowds in large halls, and must therefore be aware that her every action and movement will produce a certain effect—so she must practice striking elegant poses. In the past, attention to feminine beauty only focused on details, but now it embraces everything. Moreover, female clothing used to consist of voluminous gowns and long skirts or pants, and apart from the head, the hands and the feet that could hardly be glimpsed under such enveloping garments, the body was as if encased in a box with most parts remaining hidden. But now with the change of fashion, the beautiful shape of the body and an elegant figure are revealed. If we think about it, our clothes today have shortened to reach just below the knee, and arms are mostly completely exposed so that the shape of the bust is clearly revealed in all our actions and movements: what other possibility of concealment then remains?[6]

The article goes on to give explicit examples of the postures befitting the modern woman, warning that "crossed legs are not appropriate in grand halls and large assemblies" (Figure 3.1). Its underlying supposition is that women, exposed for the first time in their "every action" to the gaze of the crowd, have become a prime and exotic object of public scrutiny. Moreover, even a bodily posture may signal an achieved status of modernity, highlighting with its visual and moral connotations the constructed image of the new woman.

The choice of this specific bodily posture is supported by the argument proposed in this essay, which centers on the discussion of the ambiguous character of gender representation in *yuefenpai* posters. In fact, the "Modern Girl" or "Modern Woman" in these posters was presented as a symbol of progress, mirroring the way in which she was generally portrayed in popular magazines and literature; she would thus establish a "model" that fed contemporary mass culture, initiating a process of emulation among middle-class, urban females. The rehashing of this exotic icon in consumer marketing had a profound impact on modern fashion trends.[7]

In addition, the advertisers often paired beautiful women with luxury goods, reinforcing their general condition as "objects" of social and economic desires. Crossed-legged women, then, were possible reminders of sexual availability. To support this argument, I draw on magazine images and satirical cartoons, particularly of the fashionable "New Woman" in modern Shanghai, as well as explore erotic antecedents in the depictions of women from earlier periods of Chinese visual culture.

Figure 3.1   From an article by Jing Ying, "Do You Understand How to Sit, Stand, and Walk?" In *The Modern Lady* (April 1930): 4–5 (detail). The instructions read: "(A) A natural and appropriate sitting posture. (B) Crossing legs is not appropriate in public places. But if one must rest for a short while, then the position of the feet should be more or less similar to that shown in the picture (the tip of the left foot slightly inclined to the left, the tip of the right foot slightly inclined to the right). Be sure not to make the mistake illustrated in (C) with the tips of the feet positioned out of alignment in an ugly pose."

"New Woman" as Cultural Construction in the Republican Era

In her book *The Gender of Modernity*, Rita Felsky discusses women's greater visibility in late nineteenth-century European literature as "a powerful symbol of both the dangers and the promises of the modern age,"[8] an argument that can equally apply to Chinese popular media and literature during the first part of the twentieth century. Felsky states:

> In the early twentieth century the figure of the New Woman was to become a resonant symbol of emancipation, whose modernity signaled not an endorsement of an existing present, but rather a bold imagining of an alternative future.[9]

It is not surprising that the subject for the cultural and commercial negotiations at work within the calendar posters should be the figure of a woman. Females were exhibited as the most visible and direct beneficiaries of China's economic and social progress, and the modernized image of woman[10] soon became the embodiment of a new, progressive, and modernized nation "configured as a new object of modern knowledge and as a new subject of potential social change."[11]

This phenomenon had a historical *raison d'être*. Since the first attempts at political reform in the late nineteenth century, women's emancipation

had been a central issue in the cause of rescuing China from what was perceived of as an advanced stage of economic, cultural, and moral decline.
One of the first successes of women's emancipation was the abolition by
imperial decree in 1919 of foot-binding. Soon, reformers started advocat-
ing women's education, albeit for reasons instrumental to the emancipation of the Chinese population as a whole. Also in 1919, the first woman
was granted permission to attend Peking [Beijing] University, and after the
demise of the imperial examination system in 1911, women's suffrage alli-
ances were founded all over.[12]

As a result of the development of industrialization and education, more
women found employment outside the domestic sphere and greater financial independence to explore personal interests. The New Woman became
such a recurrent trope in the popular media of the 1920s and '30s that this
stereotype of the independent woman soon obscured what in fact were the
still "unglamorous" conditions of the majority of the female population.

One could easily argue that, after 1911, little had changed in women's
status in the countryside, with the exception perhaps of the banning of
foot-binding. In some rural areas, because of the deepening economic crisis
and local warfare, women's status might actually have worsened. Peasant
girls were often sent to a life of indentured labor in the factories of the big
industrial centers or sold to brothels in the red light districts of cities like
Shanghai, Beijing, and Canton.

In reality, even educated women still lived under the shadow of traditional morality. In a quite revealing statement, originally published in
1931, on the occasion of a "Symposium on Chinese Culture," a certain Miss
P. S. Tseng recounted the social history of women in China with ostensive
feminist sympathies yet displaying many of the contradictions still existing
between self-emancipation and reliance on traditional values. She ended
her speech with the following remark:

> Therefore, for the modern Chinese woman, let her freedom be
> restrained by self-control, her self-realization be coupled with self-sac-
> rifice, and her individualism be circumscribed with family duty. Such
> is our new ideal of womanhood, and to realize this is our supreme
> problem.[13]

The functional role of the Modern Girl and her relevance to the general
cultural discourses could be discerned in literature and cinema, as scholars
have extensively addressed.[14] Concerning the trope signified by the term
nüxing (lit. female sex, often translated as "woman" or "women"), prominent in May Fourth literature, Tani E. Barlow has written:

> *Nüxing* was not a self-reference. It was not initially an "identity" for
> women at all. Like the recuperation of *nü* ["woman" as employed
> before the May Fourth Movement] as a trope of nationalist univer-
> sality in masculinist discourses, *nüxing* was a discursive sign and a
> subject position in the larger, masculinist frame of anti-Confucian
> discourse...[15]

The subordinate position of women—either servants or daughters of wealthy families—is poignantly portrayed in Ba Jin's 1935 novel, *Family*. The novel describes the tragic story of the young generation in a land-owning family in Sichuan, where educated women, despite their façades of emancipation and bobbed hairstyles, are still very much pawns in the games played by their male partners.

Even the recently acquired and much publicized job independence might largely be a myth, judging from the account provided in the short story "First Morning at the Office," published in 1935 by Mao Dun, about the feeling of intimidation of a young female clerk during her first day of work in a predominantly male environment:

> "Ah—" rasped the manager. Miss Huang felt he was looking at her. She lowered her head, a bit flustered ... The interval probably wasn't very long, but Miss Huang thought it would never end. Suddenly a hand fell on her and she looked up with a start ... As Fatty pointed out various items on the document he was giving her, his beady black eyes traveled up and down her body. Appraising her clerical ability, no doubt. "You understand it all?" Fatty asked formally, in conclusion. Then, still smiling faintly, he suddenly inquired, "Tell me, Miss Huang, are you living alone or with your family?"[16]

The compromised freedom of women in the workplace emerged in several films. In the early 1930s, movies such as *Yecao xianhua* (Wild Flower, 1930), *San'ge modeng nüxing* (Three Modern Women, 1933) and *Xin nüxing* (New Woman, 1934), the narrative focuses on the different choices offered to the Modern Woman, but all efforts to attain real autonomy, as regards both career and love life, are doomed to failure. The subversive character of these emerging "independent" subjects is contained by reabsorbing the woman's role within the traditional family structure, annihilating her transgressive behavior through violent death or suicide, or channeling her hopes for "personal" emancipation into the emerging discourse of leftist ideology.[17]

Furthermore, the figure of "woman" had become the symbol of the high degree of urbanity that was to be found in modern Chinese cities—the very embodiment of "modernity." In Ye Lingfeng's *Shidai guniang* (The Girl of the Modern Era), a serialized short novel published in 1932, the protagonist, Lily, is a promiscuous and exhibitionist woman who casually shifts from one lover to the other. Her character—constructed with the specific purpose of offering her up for visual display—personifies the ultimate representation of the Modern Girl, constantly pursuing the latest fashion in all activities of her life, from clothes to sex.[18] The voyeuristic and erotic "Modern Girl as femme fatale" recurs in the neo-sensationalist fictions by Liu Na'ou (1900–39) and Mu Shiying (1912–40). The women in these novels are generally defined by a high-speed lifestyle, obsession with the latest fashion trends, and erotic inclinations.[19] Leo Ou-fan Lee has remarked how these figures are mostly constructed with the sole purpose

Figure 3.2 *Madame Ho-Tung* (1618–64). Attributed to Wu Zhuo (17th century), probably of the school of Leng Mei (Qing Dynasty, first half of 18th century). Ink and color on silk. Arthur Sackler Museum, Harvard University Art Museums.

of conveying the authors' own fascination with the city and the urban spectacle. "'Modern Girl,' like her male suitor, is but a narrative figure in a staged urban landscape… She is made to serve the larger purpose of representing the city."[20] Indeed, the fashionable and morally dubious female doubled as the head-spinning, intoxicating experience offered by the city, with the potential risk of being branded as marketable and disposable merchandise.[21]

Beautiful Ladies in Traditional Art

There is a venerable history in China of using women as the subject matter for artistic representation. Women have been depicted alone or in groups, enjoying leisure, performing music, embodying virtues, and so forth. They have also appeared in erotica and in paintings of courtesans and concubines, whose representation was indexed with codified sexual symbolism.[22] The analysis provided by Robert Maeda of a painting in the Arthur M. Sackler Museum, Harvard University, *Portrait of a Lady* (Figure 3.2), is illuminating in this context.[23] In the lascivious position of the woman who sits with one leg raised on the side of a bed, Maeda identifies the depiction of a morally unchecked attitude, in China often associated with prostitutes and women of the demimonde.[24]

> In erotic art … an artist would use certain motifs as well as figure stance to indicate the character of the subjects … the manner in which a figure was posed in Chinese figure painting could often be a subtle but important clue to determining that figure's social status.[25]

According to Maeda, the pose—"unwelcome to high-class Chinese women"—combined with the frank and bold look of the sitter, could be taken as a signifier in the representation of women of loose morals.

Classic Chinese love poetry provides some specific references for the representation of women in Chinese traditional culture. Anne Birrell has remarked that in poetry women are mostly described as being in a confined situation, waiting and longing for a reunion with their departed or estranged lover—the only excitement granted to their secluded life.[26] Likewise, in later Chinese painting, women are mostly represented in a sheltered environment, be it a room, a terrace, or a walled garden. Such representations imply a voyeuristic engagement with a world normally hidden from view. By creating an ideal juxtaposition between the open space of the viewer and the sequestered space of the sitter, these paintings evoke the idea of "visual penetration" and erotic fantasies.[27]

A later occurrence of the ankle-over-the-thigh position is found in an anonymous early eighteenth-century album, auctioned in New York in 1991 (Figure 3.3).[28] In a luxuriously decorated boudoir, a woman, seated on the edge of her canopy bed with right leg spread across left knee and her

Figure 3.3 *Figures in Interior Settings*. Album of twelve leaves. Ink and color on silk. Published in Sotheby's catalog, New York (November 25, 1991), Lot 62.

robe partly open, pulls her companion toward her, explicitly linking the position with the act of sex.

Other similar examples include late Qing decorative paintings in which the subject of beautiful women is executed in an extremely realistic style, based on conventions that were adopted in professional circles after their introduction to China by foreign missionaries in the early eighteenth century. The realistic style became quite common in "low" art thanks to its highly descriptive, "hands-on" character. Cahill has remarked how this style would actually conform with the purpose of these images, in which women "offer themselves as accessible objects of sexual desire, and are presented for inspection and visual enjoyment along with their settings."[29] The "ankle-over-the-knee" position often recurs in this style, the woman facing the viewer and resting one leg over the thigh, thus exposing the tiny lotus (bound) foot. The eroticism is heightened when coupled with partial nudity, such as in two paintings in which one of the women is coquettishly arranging a flower in her hair in an extremely seductive pose (Figure 3.4). This position is cited in a 1948 cartoon by Zhang Guangyu, representing arguably the most scandalous female character in the history of Chinese literature,

Figure 3.4 *Beautiful Women*. Late Qing Dynasty. Reprinted in *Shanghai youhuashi huaiguzhan* (Shanghai: Shanghai Art Museum, 1995), n.p.

Figure 3.5   *Figures from Jin Ping Mei: Pan Jinlian*, 1948. Zhang Guanyu. Reprinted in Zhu Jiaming, ed., *Lao manhua* (Jinan: Shandong Huabao Chubanshe, 1999) 3, no. 76.

Pan Jinlian of the novel *Jin Ping Mei* (The Plum in the Golden Vase) (Figure 3.5).

Crucial to these compositions is the resulting, close-up exposure of the bound foot, one of the most intensely erotic signifiers of Chinese sexual practice.[30] On the basis of self-presentation these images could be related to the photographic portraits of famous Shanghai courtesans circulating during the early part of the twentieth century, such as those in the 1917 collection *Haishanghua yinglu* (A Record of Images of Shanghai Flowers).[31] Another local iconographic source was *nianhua* (New Year prints), a popular genre that is closest to the calendar posters as images for wide dissemination. New Year prints, colorful woodcuts pasted on doors and walls for auspicious and decorative purposes at the beginning of the new year, often include beautiful ladies as one of their traditional subjects.[32] In a late nineteenth-century print (Figure 3.6), traditional references pack the composition, in which the richness of detail symbolizes auspicious prosperity. In this image, the lady is reclining, her tiny lotus feet in sight and surrounded by children and several erotic signifiers. Given these precursors, the erotic significance of legs and feet could hardly be ignored when examining the *yuefenpai*.

Figure 3.6   *Happy and Prosperous Family*, 19th century. New Year print. Reprinted in Yao Qian, ed., *Taohuawu nianhua* (Beijing: Wenwu Chubanshe, 1985), pl. 34.

Women as Commodities in Calendar Posters

The archetypal crossed-legged *yuefenpai* beauty is an early poster by Zheng Mantuo (1888–1961) (Figure 3.7).[33] The close resemblance of this painting to the hairstyle and clothing of the courtesans whose portraits are included in the 1917 collection suggests it was made in the early 1920s. The figure presents an interesting transition between the genre of the early professional paintings of women executed in realistic style and the later *yuefenpai* genre. Zheng Mantuo's image also functions to support the idea of a possible association between the *yuefenpai* girl and the figure of the prostitute or woman of the demimonde. Apart from the formal resemblance of this work to the photographic portraits used by courtesans to increase their visibility in the new urban context, the bunch of flowers strategically but unrealistically placed on the bent leg suggests an additional layer of meaning. *Hua guniang* ("Flower Misses") in Chinese is a term often used as a euphemism for prostitutes. In addition, flowers—fresh or in the form of jewelry—were often used as standard items of decoration by courtesans in the brothel, as Gail Hershatter remarks in her detailed study on prostitution in twentieth-century Shanghai.[34] Generally speaking, flowers are a recurring decorative item for the *yuefenpai* girl, figuring prominently both on her clothes and/or around her figure.[35] While it would be far-fetched to suggest that all the figures could be read as representations of prostitutes, it is necessary to remark how many of the attributes and visual traits employed in this genre could, in fact, equally be related to the world of sexual pleasures and the marketing of women.

Figure 3.7   Poster, early 1920s. Zheng Mantuo. Gouache on paper. National Art Museum of China, Beijing.

An advertisement of a banking institution stylistically datable to the late 1920s provides another early example of *yuefenpai* signed by Zheng Mantuo (Figure 3.8).[36] The woman, pictured alone in a modern interior, sits nonchalantly on a brightly covered armchair, her body arched and gently turned, looking out at the viewer. She has a stylish, wavy hairstyle, and her foot is crossed behind her leg. Her fashionable, short dress allows a peep at her feet, which sport a pair of trendy high-heel leather shoes. Certain iconographical references in the picture could be associated with the scopophillic tradition of Chinese painting. For example, the large hibiscus plant—which provides a foil for her body by mimicking her arched position—is commonly associated with sexual imagery because of the

Figure 3.8   Calendar Poster for a Zhejiang bank, late 1920s–early 1930s. Zheng Mantuo.

color and the carnal sensuousness of the flowers. The interior of the room is decorated with a floral art deco-style armchair and a Western-style painting on the wall; the window of paneled glass affords the view of a park; the whole place is imbued with a sense of modern luxury. This type of representation calls to mind a recurring trope in Chinese love poetry: the forlorn woman imprisoned in a luxurious boudoir awaiting the return of her lover. Anne Birrell describes this poetic motif thus:

> A woman in love is typically shown to be in her boudoir, not only isolated from her lover but also from all human contact … She spends her idle hours in luxury reminiscing about the past, dwelling on memories stimulated by certain boudoir objects … she is not free to leave, nor free to love another man, nor free to rid her mind of obsessive love … The boudoir symbolises imprisonment.[37]

Along these lines, Zheng Mantuo's image could be considered as a contemporary 1920s version of the modern woman in the boudoir. The fashionable clothing, the hairstyle, and the bourgeois interior that construct the modernity of the representation are framed by the close space of the room, whose boundaries are underlined by the open vista beyond the window. The room is depicted as modern, and yet it is couched in tradition as a limiting enclosure for women's activities. In this representation the spatial and metaphorical unit of the room becomes a gendered space, so far as it provides the ideal site for intimate encounters where a woman supposedly awaits the visit of a man. "Room" is also a spatial unit whose importance Gail Hershatter discusses in relation to the figure of the courtesan, highlighted by the recurrence of the word *fangjian* (room) in the terminology of brothel practice.[38] The representation of a woman enclosed in a luxurious room could not fail to suggest an idea of accessibility and the erotic intimacy of the figure offered for display.

Zheng Mantuo's women are generally portrayed as long and lanky figures; a certain disjunction exists between the rounder traits of the face and the more ethereal, seemingly asexual body. A relevant feature in these earlier images (Figure 3.9) is their transitional character in the representation of the body from the traditional "fleshless" kind—what John Hay has defined as "the absent body, a body lacking an objectified and solid quality"[39]—to the later Westernized and curvaceous figures (Figure 3.10).

Figure 3.9   Poster for Nanyang Tobacco, ca.1920s. Zheng Mantuo. This poster portrays one of Zheng's trademark "archaic" types of "traditionally shaped" women sitting on a railing with legs only partly crossed.

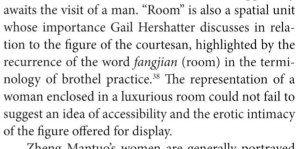

In addition to examining the iconography, it is important to expend a few words to explain the technical aspects of the calendar posters. Conceived as an amalgam of local and foreign expressions, which made it one of the most original products in twentieth-century Chinese visual culture, *yuefenpai* developed a distinct representational method to achieve heightened realism in color and anatomical definition.[40] In the first decade of the last century, Zheng Mantuo perfected the technique called *cabi dancai* ("rubbing and applying pale washes of color"), which combines techniques of Chinese *gongbi* (colorful fine-brush) painting and photographic retouching. Borrowed from ancestor photographs, the technique was made amenable to mass advertising through the addition of watercolor shades similar to the color washes applied in traditional Chinese *gongbi* painting to a charcoal sketch. The face—the central and starting point of each composition—would first be modeled through rubbing, shading, and erasing charcoal powder with the aid of a cotton wad or a paper tortillon. This would result in a soft, illusionistic effect without the use of line drawing. A pale wash of watercolor would then be added to create the rouged skin, mainly on the cheeks and the forehead.[41]

Figure 3.10   Poster for Haig Liquor, 1934. This is a highly provocative image of a woman. Note her self-contented expression, the particularly sensual pose (crossed legs and exposed armpit), the see-through dress, visible underwear, high-heeled shoes, and the Moet & Chandon champagne bottle with two glasses, underscoring the sexually charged mood of the picture.

Another example of the "crossed-legs motif" is provided by an early 1930s[42] advertisement for the Nanyang Brothers Tobacco Company[43] signed by Xie Zhiguang (1900–76), an established author of *yuefenpai* advertisements (Figure 3.11).[44] The figure poses in what can be recognized as a more Westernized stance: Dressed in a bright red *qipao* (body-hugging, one-piece dress with a mandarin collar), the woman sits comfortably in profile crossing her legs and leaning against the back of the armchair with a raised arm and a self-confident gaze. The absence of decorative props and the photographic effect of fading on the borders of the image reveal a close relation to Western advertising styles. The only concessions made to Chinese representational modes are the dress and the red, fleshy flower that she holds and with which she is visually identified. The relaxed elegance and the overall simplicity of the composition, which is focused on the sinuous curves of the body, are recurring traits in contemporary Western advertisements. In a 1930 example from *Harper's Bazaar*, the woman sits in a similar three-quarter pose wearing a luxuriously tailored silk robe and looking sideways intently (Figure 3.12).

To attempt to reconstruct the erotic impact that exposed legs might have had on the Chinese viewer at the time, it is useful to compare these images with Western advertisements of roughly the same period. A survey of two major American fashion magazines[45] has revealed a recurrent focus on women's legs in numerous advertisements (Figure 3.13). While the immediate justification for this new type of

Figure 3.11   Poster for Nanyang Tobacco, early 1930s. Xie Zhiguang. Note the photographic effect of fading the lower section of the image.

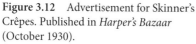

Figure 3.13   Western advertisement for Van Raalte silk stockings, late 1920s.

Figure 3.12   Advertisement for Skinner's Crêpes. Published in *Harper's Bazaar* (October 1930).

subject matter is to be connected with the recent raising of skirt hemlines to the knees and the subsequent marketing of rayon stockings,[46] the obsessive recurrence is fetishistic. Whether or not the depiction of "Chinese" legs is directly influenced by this type of representation, by exposing the legs to the knee and displaying them frankly, the Hatamen cigarettes (a brand owned by the British-American Tobacco Company) advertisement conflates a set of meanings in which the modernity of the position is linked with Western fetishistic implications while evoking the erstwhile erotic bound feet.

Two photo collages published in 1934 and 1935 in the pictorial *Liang you* (Friendly Companion) demonstrate the significance attached to the image of a woman's crossed legs. In a photo-reportage in the May 1934 issue entitled, "Such is Shanghai: Shanghai's Tall, Wide, and Big (in English "Outlines of Shanghai")," legs are displayed as one of the city's attractions, together with double-decker buses, movie theaters, a memorial tower, neon cigarette advertisements, traffic lights, and other modern wonders (Figure 3.14). The images thus come to represent both the temptations and the threats offered by the mesmerizing experience of the city, but it is still accepted as an idiosyncratic characteristic "thing" of Shanghai, one of the metropolis's inherent attractions. The second collage, from the February 1934 issue, features a seductive urban lady amid the "Excitements of the Metropolis" (the English title of the photo spread is "Intoxicated Shanghai") (Figure 3.15). The "excitements" include American movies like *King Kong*, the racecourse, variety shows, skyscrapers, and jazz bands. Whatever the context, the sexualized woman and her legs have become an intrinsic symbol of the city's modern appeal.

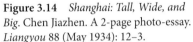

Figure 3.14 *Shanghai: Tall, Wide, and Big*. Chen Jiazhen. A 2-page photo-essay. *Liangyou* 88 (May 1934): 12–3.

Figure 3.15 *Intoxicated Shanghai*. Chen Jiazhen. A 2-page photo-essay. *Liangyou* 85 (February 1934): 14–5.

On the arousing power of feet and legs, a revealing passage is found in a 1928 short story by Ding Ling, "A Woman and a Man." The story describes the encounter between Wendy, a modern and sexually liberated married woman, and her prospective lover:

> [He] kicked lightly at the gravel on the pathway with the tips of his shoes. His feet were numb and it was still cold. Once more he caught sight of her two little feet encased in leather shoes. Her two well-rounded calves were hugged by sheer, flesh-tinted silk stockings which reached up to her knees. Once again he saw how charming they were, and felt like rubbing them.
> "Are you cold?' he asked.
> Wendy shook her head. When she noticed where his gaze was directed, her smile broadened.[47]

We have already observed how, in Chinese traditional culture, out-stretched postures and a seeming lack of control over one's body could be associated with loose sexual habits.[48] It is therefore not unrealistic to conclude that the use of Western-inspired casual positions and traditional Chinese representations of easy women could overlap in images such as the one just introduced, to create a distinctive sense of modern sexual availability. The woman exhibits her body and legs for the consuming gaze of the beholder who will enjoy the Hatamen cigarette with the pleasurable associations suggested by the images of this seemingly *available* beauty.

Another type of figure that became a recurrent model for many 1930s women representations was that of the prostitute, singsong girl, or high-class call girl. She, more than any other, could in fact "wear" the clothes of modernity, providing a direct visual reference for the images disseminated by *yuefenpai*. At the same time, it was often difficult to tell a respectable woman from a courtesan, an ambiguity that could only be discerned by the trained eye of an insider, whose tricks of the trade were disseminated through a rich literature specifically produced on the subject.[49] Ironically, the prostitute could enjoy a great amount of independence and personal freedom, and therefore it is not strange that many of her fictional representations exhibit quite a complacent attitude toward the profession. As the epitome of the fashionable girl, the prostitute accounted for one of the most visible female types in the milieu of the international metropolis.

Prostitutes, courtesans, and concubines had always occupied an important place in the social and cultural space of urban China. They can be considered among the most visible female types in the history of Chinese culture—whether in literature, poetry, or painting. In the late nineteenth and early twentieth centuries, this pattern had evolved so far that prostitutes had become ubiquitous in the urban cultural context and turned into a much-treated topic in popular cultural outlets such as gossip magazines, movies, and "Mandarin Duck and Butterfly" (sentimental love) stories. The distinctive taste for modern and Westernized items that characterized 1920s and 1930s urban culture equally affected the demand for sexual services and the way femininity was constructed. Prostitution in fact had become "a sign of China's participation in universal human history," making Shanghai, like Paris, an important symbol of its acquired modernity. Finally, prostitution was the most direct way in which women could acquire monetary value as items of consumption.[50]

The high-class prostitute figured prominently in both realist and experimental literature. In the 1935 play by dramatist Cao Yu, *Sunrise*, the main female character is an ex-country girl who becomes a shrewd and cynical courtesan kept by several wealthy men in a luxury hotel.

The short story "A Vision," by Lao She, centers on an educated woman who, after the bankruptcy of her family, has no choice but to turn to prostitution for a living. After many years of separation, the lover of her youth returns to discover the truth about her new profession:

> My tentative questions as to how she was managing were brushed aside as, lighting a cigarette, she exhaled smoke like an adept, leaning back with crossed legs to watch the smoke wreaths, the picture of empty-headed brashness.[51]

The somewhat depraved but enticing morality associated with the figure of the high-class courtesan and/or sexually unrestrained girl provides the probable context for a mid-1930s advertisement for Huadong cigarettes, which has already been referred to in Chapter 2 (see Plate 1).[52] The woman sits alluringly in the imagined setting of a Western garden with an airplane gliding pass. She wears a garish *qipao* made with a flowered fabric and is herself surrounded by flowers. The head and hands executed in a hyperrealistic mode and the extraordinarily smooth texture of the skin are justified both by the painting process—the face being the central element of the *yuefenpai* composition—and by the need to provide a quasi-physical experience of the flesh. The staging is natural and informal, but the distinct separation of foreground and background could very well suggest a photographic studio with a *trompe-l'oeil* backdrop rather than of a genuine garden scene.

A suggestive hypothesis for this disjunction between body and setting is the marketing policy that formed the basis of the success of Nanyang Brothers Tobacco. In the commercial war waged against the British-American Tobacco Company, then the leading tobacco corporation, Nanyang eventually focused on the nationalistic feelings that American anti-Chinese immigration policies had stirred up all over China. Nanyang's advertising policies thus began to promote the company's tobacco with patriotic intent by urging Chinese citizens to smoke Chinese cigarettes and boycott foreign ones.[53] In this context, the modern icon of the beautiful lady has been repositioned in a setting that looks traditional but not to the point of transforming her into an old-time beauty. Her conventional character is artificially staged, providing a fitting metaphor for the modern, pleasurable, and yet "Chinese" Nanyang cigarette.

Another interesting detail is that the lady is "consuming" the commodity that she advertises, a practice that was adopted only at a later stage in the *yuefenpai* development. Rarely, in fact, is the woman shown interacting with the product she advertises, unless the advertisement is specifically targeted to a female audience, as in the case of cosmetics, some medicines, and fabrics. The reason normally given for the absence of the advertised product within the framework of the image is related to the way in which *yuefenpai* were created, the images most often being executed in bulk and only lately selected by companies for their advertisements.[54] Equated to the status of a "beautiful object" for purchase, the *yuefenpai* girl is as passive as the object she is supposed to advertise. Whether or not she can or wants to consume the commodity is irrelevant to the product's marketing purpose.

The appeal and success of this strategy is confirmed by the marketing boom enjoyed by tobacco companies in the first part of the twentieth century, which made the market for cigarettes in China almost as large as that in the United States.[55] As stated by Sherman Cochran, in the words of a British-American Tobacco representative who later returned from China to become a successful copywriter with the American advertising agency in New York, the British-American Tobacco calendar became its "big advertising smash every year" and was distributed "in every nook and corner of the Nation."[56]

In a Chinese context, the images of beautiful and accessible women depicted in advertising were effective first because they were both reminiscent of and distinct from the Chinese tradition of women's representation and secondly, because they fulfilled society's scopophilic expectations.[57] The act of smoking a cigarette would be associated with that of "visually consuming" the beautiful woman and thus increase its pleasurable sensation. The "gendering" of the cigarette, associated with the figure of woman because of the specific advertising strategy, is suggested by the lyrics of the ballad, "Elegy to the Cigarette," composed in 1905 for Nanyang Brothers Tobacco during their aggressive campaign against their British-American rival:

> Ah cigarette,
> You have the word American in your trademark for everyone to see
> So I must give you up along with my bicycle
> Our love affair
> Today must end
> Ai, cigarette please don't harbor resentment
> Perhaps a time might come when we meet again,
> But it must be after Americans abrogate the treaty.
> Then as before I shall be able to fondle you.[58]

Conclusion

The form of *yuefenpai* was created to introduce modern commodities to China's urban market during a time of intense economic, social, and cultural change stimulated by the cultural penetration of Western mass marketing practices. Created to advertise *foreign* and *new* products to a Chinese audience, *yuefenpai* posters had to combine different sets of cultural conventions in order to suggest at the same time modernity, exotic appeal, and familiarity. To achieve such a goal, an iconographical source was provided by the genre of the "beautiful ladies": paintings or popular prints in which the images of beautifully adorned and erotically enticing women were exhibited with a set of conventions suggesting to the viewer an intimate and seductive atmosphere. In the process, the set of meanings normally attached to that traditional genre trickled down to the modern representation, creating a framework not dissimilar from the traditional way of viewing women as objects of visual pleasure.

We have noticed how the loose arrangement of a woman's body in earlier representations and more specifically the act of spreading and raising the leg could often suggest a degree of sexual availability of the sitter toward the viewer. Several markers associated with the traditional genre of erotic painting were actually encoded in the modern images: the boudoir and its sexually loaded connotations of confinement; flowers and their specific erotic associations; deep and elaborate interiors that, inviting the act of visual penetration as they did, had been tied to explicit eroticism. By translating these images into modern terms, *yuefenpai* capitalized on a combination of new forms and old contents. Establishing a kind of visual continuity with the traditional representation of the beautiful ladies, the usual flapper-like position of the Modern Woman would take on different connotations from those in the Western context.

Because of her hybrid character, the *yuefenpai* beauty expresses the sense of exhilaration created by the experience of modernity in places like Shanghai during the early twentieth century. Her glamorous veneer, her bold postures, the luxurious settings in which she is often displayed, and the exotic products that she advertises coalesce into a powerful portrait of modern life. At the same time, the subtle mixture of transgression and coyness, trendiness and historical reference, materialistic and fanciful allusions in these representations provides an appropriate metaphor for the endless and fantastic possibilities made available in the metropolis, which was buoyed by the awareness of their ephemeral quality and by the thrill of change.

With her astonishingly smooth skin, wearing a colorful and revealing *qipao*, adorned with pearl necklaces and pendant earrings, the *yufenpai* girl is both present and removed, touchable and unreachable, the stuff of reality and dreams. Her modernity has a reassuring sense of familiarity, and she is alluring insofar as she complies with a traditional iconography of eroticism, offering just the right combination of the old and the new. This is probably the most significant element to her "modernity:" a knot of tangled messages that erase and reinforce one another, capturing all the ambivalence that is a true symptom of modern times.

4

Fashioning Appearances
Feminine Beauty in Chinese Communist Revolutionary Culture*

Hung-yok Ip

When scholars address the issue of womanhood in the Communist revolution (1921–49) and under the Maoist regime (1949–76), they generally attend to such dimensions as political vocation, family, and work.[1] They sometimes briefly discuss the issue of appearance as well, but more often than not they assume that the revolutionary era and pre-Cultural Revolution stage of the Communist regime were dominated by asceticism, androgynous clothing, or both. According to Antonia Finnane, androgynous clothing was always "in vogue" during the revolution and eventually set "the tone for women's dress in China at large."[2] As for the pre-1966 regime, according to observers and insiders alike, attention to feminine beauty was mainly criticized as petit bourgeois or bourgeois and as an unwelcome outcome of gender oppression.[3] In addition, the Cultural Revolution has been identified as the high tide of "masculinization" and "puritanical asceticism."[4] It is thus no wonder that some scholars regard women's enthusiasm for feminine beauty as a "new" development in the post-Mao era.[5]

But is it true that the post-1976 interest in beauty is a departure from the revolutionary decades and the period before the Cultural Revolution? If not, the current emphasis on the "newness" of such interest obscures a significant part of Chinese women's gender-specific experience in the pre-reform stage of Chinese Communism. In this essay, I argue that the interest in feminine beauty in a broad sense—including the admiration of beauty, the belief in the desirability of being beautiful, the practice of self-beautification, and so forth—was always present in the revolutionary process.[6]

Situating the issue of feminine beauty in China's modernization, I first note that revolutionaries—men and women alike—despite fiercely criticizing women's preoccupation with appearance, did not reject but helped to sustain the interest in female beauty by mobilizing self-beautification practices and images of attractive women for political purposes. I then investigate how social-interpersonal interactions reinforced the perception that female beauty was rewarding. In addition, I demonstrate that the Communists did not always reject the concept of beauty and even accepted the practice of self-adornment. After showing how Communist men and

* A longer version of this essay was published in *Modern China* (July 2003): 329–61.

women created a milieu—political, interpersonal, or cultural—that did not powerfully challenge the interest in beauty, I focus on women themselves, venturing into the question of how women activists developed their own feminine aesthetics. Although I mainly concentrate on the revolutionary decades, I also examine how the concepts and practices related to female appearance in the revolutionary era manifested themselves in pre-1966 Communist society. I deal with the experiences of politically active women from divergent social backgrounds who joined or sympathized with the Communist movement. I will show that these women played an important role in building a most perplexing legacy of attitudes toward feminine beauty in post-1949 Communist society. Sometimes, together with men, they fought against the attention to self-adornment. Yet not only did they participate in the political, interpersonal, and cultural processes that sustained the interest in beauty, but they also beautified themselves.

Challenging the Established Model(s) of Feminine Beauty

Since the second half of the nineteenth century, Chinese historical actors have viewed female beauty as relevant to the nationalist project of strengthening China. This politicized attention led to a reevaluation of the Chinese tradition of self-adornment. In traditional Chinese society, attitudes toward women's appearance were ambivalent. Women were expected to attend to, but not be preoccupied with, self-adornment. In the Confucian discourse on womanhood, the essential attributes of a good woman—in addition to virtue, words, and work—included appearance. While traditional self-adornment had various aspects, modern thinkers and activists examining the relationship between the female condition and China's self-strengthening efforts focused mainly on foot-binding. Reformers such as Liang Qichao and Kang Youwei and revolutionaries such as Qiu Jin (a woman) believed that the female population's lack of education and bound feet made them ignorant and weak and were conditions that must be removed.[7]

In addition to criticizing foot-binding on nationalistic and pragmatic grounds, late Qing activists also castigated the practice as inhumane.[8] Arguing for women's independence and human dignity, they reprimanded those women who conformed to the traditional norms of beauty to secure men's favor. Qiu Jin declared: "When we heard that men liked small feet, we immediately bound them just to please them, just to keep our free meal tickets … Think about it, sisters, can anyone enjoy such comfort and leisure without forfeiting dearly for it?"[9]

Not only did pre-Communist activists attack the traditional Chinese norm of female beauty, but they also gradually noted and criticized the Western approach(es) to women's self-adornment. In Ding Ling's *Mother* (1932), a piece based on her family's experience in the late Qing era, the title character envies the rights and freedom enjoyed by women in the West, but she does not fail to notice the similarities between "foot-binding" and the "tiny waist," both aimed at engineering the female body: "They [Western women] don't bind their feet; they bind their waists … They can go to school, though, and are free to do all kinds of things."[10] Though Ding Ling's portrayal may not accurately represent what her mother said on the eve of the 1911 revolution, Mao's call for women's emancipation shows clearly a young radical's critical stance on both Chinese and Western approaches to female appearance. Mao wrote on July 14, 1919: "[W]hy must women have their hair piled up in those ostentatious and awkward buns? Why must they wear those messy skirts clinched tightly at the waist?"[11]

While the late Qing political actors rejected traditional norms of beauty but not necessarily the practice of self-adornment,[12] the May Fourth activists on principle opposed both. In their imagining, the Modern Woman not only should be politically active, nationalistic, and educated but should also show her independence and dignity by refusing to adorn herself.[13] In chastising both Chinese and Western ways of self-beautification, the May Fourth activists did not intend to replace them with a new model. Instead, they invented a "politically correct" appearance that they thought signified the absence of self-adornment: a face without makeup, a body without the burden of jewelry, straight short hair, and simple student uniforms in black, white, or blue.[14] Following their formulation, the view that the truly liberated woman should not be preoccupied with her appearance was shared by people taking different political stands in the 1920s and 1930s.

Confronting the commercialized version of the New Woman, the New Life movement defined a real "New Age Woman" as one who, in addition to demonstrating traditional virtues, was able to resist the lure of fashion.[15] Idealizing "Modern Woman" as patriotic, well educated, serious in political purposes, and uninterested in self-adornment, reformist intellectuals called fashionable women pseudo-modern to "regain their guardianship through debates about the qualities of the modern woman."[16] In addition, they criticized fashionable women as a group that lacked dignity, for they presented themselves as "toys" for others to enjoy.[17]

The Communist Rejection of Beauty Norms and Self-Adornment

Communists, too, held the understanding that the Modern Woman should rebel against beauty norms and forsake the notion of self-adornment. One goal of revolutionary politics, according to the Communists, was women's liberation from the male-dominated system of private property. Lack of adornment signified their liberation and dignity. Throughout the revolutionary process, quoting socialists such as Engels and Bebel, they highlighted women's humiliating existence in a male-dominated economy in which sexuality had to be traded for economic support. Within the conventional systems of private property, self-beautification, whatever its style, was a necessary device for women to gain any form of male patronage.[18]

Applying this theory to modern Chinese society, Communists proclaimed that, as the influence of the "feudal" tradition continued to prevail, women were (still) treated as undignified "playthings."[19] Moreover, in their view, there were abundant examples of "modern-style" exploitation of women. They noted that working-class women were pressed to sell their femininity to curry favor with their supervisors in the capitalist factories or to attract customers, whereas privileged and even educated women needed to adorn themselves to please their partners and thereby sustain their seemingly enviable status as warlords', bureaucrats', and capitalists' wives.[20] Russian women were presented as the opposite of their Chinese counterparts, as they were given the right to engage in the economic process and pursue a career, and thus gained freedom from all forms of oppression.[21]

In the Communist milieu, however, women's refusal to adorn themselves not only signified liberation but also was an important strategy in fighting for that liberation. Many Communist authors believed that women, especially educated young women, should take on a threefold mission of rebellion: against the patriarchal system of private property, against the disciplinary measures used to adorn the female body, and against their own attachment to self-adornment.[22]

In addition, Communists viewed non-adornment pragmatically: It was construed as an attitude and a practice that women revolutionaries should adopt so that they could contribute to the political—in this case, Communist—project of strengthening the nation and reshaping society. To understand the connection, consider a story about Fang Zhimin, the founder of the Northeast Jiangxi and Fujian-Zhejiang-Jiangxi Soviets. Circulated among and applauded by other revolutionaries, the story concerned his reason for marrying Miao Min in 1927. Reportedly, Fang explained that he simply could not settle for someone who was interested merely in "clothing, dressing up, and a comfortable lifestyle." For him, only women like Miao Min, who were indifferent to self-beautification and city frills, could become good "revolutionary wives" who not only supported their husbands but also sometimes worked for the revolution themselves.[23] Although we can hardly expect that every leading male revolutionary identified with this politicized approach to marriage, the story's popularity lay in part in its apt illustration of the Communist view on non-adornment. But that popularity was also rooted in the assumption that non-adornment had pragmatic value for the revolutionary project.

This assumption was, in fact, reinforced by the reality of the revolutionary life. Material poverty almost always, though not unavoidably, accompanied revolutionary struggle. On the eve of his execution in 1935, Fang Zhimin proudly "displayed" his poverty: "[S]ome old undergarments, a few pairs of socks… These are all I have." He then concluded: "It is our ascetic lifestyle that helps us persevere."[24] No wonder his heroic image in Communist history included his refusal to take a fashionable wife. Working in the urban areas, revolutionaries also had to wrestle with poverty. For instance, Xu Mingqing, a woman revolutionary who taught with Jiang Qing in Shanghai during the early 1930s, recalled that they were not paid any salary and that the food they ate was coarse.[25]

Under the circumstances, the will to resist fashion and self-adornment was perceived to help the CCP's (Chinese Communist Party) cause. When necessary, women revolutionaries had to give up items important not only to appearance but also to hygiene. For instance, during the Long March, female soldiers threw away many personal belongings so as not to burden themselves with their own "possessions." Many shared a single washbasin, which they used both to clean themselves and to cook. Many of these women had neither comb nor mirror, and they used their fingers to "tidy" their hair every morning (Figure 4.1).[26]

But while the Communists advocated the value of non-adornment, they also manipulated appearance strategically. That strategic use engendered disparate approaches to personal appearance and thus helped to sustain the interest in self-beautification.

Figure 4.1   *Woman Tidying her Hair.* Published in *Zhongguo Qingnian* 13 (1957): 23.

Designing Appearances I: Forsaking Self-Adornment for the Revolution?

In order to take on new institutional responsibilities, women revolutionaries found it necessary to embrace new appearances, which sometimes meant giving up self-adornment and what they personally considered pleasing. Some women became soldiers in the National Revolution when the Wuhan Central Military and Political Institute set up a training program for female radicals and recruited around 200 young and well-educated women; they included You Xi and Zhao Yiman, who later became Communists.[27] These young women were required to cut their hair,[28] a measure to which they voiced aesthetic objections (as discussed below in the section on the revolutionary aesthetic). Describing the life of the female student body in different revolutionary institutes in Wuhan at the time of the United Front, Christina Gilmartin also takes note of their "unisex" image as Amazons—their gray cotton uniforms, caps, and so forth. She asserts, writing of Xie Bingying and You Xi, that this unisex image "often expanded women revolutionaries' social space of operation and thereby facilitated their ability to command respect...in rural communities."[29]

In addition, for pragmatic reasons, the Red Army sometimes demanded that female peasant soldiers cut their braids. Meng Yu and Lu Guixiu, who became women soldiers in the Chuan-Sha'an Soviet base areas around 1933, did so when they were inducted.[30] According to Lu Guixiu, who was initially unwilling to relinquish her braid, a senior woman soldier explained to her why it was necessary: "Bobbed hair is convenient and sanitary. It is easy to take care of when you are wounded."[31]

Sometimes, women revolutionaries temporarily acted out alternative social roles. Yang Zhihua, the second wife of Qu Qiubai, was a good example. Considered by male revolutionaries in Shanghai in the early

1930s to be a very fashionable woman, she was assigned to establish connections among female workers in eastern Shanghai in 1930. To get her job done, she dressed like a woman worker.[32] In her popular novel *The Song of Youth*, Yang Mo, an author familiar with underground revolutionary life, created the image of an outstanding woman revolutionary, Lin Hong. Lin, a revolutionary intellectual who became a mill hand in a Shanghai cotton mill, always "wore a tunic and trousers" there.[33]

This strategic use of appearance meant both forsaking and employing the practice of self-adornment. Communists recognized the contribution that a fashionable and attractive appearance could make to their cause: Zhou Enlai's stylishness in the service of the revolution comes immediately to mind. Here we will concentrate on how the CCP used appearance, especially female appearance, to effectively further their political endeavors.

Designing Appearances II: Looking Beautiful for the Revolution

The Communists endorsed self-adornment for specific political purposes. Working in the city, the CCP assumed that fashion could be useful for its underground activities. Dressing up could enable revolutionaries to conceal their political identity. According to Mao Dun, his brother, Shen Zeming, and his sister-in-law, Zhang Qinqiu, were fashionably dressed because they lived in Shanghai. Shen wore a Western-style business suit, and Zhang was attired in a *qipao* and had her hair permed. They called this clothing their "disguise."[34] Such "disguises" helped revolutionaries to carry out their revolutionary mission. For instance, in 1937, one of the Long Marchers, Qian Xijun, went to Shanghai from Yan'an. She and her husband, Mao Zemin, faked their identities there: Mao claimed to be the owner of a wholesale company in the paper trade and dressed like one, and Qian naturally became the proprietress. Their main mission was to receive a substantial amount of funds, donated by the Comintern in US dollars, and then transfer the money to Xi'an. Qian Xijun and another Long Marcher, Wei Gongzi, adorned themselves in the fashion of well-off ladies, to bring the money to Xi'an.[35] Zhang Yuzhen resorted to this tactic in the early 1940s when she took a message to the Party Central for the Communists detained by Sheng Shicai in Xinjiang. Zhang, who became interested in "progressive ideas" when she was a student in Dihua, Xinjiang, dressed herself up as a rich and fashionable young woman and hid the letter written by the detainees in one of the heels of her leather shoes.[36]

Aside from using self-adornment as disguise, sometimes Communist women and men thought that, by dressing up, they could help to give the CCP a positive image. In the Yan'an period, Mao Zedong's daughter, Li Min, recalls, when Party members left their revolutionary headquarters for the Soviet Union via Xinjiang, they changed their attire in the Communist office there. Men put on Western suits, and women dresses (Figure 4.2). Westernized (and thus "fashionable") clothing was made available for children, too. When they returned from the Soviet Union, they had to return these clothes to the office. Li offered no explanation for this interesting dress code.[37] Possibly the Party wished either to present itself as a cosmopolitan contingent or to help its members fit into the Russian milieu. Less ambiguous was the case of Zhou Enlai and Deng Yingchao, who lived in Hankou. At the time of the Second United Front, they were invited by the Guomindang to join the People's National Assembly, which consisted of activists of different political stances. To represent herself as a qualified hostess and an active politician in a not-so-revolutionary context, Deng had her hair permed and, as one of her friends noted, put on a *qipao*.[38]

The Communists also realized that female beauty, created by an individual's clothing, hairdo, and style, could serve the revolution more generally. Song Qingling, Sun Yat-sen's widow, who offered significant help to the CCP, provides one example.[39] To some extent, Song's influence derived from her public persona, in which moral prestige was an important ingredient. Nevertheless, in the eyes of many admirers, Song was impressive also because of her appearance: They pointed to her dignified grace, sophistication, fragility, and tasteful but simple clothing (Figure 4.3).[40] Elegance combined with political commitment, tender beauty juxtaposed with courage: Song's image glittered in the circle of Communist sympathizers. Less eminent but similarly effective was Qiao Guanhua's wife, Gong Peng, who served as Zhou Enlai's press officer in Chongqing. Describing her as young, attractive, and intelligent, John Fairbank observed that Gong became a symbol of freedom of speech in 1943 Chongqing. As a "glamour girl," she was admired by most of the young Americans in the embassy.[41]

Pretty Women and the Revolution

It is not surprising that the Communists were aware of the political effectiveness of beauty; they also employed it aggressively in the realm of literature and the arts. Current research has emphasized the importance of the maturation of Shanghai's film studio and new film technology for the success of such actresses as Hu Die and Ruan Lingyu, and it has argued against the interpretation, dominant in the People's Republic of China, that attributed their rise to stardom to left-wing influence in famous studios in the early 1930s.[42] While this claim may be plausible, it should be noted that Communist artists used beautiful actresses

Figure 4.2 *Modern Woman in Western Dress*. Published in *Zhongguo Qingnian* 6 (1957): 33.

Figure 4.3 Song Qingling in Shanghai, 1921 or 1922. Published in Song Qingling, *Song Qingling xuanji* (Beijing: Renmin Chubanshe, 1992).

in urban media to spread pro-revolution messages and arouse popular discontent with the status quo. In the 1930s, some actresses were closely connected to the CCP and used their skills to aid its purposes. One of the popular stars working closely with left-wing playwrights and directors was Bai Yang. Born in 1920, Bai Yang achieved phenomenal success when she was only 16, cast as a young graduate of a vocational school in the film *Crossroads*. Showing how educated young men and women suffered in Chinese society, *Crossroads* was a huge success; according to a contemporary magazine, it made Bai Yang into "the girl of every high school student's dreams."[43] Thereafter, she was extremely active in a variety of stage and screen productions.[44] Viewing popular culture as a useful propaganda tool, left-wing and Communist writers also created beautiful female characters (played by attractive actresses) to be vehicles for their political messages. Around the time of the Sino-Japanese War, playwrights such as Xia Yan, Ouyang Yuqian, and A Ying employed female characters as "symbols of resistance." Hung Chang-tai argues that "in creating an effective resistance symbol, Chinese playwrights knew that they needed a character who was both visually attractive and smashingly entertaining."[45]

Apart from serving as symbols of resistance, beautiful heroines appeared as general emblems of moral integrity. Guo Moruo wrote his celebrated *Qu Yuan*, a popular play in Chongqing, in the spring of 1942, to criticize the Nationalist government's undermining of the United Front Strategy.[46] In the play, Qu Yuan is an upright official of the Chu state attacked by other aristocrats. His heroic voice is echoed by Chanjuan, his beautiful maid, who is concerned about Chu and aspires earnestly to moral perfection.[47] The play ends with Chanjuan's death: Drinking a poisoned cup of wine originally intended for Qu Yuan, she unwittingly completes her final act of devotion.

Legitimizing the Political Uses of Female Beauty

While the Communist authorities throughout the revolutionary process drew much attention to their advocacy of an ascetic style, they had not as loudly, publicly, and officially legitimated the use of feminine beauty for revolutionary purposes. Although I am not concerned here with an official theory on the use of female beauty, a careful reading of both men's and women's writings demonstrates that, in the Communist milieu, the deployment of feminine beauty for political ends was perceived to be fair and just.

The Party had already emphasized that its members should follow instructions at the expense of their own interests, long before such leaders as Liu Shaoqi and Chen Yun wrote articles to discipline revolutionaries in the Yan'an period. Since the late 1930s, the Party made it clear that, whenever necessary, CCP members should sacrifice personal concerns, including relationships, fame, power, and the like. The Communists' perennial fight against women's concern about appearance can certainly be seen as part of the required sacrifice of the personal. Conversely, the leadership's rhetoric on revolutionary commitment implied that, when the Party and Party interest demanded it, one should do everything possible—including exploiting one's appearance—for the revolution.[48]

In fact, in the 1930s and 1940s, in short stories, plays, and movie scripts written to serve the revolution, Communist authors portrayed without criticism the use of feminine beauty for political purposes. Aware of the power of feminine charm, some of them even went so far as viewing an extreme application of this charm—namely, the use of sexuality—as permissible in a righteous cause. During the Sino-Japanese War, some left-wing writers working for the CCP in the cities produced plays and movies that actively endorsed the use of the "beauty tactic" (*meirenji*). Again and again, Communist theatrical products made explicit the position that to fight for the righteous cause and to destroy the evil other justified the exploitation of feminine beauty. For instance, in the *meirenji*, Bai Yang played a young heroine who disguises herself as a lovely maiden and successfully distracts the enemy's guard.[49]

By translating self-adornment and beauty into political effectiveness in reality and in imaginative works, the Communists emphasized the power of being fashionable or beautiful. In addition, such power sometimes had a personal dimension: The audience's applause, young students' infatuation, and the enemy's softened attitude, imagined or real, toward female fighters in disguise—all these brought personal reward, in the form of social glamor, to those individuals who combined political progressiveness and feminine charm. But to understand how the interest in female beauty was sustained in the revolutionary process, we must consider interactions at the interpersonal level.

Appearance, Interpersonal Interaction, and Personal Life

Despite the Communists' rhetoric, which maintained that political qualities were the most essential in forming personal relationships, in the revolutionary context women's social standing—and marriage prospects—still to some extent depended on their appearance.

In the realm of courtship and marriage, Communists emphasized ideological compatibility but not physical attraction. For instance, in the late 1920s, many Communists living in Shanghai viewed the marriage of Cai Heshin and Xiang Jingyu, whom they considered an unfashionable woman, an ideal union based on ideological communion. Before their divorce, they were admired by others as an exemplary couple.[50] Allegedly, Fang Zhimin also stressed the importance of the ideological correctness of a revolutionary's spouse.[51] And in the early 1940s, when Deng Yingchao discussed romantic love, she presented compatibility between two youths in ideology, personality, and age as the basic criterion for choosing a spouse.[52]

Yet women who were thought beautiful by their comrades enjoyed significant prominence. Think of Mao Zedong's wife (his second, from 1930 to 1937), He Zizhen, in the Jingganshan area in the 1920s; Qu Qiubai's wife, Yang Zhihua, in Shanghai in the 1930s; Song Qingling meeting her Communist and non-Communist friends: All drew much attention from both their male and female comrades because of their appearance.[53] Their popularity indicates that women of different cultural backgrounds could be considered beautiful in settings ranging from a Communist-controlled area in the country to metropolitan Shanghai.[54]

It is also clear, however, that, beginning in the Yan'an period, as more and more well-educated people entered the revolutionary circle, educated and urbane women were increasingly regarded as being the most attractive.[55] According to the revolutionaries' gossip of the time, celebrated "beauties" in Yan'an included such women as Jiang Qing, Sun Weishi (Zhou Enlai's adopted daughter), and Zhu Zhongli.[56] Respectively an actress from Shanghai, a popular performer with Russian training, and a doctor who graduated from a medical school in Shanghai, they had one thing in common: a relatively metropolitan background.

Modern-acting and personable women enjoyed male patronage, as Communist leaders' pattern of courtship often made evident. Most attention-drawing was the relationship between Mao Zedong and his last wife, Jiang Qing (1914–91) (Figure 4.4), which generated much controversy among top Party leaders because of Jiang's problematic past and because of the close comradeship of some Party leaders and their wives with He Zizhen.[57] But Mao's preference for a young, modern, and pretty woman was echoed in other marriages elsewhere: that of Chen Yi and Zhang Xi, of Tan Zhenlin and Ge Huimin, of Xiang Ying and Li Youlan, and of Liu Shaoqi and Wang Guangmei.[58] This preference was also shared by those who occu-

pied lower rungs in the political ladder. In 1955, a woman named Liu Lequn, tormented by her husband's extramarital affair with a pretty and well-educated young woman, wrote a letter to the magazine *New China's Women*. She revealed that, in the 1940s, working as a Communist cadre in the liberated area (*jiefangqu*), her husband, Luo Baoyi, dumped his original girlfriend, whom he called a "rustic peasant-worker cadre," and married her.[59] In fact, the predilection for well-educated and urbane young women was so strong that, in the Civil War period, some male cadres saw the Communists' final occupation of the urban areas as a chance for them to grab modern women.[60] The Communist entry to the cities thus generated another new wave of divorce similar to that already seen in Yan'an.

Accompanying male revolutionaries' interest in modern women and their social visibility was the marginalization of "rustic" women. Female Long Marchers who lost their good looks and were unfashionable were excluded from Yan'an's most desirable social function—the dance party—as they did not know how to waltz and were unaccustomed to the intermingling of men and women.[61] Intertwined with their

Figure 4.4   Jiang Qing and Mao Zedong in Yan'an, 1945. Published in Rose Terrill, *The White-boned Demon: A Biography of Madame Mao Zedong* (New York: Morrow, 1984).

sociocultural marginalization were tragedies in their personal lives, when educated young women from big cities migrated to Yan'an and "business soared at the Divorce Office."[62] Observing what happened at that time, Ding Ling, who herself was not much liked by many female veterans, described sarcastically in *Thoughts on March 8* (1942) how revolutionary men used the excuse of "political backwardness" to divorce their unattractive wives. She noted: "Even from my point of view, as a woman, there is nothing attractive about such 'backward elements.' Their skin is beginning to wrinkle, their hair is growing thin, and fatigue is robbing them of their last traces of attractiveness."[63]

In the Yan'an period and after, many female Long Marchers enjoyed prestige and even influence.[64] However, some, including He Zizhen, were confronted with the irony that, despite being politically esteemed, they were personally punished for their lack of attractiveness. While the Communists invested much effort in deprecating self-adornment and the pursuit of beauty, they also acted politically and personally in ways that counteracted this effort. Their ambivalent attitude provided little support for their rhetoric, which sang the praises of indifference to appearance.[65]

The Revolutionary Aesthetic of Femininity

Revolutionaries did not reject the concept of beauty and sometimes even demonstrated an acceptance of female pursuit of self-adornment.[66] In the May Fourth and Communist Movements, radicals argued that a new female appearance created a new kind of beauty. In Ba Jin's popular novel *Family* (1931), Qin, a young woman radical, viewed short hair, which signified the "removal of discrimination against women," as pleasing: It "carries with it freshness of style and beauty in simplicity."[67] Qin—or rather Ba Jin himself—saw aesthetic value in the new look. In real life, some women activists were indeed impressed by the aesthetics of radical appearance. In 1923, Ding Ling met her mother's good friend, Xiang Jingyu, and saw "gentleness and quiet grace" in the latter, whose appearance—short hair, plain jacket, and dark skirt—was a far cry from that of fashion-conscious women.[68]

Aside from embracing this alternative notion of beauty, revolutionaries sometimes also accepted women's interest in appearance. This acceptance was revealed in their recognition of women's right to self-adornment, always expressed in class-based rhetoric that sympathized with those women whose longing for self-beautification was thwarted by unjust economic realities. By the early 1950s, Communist writers and artists were clearly using women's new access to what they wanted—self-adornment—to sing the praises of the revolution. The authors and artists transformed the issue of self-adornment into a site where revolutionary struggle could be made to seem more admirable to the suffering masses.

Take, for instance, the masterpiece of Yan'an's "new opera," *The White-Haired Girl*, rewritten continuously from 1944 until 1950. To highlight the poverty throughout the countryside in the 1930s, it showed the poor peasant girl, Xier, deprived of resources that she might use for self-adornment. Unable to afford flowers, she is excited by a simple red string that her father bought for her.[69] This condemnation of the unjust class system that denied some women access to self-beautification was accompanied by praise for the emancipation that gave women their right to self-adornment. Although *The White-Haired Girl* did not follow up on the changes that might be expected in poor peasant women's ornaments and clothing, another piece, intended for a more sophisticated audience, did. In *The Sun Shines over the Sanggan River*, which examines the unfolding of land reform in 1946, Ding Ling presented all the little details involved in Chinese peasants' participation in the revolutionary process. In portraying their joy, she approvingly describes peasant women looking for nice clothes (by rural standards) as they search well-off people's confiscated property.[70]

The Communists thus did not suppress interest in beauty, as they recognized the pragmatic value of beauty and self-beautification for the revolution, adored beauty themselves, saw beauty in a radicalized appearance, and accepted women's practice of self-beautification. While the question of how women responded to all this awaits further investigation, clearly some women did practice self-beautification in a revolutionary context in which the political value and personal rewards of beauty were confirmed, and beauty and beautification were to a certain degree endorsed. How, then, did women beautify themselves? In the revolutionary process, there gradually emerged a set of principles and practices pertaining to self-beautification, which I call "the revolutionary aesthetics of femininity."

The revolutionary aesthetics of femininity was marked by women radicals' attempts to adorn themselves in ways befitting their political identity and activities. In settings where they did not have to hide their political orientation, some adorned their radicalized image, despite its being rooted in the revolutionary spirit of non-adornment. For instance, when female students put on politicized attire at the military institutes during the National Revolution, they followed a modest approach to beautification, creating a look that would go along with their politics. A revolutionary appearance was attained by wearing unisex clothing made of rough, cheap cloth and cutting their hair short. But not wanting to be plain, they transformed their short hair into a form of ornamental display: According to Hu Lanqi, then a student at the institute, when the members of the women's training program as a collective decided to cut their own hair, some had their short hair styled. As for the feminine military uniform, one student found a tailor to make it more stylish.[71]

In the rural areas, young peasant women who enlisted in the army also modified their uniforms. Li Min, who was born into a peasant family and joined the Red Army in the Chuan-Sha'an Soviet Area in 1933, recalls that, when women soldiers were given the assignment of making uniforms, they took advantage of the chance to beautify themselves. Although they did not have good fabric, as Li remembers, they tailored the unisex uniform carefully to their figures. They used linen strands to cover the buttons, sewed decorative patterns onto their leg wrappings, and tied little red balls made of thin threads to their straw sandals.[72] Like women students in the National Revolution, these women peasant soldiers maintained but polished their radicalized appearance.[73] But unlike them, peasant women could not afford such luxuries as hiring a tailor; frugally, they used their limited resources to create aesthetic effects.

Frugality as an aesthetic principle was also sometimes adopted by educated and modern women radicals. Consider what happened in Yan'an, a stratified society whose limited resources forced the Communist leaders to live on rations and in caves: Women had little chance to wear chic clothing or to purchase expensive cosmetics.[74] Moreover, in Yan'an many revolutionaries—veteran female revolutionaries and peasant cadres in particular—did not approve of those who were eager to pursue beauty.[75]

Under the circumstances, even Jiang Qing, as first lady of the CCP, wore only what every woman cadre wore: a short jacket and pants. But according to a reporter for the *New York Times*, the way she wore them showed her "good taste" as an actress and thus her feminine charm.[76] The recollection of Mao's personal guard, Li Yinqiao, authenticates the American journalist's observation.[77] Jiang's concern for her appearance was not unique, however. In the Yan'an period, "peasant-worker" cadres who noted young women cadres wearing "revolutionary" military uniforms with ropes tied around their waists criticized this practice as coquettish.[78] Undoubtedly, these young women's approach to accentuating their femininity was very different from that of the Red Army's women soldiers in the Chuan-Sha'an Soviet Area. But they, too, were practitioners of the aesthetic of frugality.

Although the term "frugality" suggests plainness, restraint, prudence, and low cost, it is an elastic concept, differing with individuals' social, geographical, and cultural backgrounds; what people in one place found fashionable and extravagant may have looked homely and outmoded in another. The principles of modesty and frugality, adopted since the 1920s in openly revolutionary settings, were followed differently by some women activists who worked in the urban areas under the rule of the Nationalist government. These women activists did not put on revolutionary clothing, and those who were performers had professional reasons to pay attention to their appearance. However, by keeping their adornment frugal and modest (by urban standards), they made themselves look beautiful and made their image "politically progressive." For instance, according to an anti-Communist source, Yuan Xuefen, a famous Yue opera star who openly cooperated professionally with the left-wing playwrights Tian Han and Ouyang Yuqian and helped to organize underground Communist activities in Shanghai in the 1940s, looked serious and wore simple clothing.[79]

Simple clothing appears to have served as a political symbol, highlighting the difference between left-wingers' idealism and the establishment's decadence; performing with her comrades in wartime Sichuan, Bai Yang relied on her unpretentious appearance to impress her fans, presenting herself as a patriotic heroine.[80] It certainly is difficult to determine if there were any political reasons for Song Qingling to embrace a style that was both exquisite and simple. But evidently, her unassuming elegance matched her image as a righteous political fighter well. If she had looked like Chiang Kai-shek's wife, Song Meiling, her political idealism would have appeared much less convincing.

By the time of the founding of the People's Republic, the Communists had developed a complex legacy regarding female appearance, strongly influenced by politics and marked by contradictory attitudes toward and interest in self-beautification and beauty. In the following section, I briefly examine how this legacy operated in a different context: the pre-Cultural Revolution regime.

The Legacy of Female Beauty in the Communist Regime

Maoist China has been known for its advocacy of a simple, revolutionary appearance.[81] The media always encouraged Chinese citizens to struggle for political correctness and to put aside the pursuit of self-adornment. For example, in *Zhongguo qingnian* (Chinese Youth), a magazine targeted at young readers, a writer introducing the life and personality of Zhao Yiman described how this famous woman martyr showed little concern about her appearance and wore extremely short hair when she was in Moscow.[82]

In commenting on young men and women who paid attention to their own or others' looks, the Party was always critical. It did not hesitate to show its disapproval of what it called a deviant phenomenon: "Now, among the youths, those plainly dressed were looked down upon as being 'conservative' and 'shabby'.... Young men and women always envy those who wear beautiful clothes."[83] Party authorities de-emphasized the importance of appearance for love, stressing instead ideological compatibility.[84] When it identified men who intended to leave their rustic wives for pretty, modern women, it forced them to give up such bourgeois individualism and reform themselves.[85]

But at the same time, the state allowed the spread of messages that endorsed the concept of beauty and the practice of self-beautification. The political, pragmatic strength of beauty and self-beautification continued to be celebrated. In literature and the arts, heroic female characters sometimes employed self-adornment and beauty to achieve their political goals. In *Revolutionary Struggle in a Historic City*, a devoted revolutionary named Jin Huan uses her beauty to subvert a Japanese military officer.[86]

Whereas in the revolutionary past, nice-looking revolutionary women drew attention only in revolutionary circles, the social glamor of beautiful and politically eminent women was now nationally publicized. In state-sponsored media, positive representations of feminine beauty abounded: Images of such attractive and well-groomed elite women as Song Qingling were frequently seen nationwide in newspapers from the 1950s to 1960s. That beauty combined with political correctness or accomplishments was admirable was further reinforced by revolutionary novels and movies, whose heroines were often beautiful. While we cannot be sure how members of the Chinese audience responded to all this information, they were obviously aware of the connection between beauty and political worthiness. One author notes that, when she was growing up in the 1950s, female revolutionaries in varied cultural manifestations were always attractive.[87]

In addition, women's self-beautification, as before, was used to glorify the Communist revolution. In the new regime, female self-adornment was exploited to symbolize the fruits of the revolution—now redefined as the new China's prosperity. One author boasted: "as our economy develops, and our salaries are raised, we can certainly improve our lifestyle. In the past we only wore plain clothes, but now we can afford to buy one or two things made of velvet."[88] Propaganda films also used images of women trying on new clothes, to highlight the Communist state's impressive growth.[89] As beauty and beautification were endorsed, beauty tips filled women's magazines.

In the magazine *Chinese Women*, articles were dedicated to such subjects as the effect of colors on one's image and how to protect one's skin.[90] The article in *Chinese Women* on skin care said little about applying different kinds of cream, emphasizing instead the use of water and ordinary soap. It seems that, despite the Party's claims about China's prosperity, the principle of frugality was still at least partly in force. In the 1960s, after the Great Leap Forward, articles showed women how to make stylish clothes for themselves out of men's worn-out jackets or scraps of fabric.[91]

In the Communist milieu, hence, there was room, however limited, for women to beautify themselves. Their experience with self-adornment was determined by such factors as their class, education, and location. Among wives of central or provincial leaders, dressing up was, after all, not so unusual. As the regime became more stable, many paid more attention to beautification. To some extent they used politics to explain their interest in beauty. Shui Jing, the wife of the Jiangxi Party Secretary, reports that Zhang Xi, the wife of Chen Yi, was an amateur fashion designer who zealously took on the mission of modifying the *qipao* for the wives of Chinese diplomats so as to keep them warm and make them look beautiful.[92] Sometimes their public roles helped legitimize their self-beautification: They donned a *qipao* and makeup on "important occasions" without being criticized by authorities for being bourgeois. But they themselves wanted to look beautiful. Zhang Xi enjoyed trying on Romanian costumes; Wang Guangmei's dresses looked so beautiful that Shui Jing and Yu Shu, Zeng Xisheng's wife, eagerly borrowed her patterns.[93] Top leaders' young wives were not the only group of elite women who dressed up. Once the time of revolutionary military struggle was long past, veteran revolutionaries like Cai Chang were also interested in dressing well.[94]

In the face of this evidence, it is hard to conclude that upper-class women continued to adopt the revolutionary aesthetics of feminine beauty. Those outside the elite circle also retained their interest in self-beautification. Ordinary cadres and students always wore dark Lenin jackets and sometimes dressed in traditional-looking clothing and shirts;[95] rural women were always attired in high-collared tops and loose pants. But before the Cultural Revolution, in the urban areas, some women still wore makeup and perfume; others put on floral-patterned cotton blouses under their Lenin jackets.[96] While permed hair was certainly not praised as a sign of political correctness, it could be seen even among politically progressive students.[97] Rural young women who were praised as good models were certainly dressed in simple clothing, but they also tied their hair with ribbons.[98]

I have sketched the interest in female beauty during the revolutionary process and to some extent during the pre-Cultural Revolution regime, arguing for a more comprehensive approach to the analysis of womanhood under Communism. In addition to paying attention to such facets of women's experience as family, career, and political performance, we should consider how questions of appearance affected them both during the revolutionary process and in the Communist regime. Historians have already drawn attention to the Maoist regime's ambivalent attitudes toward career and domestic obligations.[99] But to understand better how Chinese women's femininity was constructed in the Maoist state, we have to examine in more detail how women lived their lives amid a complex legacy that both disapproved of and reinforced the interest in beauty.[100] How did women respond to and reflect on the practical and personal value of attractiveness? How did they create their own concept of beauty and sense of fashion within a culture that emphasized beauty in simplicity, modesty, and a politically correct appearance? How can we expand our understanding of women's lives in the Communist regime by integrating the issues of appearance, family, and career? These are important questions for those committed to the mission of reconstructing women's gender-related experience in the Communist state.

The Modern Girl (*Modeon Geol*) as a Contested Symbol in Colonial Korea

Yeon Shim Chung

In colonial Korea, the Modern Girl symbolized a sexual revolution, a revolution that began literally from the head. To become a Modern Girl, a woman should first cut her long hair—a signifier of tradition and Confucianism. Prominent female intellectual women at the time promoted the short hairstyle as practical and "modern." But what did modern mean? Starting in the 1920s, the adjective "*geundae*" (modern) appeared with frequency in Korean sources. Im In-saeng noted its widespread and seemingly random usage in his article "Modernism":

> Modern, modern … everything is modern. America is modern, so all the European countries are modern, as Shanghai and Japan were. Lucky enough to be close to the Asian cities, Joseon Korea is modern as well.
>
> Modern, everything is modern!
>
> Modern girl, modern boy, modern state ministers, modern prince, modern philosophy, modern science, modern art, modern suicide, modern theater, modern style, modern police, modern thief, modern magazines, modern love, modern architecture, modern boutiques, modern courtesan *gisaeng* (just in Korea) … endless … However, when asked what "modern" is, nobody answers.[1]

Because so many things were labeled "modern," it is difficult to render a definitive analysis of the Modern Girl. The short hairstyle is but one aspect of the iconography that opens up discussion regarding conflicts between tradition and modernity. Cutting hair represented a gesture of revolt/ reform because Confucians had previously banned this act in any public or private arena as a social offense, regardless of whether the individual was male or female. For women in early twentieth-century Asia, short hair strongly signaled Western-style feminist revolution. In Korea at this time, Henrik Ibsen's character Nora was emerging as a gender icon, a symbol of women's rights and women's liberation from domestic obligations. An anonymous writer in *Donggwang* (East Light) in August 1932 noted that Korean women should look to the example of Chinese modern women who had fought against foot-binding and long hair and who finally gained healthy feet and appropriate hairstyles.[2] The author claimed that, while the modern look might be associated with red lipstick, café waitresses, and vulgar dance girls, any society of "sports, speed and senses" would eventually require the cropped hair to keep up with the pace of modernity. Likewise, Western shoes and short skirts would be necessary conveniences and visual tropes for modernity's defiance of convention.

Because of its European origins, the Modern Girl, like the Modern Boy, some of whom particularly enjoyed their intellectual life as an idle lumpen, also symbolized the decadent, profligate, and conspicuous descendants of the bourgeois or nouveaux riches, now became a young urbanite sporting Western attire, hairstyles, and shiny shoes. This stereotype appeared in a cartoon from the magazine *Byeolgeongon* (Another World), featuring a male and a female who bemoan the pressure to dress like Hollywood sexual icons (Figure 5.1):

> [Rudolf] Valentino: It's not easy to be an actor, because nobody recognizes me if I don't dress like this.
>
> Pola Negri: Oh! I am suffering more than you. With hips upward, how shall I control my ankles in these tiny shoes!

For the Modern Girl, the indignity of decadence is compounded by physical discomfort. In similar depictions of this period, while the Modern Boy at least acquired the trappings of an intellectual, such as eyeglasses and a Western suit, the Modern Girl had little to show for it except a frolicking sexual attitude. A woman drawing attention to her own sexuality—body and desire—was frowned upon in traditional Korea.[3] The Modern Girl (in Korean, *modeon geol*) not only aroused moral censure but came to embody the fracturing of class (poor/bourgeois) and citizenship (Korean/Japanese), as this essay seeks to demonstrate.

Figure 5.1 *Modern Boy, Modern Girl.* Published in *Byeolgeongon* (July 1927).

Western literature and culture undoubtedly influenced the Korean Modern Girl, but Japanese sources played an important mediating role and in some cases served as the direct informant.[4] The Korean Modern Girls in some cases identified themselves with both Western and Japanese types, who achieved free love but rarely the freedom to pursue a public life outside the family. Modern Korean women might also have been aware that the first generation of college-educated Western women in the 1890s, having been raised in financially secure and liberal upper-middle-class households, could realistically choose career over marriage and advocate women's public activity without losing social respectability. Such professional and educational opportunities further improved Western women's chance to shape their own social and political destiny.[5]

In contrast, the Modern Woman in colonial Korea remained awkwardly wedged between moral anxiety and the anti-feminist sentiments of the Korean patriarchy that mistrusted foreign ideas.[6]

The *modeon geol* as a theme in Korean modernism and modernity has been the subject of much recent scholarship, notably the writings of Kim Youngna and Kim Jinsong.[7] Kim Youngna's "Modernity in Debate: Representing the 'New Woman' and 'Modern Girl,'" elucidates the rise of the Modern Girl phenomenon in connection with another female type: the "New Woman." Kim Jinsong's *Formation of Modernity: Allow a Dance Hall in Seoul* compiles primary texts and images from newspapers, journals, and other mass media resources dating from the 1920s and 1930s. These scholarly contributions shed light on the intricacies of colonial culture, informing subsequent research on Korean modern art.[8]

According to Kim Youngna, the Korean Modern Girl was an offshoot of the "New Woman" discourse of the 1910s, which described the material life of a woman belonging to the affluent class. But before long, attributes of the New Woman—cigarettes, Westernized fashion, etc.—began appearing in posters, advertisements, and newspaper illustrations and had a direct impact on female desires and attitudes across the economic spectrum. The New Woman and the Modern Girl, the latter having more working-class associations originally, eventually became indistinguishable.

Western literary and visual products guided Korean cultural trends to be sure, but the *modeon geol* was also directly derived from Japanese concepts. In Japan, the "short-haired missy" who wore Western-style makeup and fashion such as slacks and broad-brimmed hats was called *modan gāru* or *moga*,[9] a term coined in the Taishō period (1912–26).[10] This character type provided the visual and behavioral models for the Korean *modeon geol*.

Like the *moga*, the *modeon geol* brought to mind particularly women employed in cafés, Western-style bars, theaters, and so on. Even so, as Yu Kwangyeol indicated in his essay in 1927,[11] the Modern Girl phenomenon was not merely a trend imitating the Japanese counterpart of *moga* or the American version of the flapper. Rather, it mirrored the changing social consciousness, the collective identity of traditional womanhood as an aspect of modernity and modern conditions in colonial Korea. In Yu's account, modernity is not about the visual elements of fashion and hairstyle but about the new psychology of accepting modern changes. The enlightened being is the essence of the true Modern Girl. In the end, both the Korean pronunciation of *modeon geol* and the Chinese characters for *sichea* (meaning "the child of the current body") were alternatively used to signify the Modern Girl.[12] The *modeon geol* contained the contradictory notions of both the bad girl and the ideal of lifting women from domesticity to emancipation.

Korean male writers predominantly criticized the *modeon geol* trend, but it took hold under the powerful capitalist economy, buoyed by the rising tide of women's consumer culture. Shopping girls challenged traditional gender roles and centuries of Confucian morality by accumulating products that enhanced female beauty and sexuality. In addition to the massive influx of Japanese commercial products for the Modern Woman, such as white powder and other cosmetics,[13] Japanese women's publications inspired several Korean female students and readers to further their *modeon geol* aspirations. Numerous Japanese popular or literary magazines, such as *Shinseinen* (New Youth), *Modan Nihon* (Modern Japan), *Bungaku Jidai* (Literary Times), *Seitō* (Bluestockings), and *Tokyo Puck*, disseminated not only modern consumer commodities but also modern ideas about femininity and masculinity. This cultural influx promoted a new social consciousness of gender equality in addition to other more prosaic Western trends.[14]

Commerce and feminism intersected with colonialism in controversial ways. Facilitating Korea's access to Japanese and Western goods was one vehicle for Japan to prove its utility as a civilizer and modernizer. As voracious consumers of these goods, Modern Girls inadvertently participated in Korea's colonial subordination to Japan, which entailed promoting progressive images of Japan while denigrating Korea as a remote, pre-industrial land. As Kim Jinsong noted,[15] the Joseon Exposition, which started in 1929, was one instance when handmade Korean objects were displayed to look inferior to the sumptuous Japanese commodities. Both the Japanese consumer goods and their idea of modern womanhood fed colonial material and intellectual oppression. In Kim's account, Yu Kwangyeol argued in 1923 that the Korean masses were so blinded by the glittering, seductive products that they failed to recognize Japan's assault on Korea's economy. Writers such as Yu vigorously condemned both modern commodities and the Modern Woman as byproducts of an insidious colonial policy.

During the occupation, the Japanese government distributed annual reports on its administration of Korea. They typically included photographic images of Koreans as a pre-industrial people in a primitive land. These reports furnished evidence of "the great change that has taken place in this corner of the Far East, as it shares [in] the advancing prosperity of the mother country, Japan."[16] Mass-marketed to the West as colonial propaganda, these reports, or pamphlets, were often written in English and contained photographs to illustrate the "before" and "after" states of the annexation. These images showed the world the benefits of colonialism.

Photography, thought to be an "honest" medium, exaggerated Japanese contribution to Korea's industrial and urban advancements. To enhance the fiction of the good shepherd, the Japanese supplemented the reports with favorable data and transcripts of interviews with contented subjects. These annual reports misrepresented Koreans as a lazy and corrupt people unable to modernize on their own, and who therefore must be saved by Japanese colonialism. Conceptually, this approach was derived from the *mission civilisatrice* of French imperialism. Japan initiated a policy to assimilate the Korean people and culture into Japanese culture by promoting a common language and culture. This was a part of Japan's Pan-Asian plan for a unified

Asia. The Koreans and the Japanese did share some similar cultural sources, including the adoption of Chinese characters in their writing systems. But while bringing changes with ostensive benefits, Japan contrived a hierarchical differentiation between the colonizer and the colonized.

Japan was mostly interested in extending its own geopolitical influence and the resulting opportunity for material exploitation. Developments in manufacturing, finance, mining, agriculture, education, commerce, health, and even sports often served the auxiliary goal of Empire consolidation by enticing and molding docile colonial citizens.[17] The colonial authority repeatedly defended its exploitation in the name of Korea's future prosperity. A caricature called "Goddess of Peace," included in *Tokyo Puck* on October 1, 1919 (see Plate 2), showed Japan and the League of Nations consuming greedily the Peace Treaty in an attempt to satisfy their endless appetite.[18] The perceived threat that the Modern Girl posed in this colonial fetishism of Japanese and Western imports perpetuated the erosion of indigenous pride.

The image of modern womanhood proliferated as the publishing industry blossomed in the 1920s and 1930s. This period coincided with the climax of Korean nationalism, which began with the March First Independence Movement of 1919.[19] This movement came in the wake of the February Eighth Declaration of Independence by Korean students at Waseda University in Tokyo, following the sudden death of former Korean Emperor Gojong. These two events incited Korean nationalist emotions even "in the absence of a nation." As an appeasement measure, the Japanese colonial government permitted the establishment of Korean newspapers and magazines through an "enlightened policy." In a short time, the number of Korean journals tripled, from 490 to 1,240, under the new Publication Law. *Sin yeoja* (New Woman) and *Buin* (Madame, which changed its name in 1923 to *Sin yeoseong*, also New Woman) were major women's magazines that came into being at this time.[20] These publications popularized the latest images of modern womanhood as well as new decorating trends for household interiors.[21] Many of these popular magazines promoted the *hyeonmo yangcheo* (wise mother, good wife) ideal, especially as Japan moved closer to war in the 1930s.[22] *Hyeonmo yangcheo*, similar to the original Japanese concept of *ryōsai kenbo* (good wife, wise mother),[23] could be seen as the heir to Confucian virtues but reinscribed in the rhetoric of colonialism, which emphasized duty and loyalty to the ruling regime.

The Modern Girl phenomenon evolved in the framework of this cultural and economic subordination of the era, which led to its conflicting popular reception. Urban culture accelerated the circulation of the *modeon geol* image. During the interwar period of the 1920s and 1930s, in particular, office women, housewives, and shoppers regularly encountered the Modern Girl or the New Woman in shop windows and advertisements. A drawing by Choe Yeong-su for the magazine *Yeoseong* (November 1936) depicts four young women looking at a window display outside a newly established department store, admiring and discussing its contents.[24] These modern women are shown wearing traditional Korean dresses but in a modified style complemented by short hair and pointy Western shoes. In *Painter of Modern Life*, Baudelaire called fashion "a symptom of the taste for the ideal which floats on the surface of all the crude, terrestrial and loathsome bric-à-brac that the natural life accumulates in the human brain: as a sublime deformation of Nature, or rather a permanent and repeated attempt at her reformation."[25] One might interpret the "deformation" of the Modern Girl's fashion as an undesirable social consequence of imperialist capitalism.

The *modeon geol* roused tension between traditional and modern concepts of femininity, and between the rich and the poor. For those with limited income and leisure, fashionable women who had nothing better to do than to shop for self-adornment were objects of envy and resentment. In an essay on "*Modeonijeum*" (Modernism) published in *Sinmin* (New People, June 1931), O Seok-cheon argued that the Modern Girl was symptomatic of social decadence, which was the inevitable result of the vulgar influences of Japanese and American bourgeois capitalism:

> The social members of Modernism are Modern Boy and Modern Girl: their lifestyle is drawn to Jazz, dance, speed, and sports. Their expression is the *ero* (erotic), the *gro* (grotesque), and nonsense. They live as bourgeois and they are born out of modern capitalism. Socially, Modern Boy and Modern Girl depend on the rapid development of the machine. The leading principle of the Modern Boy and Modern Girl is based on the vulgar predilection, worldly taste, and the first class, which I would define as "Americanism."[26]

Miriam Silverberg pointed out that the "*eroguro nansensu*" (erotic-grotesque nonsense) or "Ero-Gro" was a recurrent theme in Japanese modern popular culture, partly identified with the value system of Western consumerism and Hollywood.[27] Borrowing this Japanese expression to characterize the Korean Modern Boy and Modern Girl, O criticized their mindless consumption as debased, disgusting, and ignorant. He added: "How much do they understand the essence of modern culture and tradition? I think it's 'Zero.'" Yet, the ingredients of the erotic and the grotesque effectively spurred voyeuristic participation in mass culture, titillating the public while inviting condemnation at the same time. Advancing his own theory of Ero-Gro, meaning "debased" and "disgusting," the writer also notes that the Modern Girl and Modern Boy produced the modern ideals of femininity and masculinity to which the culture increasingly subscribed. Ero-Gro placed the Modern Girl as a commodified object of desire at the center of the public gaze; as such, she signified modernity.

The arousing mixture of erotic and grotesque elements made the viewer into a voyeur, who secretly participated in mass culture while at the same time bitterly condemned its materiality. In some cases Modern Girlhood was portrayed as a psychosis. The author of "Modeon suje" (Notes on the Modern) in *Sinmin* in July 1930, pinpoints this macabre yet ambivalent quality of the Modern Girl:

Although there would be some people indignant at my comparison of the Modern Girl and Modern Boy to patients, I don't think this is an insult. As some geniuses are treated as madmen, these girls who behave against the grain in spite of their normal consciousness, wouldn't they be psycho perverts? However, I am not railing against the Modern Girl, neither am I commemorating her... Who wouldn't feel disgusted and want to spit in the face of these girls with modern symptoms? However it's also true that you want to caress her like a lovely cat.[28]

Appropriating the sensuous language of decadent literature, the writer saw the Modern Girl as a revolting attraction. Novelist Yeom Sang-seob explored this paradox in *Samdae* (Three Generations, 1931). One male protagonist distances himself from girls who wear garish garments and shoes in the stereotypical Modern Girl style, while another delights in them as novelties.[29]

As censorship grew stricter in the 1930s, and public "morality" was more closely watched, slowly the Modern Girl herself became the focus of ideological and political debate.[30] However, the sexualized shell of the Modern Girl made her less susceptible to colonial policing, as she was seen as luring people towards erotic indulgence and away from sociopolitical dissension. This may be why the Modern Girl was able to stay in the mainstream of popular culture well into wartime. Whereas her earlier incarnation as the New Woman had a certain aura of intelligence, the Modern Girl emitted a frank eroticism that seized the gaze and incited sexual impulses. The colonial Japanese government thus tolerated this form of cultural decadence in order to avoid direct political challenges to its hegemony.

The similarity between the Modern Girl and the American flapper in the 1920s was noted, as the Ero-Gro seemed to have derived partly from America and not completely from Japan.[31] Just as the modern American flapper celebrated the death of the Gibson Girl, an earlier cultural icon, and rejected traditional family values with her assertive sexuality in order "to liberate destructive sexual fires and to let the fire of civilization die out for want of tending,"[32] so too the Modern Girl in Korea challenged the way in which men took for granted being the initiators of sexual advances, women being the passive recipients.[33] For the first time with the Modern Girl, a woman's sexuality and her very body assumed active roles in the social structuring of Korea.

In sum, in colonial Korea, the social site in which the Modern Girl was a heroine in the development of modernity produced a Korean version of the French *flâneuse*, whether consciously or not. The collective body of the Modern Girl combined the cynical, the bizarre, and the nonsensical, culminating in what Richard Gilman terms "decadence":

Before any specific associations arise, "decadence" gives off a feeling of age, of superseded behavior, something almost quaint and even faintly comical. Going further, allowing this strange and marginal word to declare itself more fully, one can detect in it a quality of languor, of debility, a suggestion of repletion but also of continual striving toward pleasure of a bizarre, peripheral kind…Another and related sense of transgression clings to the word. But it has to do with taboos violated not out of surging passion or grim philosophy but out of cynicism or what one might call a surfeit of the licit. One thinks of an irritated ennui stealing over those of the rich or powerful who don't feel themselves bound by prevailing states or standards, or even regard it a sane obligation to break with them. And finally there is a nuance of distemper, of being out of sorts, neurasthenia producing an exquisite itch for whose relief no habitual or straightforward remedy will do.[34]

The Modern Girl, like the Modern Boy, is a city dweller who thrives in the world of speedy cars and trains, glittering lights, and American jazz. Some modern girls from poor backgrounds, as alternatives to working in a factory or in the traditional red light district, took up employment as bus girls, or ticket girls. Working as bartenders, waitresses, or other low-skilled labor in the service sector, these modern girls became sexually desirable and sexually available objects. The nickname "Ero-Girls" was given to those who earned tips for erotic services. In cafés, a new consumer institution that mushroomed in cities as fast as pawnshops, male customers could pay to touch the waitresses' bodies or to engage them in other carnal transactions: "The café would be a market selling love, not true love. [The] café waitress is entitled to sell love, although she could sell much more than that. Alcohol is the gateway to that love and tip is the price of the love."[35] These women were not all sordid and depraved. Some of them came from a *gisaeng* background of professionally trained entertainers (the Korean equivalent of the Japanese geisha).[36]

Proletarian writers incessantly attacked the commercialism of the Modern Girl. KAPF (the Korean Proletarian Arts League) was founded in 1925, after the model of Japan's NAPF (Nipponia Artista Proleta Federaciao, in Esperanto;[37] the Japanese Proletarian Arts League).[38] Such groups sympathized with the suffering poor and did not recognize the Modern Girl as a part of the struggling class. Names such as "Marx's Girl" or "Engels's Lady" were invented for the proletarian heroines who fought for sociopolitical equality in workers' clothes and sensible shoes.[39] These terms were used to promote the sociopolitical equality of woman, not like the capitalist Modern Girl, whose sociopolitical equality was not an issue.

The complexity of Korean society during the interwar period is precisely captured by the image of Modern Girls sharing the urban landscape with traditional Confucian ladies and female workers and laborers.[40] However, despite the increased participation of women in public life, Korean society overall was not yet ready to overthrow the patriarchal ideal of the submissive woman.[41] The Modern Girl, therefore, was represented in essentially grotesque terms, as was typical in France at the turn of the nineteenth century.

The tragic life of the first Korean woman oil painter exemplifies the fate of those who dared to challenge the status quo. Na Hye-seok (1896–1948) was a pioneering feminist writer, artist, and world traveler.[42] After her divorce from a prominent politician in 1934, Na was viewed as an outcast by both her family and society.[43] Her writings told of the irrational treatment of women and her yearning for free love and gender equality. In *Confession of Divorce* (1934) and *The Domestic Life of a French Matron* (1934), Na ponders the constant conflict between tradition and new morality in the changing Korean society.[44] She writes: "The psychology of the Korean man is very hard to understand. Although he isn't chaste himself, he demands chastity in a woman and feels free to take it from her. Western men or men in Tokyo still understand and respect me if I am not a virgin."[45]

Several literary writings reevaluate Na's ambiguous status, but there is no argument that she was one of the early feminists in modern Korea.[46] She illustrated Henrik Ibsen's *A Doll's House*[47] and authored many stories and poems celebrating the Modern Woman, as a regular contributor to the journal *Sin yeoseong*. Born to a wealthy family in 1896, she identified with the New Woman and advocated women's rights early on, as evidenced by her essay "The Ideal Wife" (1914), which appeared in the progressive magazine *Hakjigwang* (Light of Learning) (founded by Korean students in Tokyo). From 1915 to 1918, Na studied Western-style painting at the Tokyo Women's Art School. She continued to paint after graduation, but few of her paintings have survived.[48]

Na's *Self-Portrait* (1928) best captures the intensity of her art (see Plate 3). Her penetrating eyes meet those of the viewer. Shadow darkens her left cheek and neck; a pale, mask-like face stands out against the strongly outlined eyes and somber jacket. The viewer's gaze moves naturally from her mask-like face, down the Y-shaped collar, to meet her large but simply brushed hands. The frontal rigidity and the symmetrical arrangement of her image, which is abruptly broken at the bottom of the painting due to the off-center placement of the hands, expertly convey her own psychology as a woman artist, the New Woman, and bourgeois intellectual. The work reveals her attraction to the new Western femininity and her intention to create her own image outside the traditional sphere as a Modern Woman. In fact, she presents herself more or less as a Western woman in her facial bone structure. In the near absence of self-portraits by women in traditional Korea, Na has created a provocative first statement of female subjectivity. In addition to its bold abstraction and frontality,[49] this painting may be the only woman's self-portrait in modern Korea. Na was also one of the earliest known Korean women to paint in oil.[50]

In *Portraiture*, Richard Brilliant argues that portraits incorporate various indexical properties whose primary function is to signal an individual's presence, often by highly concentrated symbolic means, so long as the image has a proper name.[51] When viewing Na's self-portrait, the contemporary observer might not have comprehended this underlying code of the proper name and the image, because this is a novel representation. Again, if "portraits stand to their subjects in the same relation as proper names stand to the objects denoted by them, then denotation is the special case of reference exemplified by proper names and portraits."[52] Because of the absence of traditional or preexisting images of "subjective" women artists or intellectuals, equal to the power, ability, and authority of male artists in the West (and in Japan), Na must have had difficulty portraying herself. In addition, the representation of her self-portrait does not correspond to the types that were familiar and, therefore, accepted in modern Korea, because the medium was oil and the subject matter was a female with an aggressive gaze.[53]

The mask-like face, massive torso, and dramatic chiaroscuro of *Self-Portrait* recall Pablo Picasso's picture of *Gertrude Stein* (winter 1905–autumn 1906). Like Stein, a literary icon and a liberal woman, Na searched for the ideal point of departure to formulate a womanhood that spoke to her own professional and personal aspirations. Of course, Na wasn't a lesbian, but Robert Lubar's concept of Gertrude Stein as "Modernism's M(Other)" takes place in the painter's masculine, solid representation of her body and the representation of her identity.[54] In particular, Na deconstructs the submissive image by emphasizing her social class and occupation and challenging the hegemonic masculine power and stereotypical representation of gender. In this way, Na creates a gendered space, which can be read aesthetically and sociopolitically. The very question of how society discursively controls sexuality, class, and gender is visible in her own dark, formidable portrait. More than a private image of the artist, *Self-Portrait* furnished a potent icon for the New Woman movement and sealed Na's reputation as a modernist.

In *Two Dancers* (1927–28), by contrast, Na portrays the Modern Girl as a mechanical mannequin by placing two dancers in an identical position, one imitating the other (see Plate 4). Their presence and gestures are theatrical, as if they have been placed in a department store window. Both dancers are stylized and cartoon-like. Their bodies are overwhelmed by the heavy furs they wear, while they look upward and beyond the restricted theatrical space. Their black outlines and the dark brown curtain contrast with the white fur. Their eyes, lips, and their very style exclude traces of individuality, such as those we read in Na's self-portrait. The contrast between her self-portrait and the depictions of the Modern Girl intentionally represent the artist's own, conscious, intellectual bourgeois identity, and the interior of her mind. In other words, Na's self-portrait, highlighting her mask-like face accentuated by shadows, is a manifesto of her identity as a feminist painter and a New Woman—not a simple victim of modern womanhood or new fashion styles. It is significant that Na's *Self-Portrait* was created in 1928, after coming back from an eight-month trip to Paris with her husband Kim Wu-yeong. The following year, she extended her sojourn to Berlin and other European cities, where she opened herself to diverse art styles and cultures. Her husband was a modern intellectual, who had studied law at Kyoto University and respected the Modern Woman's thoughts on marriage and love. At Na's request, he had erected a tomb stele for her late fiancé, who died of pneumonia in 1917.[55] Returning to Paris in

1928, Na had a reunion with her lover, Choe Rin. Her liberal ways eventually led to divorce. She made no apologies for her action: "To my four children! Don't blame me; rather blame the social system, morality, law, and convention. Your mother as a pioneer of social transformation is victimized by destiny. If you should come to Paris as diplomats, put a flower in front of my tomb."[56] In 1948, Na Hye-seok died with neither her children nor any other family at her side.

As we have seen, the Modern Girl and the New Woman were pioneers in the development of Korean modernity and represented the confluence of femininity and social consciousness. Although these new types of womanhood became pervasive internationally, the Korean version was quite distinctive due to the complicated political situation in the colonial period. The *modeon geol* not only fought against male authority and convention but also struggled in the crossroads between the capitalist and the proletariat, the colonialists and the nationalists. While the New Woman was progressive politically, the Modern Girl was decadent, and so the identity of the *modeon geol* remained divided and conflicted.

Plate 1 Cigarette poster featuring a Modern Girl. Hang Zhiying. Shanghai, early 1930s.

Plate 2 *Goddess of Peace*. Published in *Tokyo Puck* (October 1, 1919).

Plate 3 *Self-Portrait*, 1928. Na Hyeseok. Oil on canvas. Private collection.

Plate 4 *Two Dancers*, 1927–28. Na Hye-seok. Oil on canvas. The National Museum of Contemporary Art, Korea.

Plate 5 *Portrait of Chunhyang*, 1939 (second version, 1960). Kim Eun-ho. Color on silk. Chunhyang Shrine in Namwon, Jeollabuk-do, Korea.

Plate 6 *Painting of a Beautiful Woman*, 18th–19th century. Sin Yun-bok. Color on silk. Kansong Art Museum, Seoul.

Plate 7 *Painting of a Beautiful Woman,*
19th century. Anonymous. Color on paper.
Donga University Museum, Busan, Korea.

Plate 8 A cover of *Jeolsae Mi-in-do*
(*Painting of A Fair Lady*), 20th
century. Anonymous.

Plate 9 *Portrait of Chunhyang*, 1937. Jo Yong-seung. Ink
and color on silk. National Museum of Contemporary Art,
Korea.

Plate 10 *Portrait of Unnanja*, 1914.
Chae Yong-sin. Color on paper.
National Museum of Korea, Seoul.

Plate 11 *Silent Listening*, 1934. Kim Gi-chang.
Shown at the 13th Joseon Art Exhibition. Color
on paper. Private Collection.

Plate 12 *Portrait of Madame Sin Saimdang*, 1938. Lee
Yong-woo. Color on silk. Ewha Woman's University
Museum, Seoul, Korea.

Plate 13 *Island Women*, 1912. Tsuchida Bakusen. Color on silk. The National Museum of Modern Art, Tokyo.

Plate 14 *Flower Basket*, 1913. Fujishima Takeji. Oil on canvas. The National Museum of Modern Art, Kyoto.

Plate 15 *Rose Vendor*, 1889. Carolus-Duran. Frontispiece of *Bijutsu* 3, no. 7 (May 1917). Tokyo: Shichimensha. Present location unknown.

Plate 16 *Woman with an Orchid*. Fujishima
Takeji. Published in *Bijutsu* 14, no. 1 (1939).
Tokyo: Bijutsu Hakkosha.

Plate 17 *Women Peddlers from Ohara*, 1927. Tsuchida
Bakusen. Color on silk. The National Museum of
Modern Art, Kyoto.

Plate 18 *Flat Wooden Bed*, 1933. Tsuchida Bakusen. Color on silk.
Kyoto Municipal Museum of Art.

Plate 19 *Abstracts of Women's Life in Korea: Processing Herbs*, 1933.
Hayami Gyoshū. Color on silk. Published in Yoshida Kozaburo, ed.,
Hayami Gyoshū (Kyoto: Benridō, 1975).

Plate 20　Nakagyō Post Office, 1903. Mitsuhashi Shirō and Yoshii Shigenori. Kyoto. Photograph by Sarah Teasley.

Plate 21　Bank of Japan, Kyoto Branch (now the museum of Kyoto Annex), 1906. Tatsuno Kingo and Uneji Nagano. Photograph by Sarah Teasley.

Female Images in 1930s Korea
Virtuous Women and Good Mothers

Yisoon Kim

A significant trend in Korean art during the colonial period was the emergence of non-religious figure painting as a major genre. Representations of women, not highly regarded in the past, grew in number and in variety. Young beauties, mothers, and housewives were particularly prevalent. How should we understand this new repertoire? What was its relationship to the earlier *mi-in-do* (Paintings of Beautiful Women) and to traditional genre pictures? To answer these questions, this essay considers works produced for the Joseon Misul Jeollamhoe (Joseon Art Exhibitions) that were held under the auspices of the Japanese colonial authority.[1] Most of the original paintings and sculptures were destroyed during the Korean War (1950–53), preserved only in black-and-white reproductions. Nevertheless, these exhibitions stood as definitive moments in modern Korean art history. Held yearly between 1922 and 1944, the Joseon Art Exhibitions celebrated many local artists and were instrumental in shaping public perception of what constituted acceptable subjects in modern fine arts production. These high-profile, official events drew audiences of all ages. Attendance was in fact mandatory for middle and high school students. All the exhibits, including the female images, necessarily conformed to the ideals of an obedient colonial subject. Fueling the politics of control was the complicity of Korea's own male-dominated society, which harbored anti-feminist sentiments.

The present analysis concentrates on the 1930s, the height of colonialism, when conservatism and progressiveness coexisted. During this period, department stores, cafés, and theaters flourished, and women who patronized or worked for these modern institutions were branded "Modern Girls," a designation that was by then used interchangeably with "New Women" but with a somewhat negative connotation. Fine artists tended to depict their opposites, that is, virtuous women who demonstrated chastity and sexual restraint. Modernization was underway, particularly in Gyeongseong (now Seoul), but unfavorable economic conditions inside and outside the country made Koreans wary of change. The Great Depression affected the whole world, and Japan was starting a fifteen-year war with China. Under these conditions, the colonized and impoverished Korean nation took comfort in the idea of women carrying out their motherly duties and grooming the next generation for a more prosperous future.

In that age, Korean women themselves in general conceded that, even in highly educated, elite households, females should handle sewing, child-rearing, and cooking. They would say that, as candidates for wives, "traditional women are far better than New Women."[2] This bias drowned out a fledgling discourse in the 1920s that had posited that "Educated, New Women Make Better Wives."[3] What remained unchanged, whether in the nationalist or colonialist framework, was the normative status of the patriarchal system. Artists, mostly men, were instrumental in idealizing women's domestic servility as a cornerstone of national well-being. Their portrayals of good wives and responsible mothers provided the behavioral template for a new generation of women who were encountering the many distractions of modern life.

This essay's chief intention is to cast light on the relationship between colonialism and Korean gender experiences. In analyzing constructs of womanhood through art and print culture, it sets out to demonstrate how public discourses imposed upon the Korean female a seemingly innocuous but in fact highly charged role as keeper of family and national values. Making sacrifices for the greater good and not yielding to personal desires were certainly not ideals exclusive to women but when projected onto the familial mothers and housewives, such sacrifices found widespread acceptance. The general appreciation in Japan of the homebound female types also lent legitimacy to their visual representations in the colony, even as Korean nationalists interpreted these images as expressions of anti-colonial aspirations.

Two specific kinds of female images were common: breast-feeding mothers and housewives performing needlework. They were ubiquitous in the 1930s when both Japanese colonizers and Korean nationalists embraced the dutiful woman as model citizen. As dominant female types in the Joseon Art Exhibitions, these mothers and housewives hold the key to understanding the entwined discourse of gender and colonial politics.

Beautiful, Young Women Faithful to One Man

In the 1930s, the archetypal females were Baekhwa (White Flower) and Chunhyang (Fragrant Spring), virtuous heroines from Korean literature known for their obdurate faithfulness to only one man. The fictional protagonist Baekhwa lived in the late Goryeo period (918–1392). Her family forced her to become a *gisaeng* (a singing and dancing entertainer similar to a Japanese geisha) even though she was already betrothed. She tried to stay faithful to her fiancé but in the end committed suicide. *The Story of Chunhyang*, a widely read Korean classic, tells of the eighteenth-century romance between a former *gisaeng*'s daughter (Chunhyang) and a nobleman's son (Lee Mongloung).[4] The two could not marry because of class differences. While pining for her beloved, Chunhyang suffered physical abuse as she refused the advances of a lascivious new governor in town.

Both Baekhwa and Chunhyang became prominent subjects in the visual arts. Kim Bok-jin's sculpture of *Baekhwa* was shown twice at the Joseon Art Exhibition, first in 1938 (Figure 6.1) and again in 1941 (by his widow).[5] The model for the image was actress Han Eun-jin, who played the role in a contemporary theater production.[6] In 1939, a *Portrait of Chunhyang* was produced by Kim Eun-ho (see Plate 5), the highly regarded painter who was a one-time portraitist of Emperor Sunjong (1874–1926). This picture was placed in the Chunhyang Shrine in Namwon, Jeollabuk-do (built in 1931), but eventually lost. The artist made a second version in 1960 for the shrine, where it has acquired the status of a quasi-religious icon.

Women were depicted infrequently in traditional Korea, even compared to other Confucian societies such as Japan and China. Their visibility grew somewhat towards the beginning of the eighteenth century, when a new genre called "Paintings of Beautiful Women" came into existence.[7] In these paintings, as exemplified by a work of the renowned Sin Yun-bok (ca. 1758–1813) (see Plate 6), the figure typically stands facing forward, wearing the traditional Korean costume called the *hanbok*. Her *chima* (skirt) falls all the way to the ground while her *jeogori* (shirt) is tight and short enough to expose the upper part of the skirt. The woman's averted gaze suggests shyness, but her luxurious outfit and hair ornaments beckon the viewer's attention. From the Donga University Museum's collection of "Paintings of Beautiful Women" (see Plate 7), one picture recalls Sin Yun-bok's style except for the absence of ornate hair accessories. Donning a short shirt, which tantalizingly reveals the breasts, the woman lifts one hand to adjust her hairdo. Although the *hanbok* is designed to fully cover the body, these paintings expose the flesh in strategic places. Sin's picture includes a silver knife, a traditional symbol of chastity, hanging from the shirt as a reminder of the sexual potential of the image. "Paintings of Beautiful Women" facilitated carnal fantasy. They could be made to hang on walls like Western pinups or as portable scrolls for the convenience of private viewing, presumably at men's leisure (see Plate 8).

In the colonial period (1910–45), titillating "Paintings of Beautiful Women" all but ceased, giving way to more modest, morality-laden female types. The images of *Baekhwa* and *Portrait of Chunhyang* discussed above, for example, depict these iconic women as neither extravagantly accessorized nor overtly sexual. Their figures and poses are dignified, unostentatious, and innocent, befitting the characters' virtuous personae. Kim Bok-jin's *Baekhwa* wears a *jokduri* (Korean crown worn by the bride at a traditional Korean wedding) with her hands clasped in front. Her bare foot may be a vestige of the "Paintings of Beautiful Women" tradition, but overall, the sculpture draws little attention to ornamentation and contains no risqué elements. Here, the heroine stands for the upright bride, who will steadfastly adhere to her marital commitment.

Kim Eun-ho's *Portrait of Chunhyang* presents a figure dressed in the traditional fashion of a newly married woman.[8] A green shirt and a red skirt cover her entire body. References to marriage and domesticity were

Figure 6.1
Baekhwa, 1938.
Kim Bok-jin.
Exhibted at the
17th Joseon
Art Exhibition.
Destroyed. Plaster.
Published in
the catalogue of
the 17th *Joseon
Art Exhibition*
(Japanese
Governor-
General in Korea,
1938), 109.

recurrent features in images of women in colonial Korea. Before Kim Eun-ho, Jo Yong-seung submitted a *Portrait of Chunhyang* (1937) to the Joseon Art Exhibition (see Plate 9). In this version, the figure sits with a book in front of her but does not read. Flirting with the possibility of the role of an intellectual, she nevertheless remains most comfortable as guardian of the home.

Public discourse at the time overwhelmingly favored conservative gender roles. Nam Man-min, one of the writers for the popular magazine *Woman*, contrasted Chunhyang with Nora of Henrik Ibsen's *A Doll's House*. He accused Ibsen's heroine of arrogance as she tries to find herself and seeks to be a "true human being," while praising Chunhyang for already possessing the qualities of a real human being: sincerity and loyalty.[9] He regarded Chunhyang as the antithesis to Nora and blamed the latter for being a harmful model for modern girls who indulged in vain pretenses and disloyalty.

Women as Mothers and Housewives

In the early twentieth century, Korean women were expected to stay home to fulfill their duties as mothers and wives. Pictures of mothers and their children began to appear in the second decade, such as *Portrait of Unnanja* (1914) (see Plate 10) by Chae Yong-sin (1850–1941),[10] but it was not until the 1930s that they were produced in large numbers. The women illustrated in these paintings wear the *hanbok* with a neat, traditional hairdo. These domestic women are usually doing chores such as sewing and ironing, and in the most distinctive mothering gesture, breast-feeding.

Although the motif of a breast-feeding mother can be found in Korean genre paintings dating to the eighteenth century, such as *Jeomsim* (Lunch) by Kim Hong-do (Figure 6.2), it had tended to be only one aspect of a larger composition. Not until towards the end of the 1930s did breast-feeding women take center stage, such as *Moja* (Mother and Child, 1939) by Im Eung-gu (Figure 6.3) and another *Mother and Child* by Im Hong-eun (1940) (Figure 6.4).

Some scholars contend that such paintings of breast-feeding mothers served Japan's war interests: Japan wanted Korean women to stay home and devote their lives to bearing and rearing future soldiers who would fight for Japan.[11] However, it would be premature to impose this kind of meaning on all Korean artworks that explore the image of mother and child, especially those portraying breastfeeding mothers. Before the invasion of Pearl Harbor, imperialist Japan did not force a draft onto the Koreans, partly because the Japanese government did not completely trust their loyalty. It seems that Japan had little need to require or demand maternal devotion from Korean mothers in the 1930s. However, Korean nationalists used magazines and newspapers to display images of maternal devotion to goad Korean women to be good mothers. They saw maternal devotion as vital to raising strong citizens, who might one day overthrow the colonizers.

Figure 6.2   *Lunch*, 18th century. Kim Hong-do. Ink and light color on paper. National Museum of Korea, Seoul.

Figure 6.3   *Mother and Child*, 1939. Im Eung-gu. Shown at the 18th Joseon Art Exhibition. Present location unknown. Published in the catalogue of the 18th *Joseon Art Exhibition* (Japanese Governor General in Korea, 1939), 48.

Figure 6.4   *Mother and Child*, 1940. Im Hong-eun. Shown at the 19th Joseon Art Exhibition. Present location unknown. Published in the catalogue of the 19th *Joseon Art Exhibition* (Japanese Governor-General in Korea, 1940), 142.

A typical example is seen when a famous novelist and frequent columnist for female magazines, Lee Gwang-su, went so far as to associate breastfeeding and toilet training with world peace:

> It will be a disaster if women like having [sexual] relationships, but hate bearing and rearing children … It will be a disaster if women have children, but avoid breast-feeding them. Avoiding breastfeeding children is an unforgivable crime … It will be a disaster if women dislike all the motherly duties entailed in rearing children such as hugging and toilet-training them. Only those who are unhealthy or unfaithful would want to consign their motherly duties to others. They are psychologically disabled women, who lack maternal love, the most valuable and strongest emotion humanity can have. If all the women in the world practice maternal love, the world will see a better future. If all the women in Korea practice maternal love, Korea will see peace and prosperity. Women should realize that becoming a good mother is what this country wants of them. If they realize this today, we will have a chance to usher in a new era.[12]

This strongly worded passage reflected a sense of urgency in the politicized ideology of motherhood in Korea at the time. Its author, Lee Gwang-su, vilified women who shirked their breast-feeding duties, judging them to be somehow mentally deficient. Lee and many intellectuals in colonized Korea argued that part of women's responsibility as citizens was to build loving homes, starting with the care of their babies. This rhetoric emphasized women's importance in society-building without undermining the patriarchy that underlay the colonialist and nationalist discourses.

Lee Gwang-su was not alone in exalting maternal love. Another renowned writer, Lee Gi-yeong, opined:

> Becoming a mother and practicing maternal love is the most meaningful work women can have pride in… We see those who challenge this idea. They are nothing more than rebels who have grown out of social difficulties … What mothers do is nurturing human resources. Their role is more important in a society which lacks cultural facilities and educational infrastructure.[13]

When Korea adopted an open-door policy in the late nineteenth century, there had been discussions of women entering the workforce and contributing directly to the nation's economic development.[14] Starting in the mid-1920s, however, this way of thinking became overshadowed by the "good mother" ideal, discouraging women from fulfilling themselves outside the domestic confines.[15] As colonial oppression grew stronger in the 1930s, the doctrine of dedicated mothering gained even greater traction.[16] More and more Koreans came to believe that their people's future, including freedom from colonialism, depended on women's willingness to sacrifice themselves to stay home and raise good sons and daughters. Becoming a mother was promoted as the most sacred duty, and females who veered from this paradigm were accused of being oversexed and vain.[17] Popular women's magazines repeatedly reminded readers of the inviolable sanctity of motherhood.[18] In these magazines there were many "mother and child" images, including reproductions of contemporary paintings.

Before the twentieth century, the subject of a mother taking care of her child was a rarity in Korean art.[19] In the depiction of upper-middle-class households, for example, mothers are not shown tending or playing with their children themselves. The job usually went to maid-servants, as that was the reality of elite families in the old days. Beginning in the 1930s, scenes of a mother playing with her child in a well-to-do household suddenly surged in popularity. Examples include *Huihui* (Happiness and Fun, 1936) by Baek Yun-mun (Figure 6.5) and *Gibbeum* (Pleasure, 1938) by Jin Se-mu (Figure 6.6). Some historians perceive these images as indicative of a general elevation of children in modern times. This theory is too simplistic and ignores the vexed gendered politics in the 1930s, which compelled the conservative elements in society to define women exclusively by their roles as good mothers and virtuous wives.

The woman in *Pleasure* is beautiful and refined, reminiscent of *Portrait of Chunhyang* and *Baekhwa*. She is playing with her child and making bubbles. The Western-style clothes of the child and the radio in the background suggest an upper-middle-class setting.[20] The spotlessness of the room and the embroidered cushion point to the mother's devotion to domestic duties. Befitting the title *Pleasure*, her smile shows that she is satisfied with her life. The painting reminds us of Berthe Morisot's *Hide and Seek* (1873), but the two works differ in one fundamental way: While *Hide and Seek* was painted by a female artist based on her own experiences, *Pleasure* was created by a male artist reflecting men's demands and expectations of women.

Figure 6.5 *Happiness and Fun*, 1936. Baek Yun-mun. Shown at the 15th Joseon Art Exhibition. Present location unknown. Published in the catalogue of the 15th *Joseon Art Exhibition* (Japanese Governor-General in Korea, 1936), 28.

Figure 6.6 *Pleasure*, 1938. Jin Se-mu. Shown at the 17th Joseon Art Exhibition. Present location unknown. Published in the catalogue of the 17th *Joseon Art Exhibition* (Japanese Governor-General in Korea, 1938), 15.

Jeongcheong (Silent Listening, 1934) (see Plate 11) by Kim Gi-chang (1914–2000) similarly idealizes the life of a devoted housewife. Attired in a type of reformed *hanbok*, a seated mother and daughter listen to music from a gramophone, another attribute of bourgeois affluence, along with the Western-style chair and the framed picture on the wall.[21] The mother looks modern in her relatively short skirt (compared to the traditional trailing attire) and Western-style shoes but is not the radical Modern Girl. Wearing a *hanbok* and an old-fashioned hairdo, she represents a housewife in a good family who has the taste and temperament to bring up fine off-spring.[22] Numerous other paintings in the 1930s and early 1940s center on woman-child interactions, including scenes of intimate conversations and children bowing to grandmothers.

Shown at the Joseon Art Exhibitions and widely disseminated through women's magazines, paintings of the "good housewife" illustrated the doctrine that stated that women were born to become mothers. Even the female writer Hwang Sin-deok declared in her article "Joseon [Korea] Wants Mothers Like This" that women should devote themselves to rearing children and doing housework for the country's future, whose leaders are "the babies sucking at their mother's breasts."[23] One after another, leading intellectuals chimed in to make motherhood a top priority for Korean women. "Mothers, you are carrying out the most significant responsibility in the world," said Yu Eok-gyeom. "Maternal love is another form of the sun which Mother Nature grants to Humanity," according to Kim Lim. Constantly bombarded by rhetoric like this, the majority of upper-class Korean women also embraced the model of good wives and mothers as the social norm, as they sought to glorify their status with new consumer goods. Of course, few of the images that reinforced this role were made by women.

Women Doing Needlework

In colonial Korea, needlework loomed large in the ideal housewife's routine, and accordingly, women with the accoutrements of needlework became a popular iconography in the art of the period. Doing needlework, spinning thread, and weaving cloth are traditional female work that teaches the "feminine" virtues of patience, silence, and obedience. The first iteration of this image type presented to the Joseon Art Exhibition was a 1923 work by Ji Seong-chae (Figure 6.7). The needlework is set in front of the woman rather than being manually handled. The setting, which includes a scroll of calligraphy in the background, identifies the woman as member of a gentry family. In accordance with the visual convention for women of this class, her outer beauty indexes her inner virtue.

Korean art created circa 1930s seldom underscored women's artistic or scholarly achievements, even when the subject was an educated woman. A case in point is *Sin Saimdang buin-do* (Portrait of Madame Sin Saimdang) by Lee Yong-woo (see Plate 12). The woman spinning threads is the historical figure Sin Saimdang, mother of the Confucian scholar Yulgok and a respected artist herself, who excelled in calligraphy, painting, and writing. Praised as one of greatest women artists of the Joseon Dynasty, her works are treasured in Korea even today. In Lee Yong-woo's painting, however, Sin is reduced to a regular housewife, stripped of all scholarly and artistic associations.

Mo (Mother, 1935) by Jeong Do-hwa (Figure 6.8) is a fusion of a breast-feeding woman in *hanbok* and a needle-worker. The cloth and the spool scattered in the foreground suggest that she has temporarily stopped sewing in order to feed the child. In *Moja* (Mother and Child), Im Hong-eun also paints a woman with a reel in front of her. Consistent with paintings of this type, the female characters display no strong emotions; their placid faces convey contentment and quiet acceptance of their lot.

At the same time as the model of the dutiful housewife was being promulgated, the Modern Woman, an incarnation of the New Woman, drew repeated criticism. Until the 1920s, the term "New Women" referred to highly educated, Westernized females with strong self-esteem who challenged traditional moral values.[24] By the 1930s, however, New Women were no longer seen as positive embodiments of modernity or Westernization but rather as materialistic, urban idlers.[25] The writer Sim Hun used the adjective "frivolous" to describe them.[26] An illustration printed in the magazine *Sinsegye* (A New World) by An Seok-yeong, *Yeoseong seonjeonsidae ga omyeon* (If the Age of Advertising Women Arrives), depicts Modern Women with signs that say they would have sex with anyone who is willing to buy them what they want (Figure 6.9). These women think little of chastity and will sell their bodies for material satisfaction and vanity. Another magazine illustration (Figure 6.10) portrays Modern Girls in high heels and shortened *hanbok* staring at a department store window. Rather than becoming individuals who set out to be active participants in society with the hope of realizing their full human potential, they tended to be portrayed as mindless consumers by the public discourse of 1930s Korea.

The ideal colonial woman was characterized by conformity, innocence, obedience, diligence, and self-sacrifice. She assumes the guise of a newly married woman, mother, and/or housewife. While numerous paintings describe breast-feeding women, none of them shows labor pains or emphasizes the endless drudgery of running a household and rearing children. Caged inside their homes, the good wives and mothers

Figure 6.7 *Painting of Beauty Doing Needlework*, 1923. Ji Seong-chae. Shown at the 2nd Joseon Art Exhibition. Present location unknown. Published in the catalogue of the 2nd *Joseon Art Exhibition* (Japanese Governor-General in Korea, 1923), 2.

Figure 6.8 *Mother*, 1935. Jeong Do-hwa. Shown at the 14th Joseon Art Exhibition. Present location unknown. Published in the catalogue of the 14th *Joseon Art Exhibition* (Japanese Governor-General in Korea, 1935), 31.

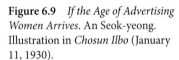

Figure 6.10   *A Streetscape in Late Autumn*. Choi young-su. Illustration in *Yeoseong* (1936) 11.

Figure 6.9   *If the Age of Advertising Women Arrives*. An Seok-yeong. Illustration in *Chosun Ilbo* (January 11, 1930).

were denied the choice of leading alternative lifestyles, doing creative things that bring personal fulfillment.

The idea that it is women's heavenly ordained duty to be mothers represses women. At the height of colonialism, Korean nationalists prescribed to the notion that women should stay home to safeguard the integrity of the family and, by extension, the integrity of the nation. Why this duty should fall uniquely on the shoulders of women and not of men was not clearly explained. Partly, this had to do with the perception that female consumption, unless directed towards the home, used resources in frivolous and unseemly ways. It also partly reflected a persistent hold of Confucian patriarchy on a society that saw gender conservatism as an avenue of political mobilization. Hence, the iconography of good mothering always stressed productivity, from giving milk, to sewing, to educating children.

Japanese Images of Asian Women in "Traditional" Clothes in the Age of Empire

Kaoru Kojima

In 1876, the Meiji government founded the Kōbu Bijutsu Gakkō (Technical Art School), which became Japan's first national institution dedicated to the teaching of Western-style art. Both males and females were eligible to enroll. Six years later, the government closed the school due to rising tension between indigenization and Westernization in Japanese art trends. It was only after 1896 that the Tōkyō Bijutsu Gakkō (Tokyo School of Fine Arts, founded in 1887 with the support of the Ministry of Education) renewed official approval for Western-style painting, creating a special department for its instruction with a curriculum that included life drawing and *plein-air* sketching. Admission, however, was limited to men until as late as 1946. Among the favorite subjects of this generation of artists was the female nude, which overcame initial moral controversies to become a mainstream subject. Concurrently, there was a steady interest in images of women wearing the kimono, not only in *nihonga* (Japanese-style painting), which overtly harked back to tradition, but also in oil-on-canvas *yōga* (Western-style painting). These images were primarily works of male artists, and their repertoire beginning in the 1910s expanded to depictions of the Traditional Woman in Chinese-and Korean-style dress. Through visual strategies that claimed Japan's superiority, these Japanese male representations of non-Japanese Asian women reflected the ideology of empire-building.

Japonisme and the Japanese Woman in Kimono

Japanese women in kimono were prevalent in European and American *Japonisme* of the late nineteenth and early twentieth centuries. In these images artists found a representation of beauty that was at once sensual and exotic.[1] In addition to paintings, other media made memorable uses of the iconography of "woman-in-kimono," popularizing the idea that Japan was a land of beauties and the beautiful. *Madame Chrysanthème* (1884) by Pierre Loti was the most famous example in literature, and it is perhaps best remembered today for its operatic adaption by Puccini (premiered in 1904). Several comedies with Japanese subjects with an imagined "Japanese" girl had also appeared in Paris as early as the 1870s.[2] The huge success in 1896 of Sidney Johns's operetta titled "The Geisha: A Story of a Tea House" helped put the word "geisha" in the Western lexicon.[3] Historically, the geisha was primarily a musical performer, but as Saeki Junko points out, Westerners often confused this profession with the gorgeously dressed *oiran* (the highest-ranked prostitute in the Edo period).[4] In time, the Japanese woman in kimono also became sexualized as an object of European (male) fantasy. Indicative of this trend were the romantic tales about Western men and young kimono-wearing Japanese women, and in most cases these stories implied a gendered conquest by the male West of the yet "undeveloped" female Japan.

The first international exhibition in which Japan officially participated was the 1867 Exposition Universelle in Paris. For the event, the waning Tokugawa Shogunate constructed a Japanese-style pavilion where three Japanese women served tea. Henceforth, even under the modernizing climate of the Meiji period (1868–1912), a tea room with female receptionists dressed in kimono remained standard Japanese fare at international exhibitions; these women were "exhibited" along with lacquerware and other Japanese artifacts displayed for foreign consumption.

After the Sino-Japanese War of 1894–95, the Mitsui Kimono shop started a campaign to market luxurious kimono to urban bourgeois women. Such companies played an important role in reinventing the kimono as a "national dress" or *wafuku* (Japanese clothes) that indexed both Japanese tradition and cultural identity. It is worth noting that only women were expected to wear traditional attire, not men. Urban businessmen and government officials had since the late nineteenth century been donning Western clothes daily for their public duties as a sign of modernity, while Western dress for women only started to have an appreciable market around the 1930s. One could think of the occidentalization of the bourgeois Japanese male as a way to secure for him parity with the Western male who consumes the Japanese female as an artifact of desire.

The Japanese government allocated a very large budget for the 1900 Exposition Universelle in Paris and sent officials, scholars, and artists to Paris. Kuroda Seiki (1866–1924) had studied in the French capital from 1884 to 1893 under the Salon painter Raphaël Collin. After his return to Japan, Kuroda was appointed professor at the Tokyo School of Fine Arts and placed in charge of selecting Japanese oil paintings for the Paris Exposition. Kuroda's own works included one depicting a young Japanese woman in kimono in natural surroundings, titled *Kohan* (Lakeside). Among other paintings was *Chihan Nōryō* (Summer Evening at Lakeside) by Fujishima Takeji (1867–1943), which shows two young women in kimono enjoying a cool evening. There was also a painting titled *Keiko* (Music Lesson) by Shirataki Ikunosuke (1873–1960) that featured a group of young women and female children practicing the Japanese shamisen and songs. The last, in particular, was a scene of ordinary life in contemporary Tokyo. However, the image of Japanese young women playing music also recalled the iconography associated with the geisha. These works of kimono-clad Japanese women no doubt resonated with Western audiences at the height of *Japonisme*. In this instance, it was Japanese male painters who depicted this "exotic" theme. A group photograph taken in Paris of Kuroda and his colleagues wearing Western suits illustrates the receptiveness of these Japanese men to European culture and fashion. In art, they readily adopted the Western gaze to objectify kimono-clad Japanese women.

"Kimono Beauty" Imperialism

The colonization of Korea in 1910 marked a major expansion of Japanese imperialism in Asia. It aroused interest in images of women dressed in the traditional Korean *chima jeogori* (skirts and shirts). Fujishima Takeji, a professor of the Tokyo School of Fine Arts, was sent to Korea in 1913 by the government, probably to inspect local culture, though the exact reason was unclear. His published impressions of Korea drew analogy with Italy:

> Korea, whose form juts out from the continent, immediately reminds me of Italy, [the two places having] much in common in terms of scenery. The bright color of the earth and the bare mountains studded with pine trees make the landscape so beautiful. Mild sunshine illuminates the bare mountains and the earth in bright colors, and they show good contrast with the clear blue sky whose color seems to be deeper .... If we could compare the Japanese landscape with that of Switzerland, then the landscape of Korea should be compared with that of Italy.[5]

Korea and Italy are both peninsulas, and besides this geographic resemblance, Fujishima contended that their bright light and colors were alike and similarly charming. He wrote that Korean art had attained its highest level during the Three Kingdoms period (first century BCE–mid-seventh century CE) and declined gradually through the Unified Silla period (668–935) and the Goryeo Dynasty (918–1392),[6] just as Italian art reached a high point in the Renaissance but has lost its luster in recent centuries. Fujishima's view that Korean history was only worthy of esteem in the remote past echoed the well-publicized colonial scholarship of the architecture historian Sekino Tadashi (1868–1935).[7]

Fujishima's paintings in Korea sought to capture, in his words, "the bright colors of the earth" and "good contrast with the clear blue sky." One picture shows two females walking in the countryside wearing the traditional clothing of the last three centuries of the Joseon Dynasty (1392–1910). His focus is on the exotic beauty of the women's fashion:

> The clothes of the Korean people are interesting. While men are usually dressed in white, female dresses are made with combinations of simple colors, such as a red blouse with a white skirt or [clothing with a mixture of] green, purple and yellow. When viewed from a distance, they look like color spots—very lovely. Korea, in all respects, has not changed or progressed much, and the clothes still seem to be reminiscent of ancient ages. I was deeply impressed with the beauty of the green cloths that women used to cover their heads with and

of their pale-colored skirts that flutter in the wind. I feel as though
I were seeing a handscroll from around the twelfth century in Japan
displayed before me.[8]

The colorful Korean fashion reminded Fujishima of Heian-period Japan.
Although the Joseon-style female dress indeed exhibits certain design elements evocative of Japanese clothing of the past, the suggestion that Korea
"has not progressed much" smacks of the condescension among many
Japanese who traveled to Korea during occupation. Subsuming Korean
culture in Japan's historical past had become a trope for justifying Japanese
imperialism.[9] Fujishima's Korea, as he wrote in the same article, was comparable to colonial Algeria, which had fed the imagination of Delacroix
and other nineteenth-century French painters. Inhabiting the position of
an Orientalist, Fujishima argued for the artistic benefits of colonization.[10]
Korea appeared, in his art, mostly as an "exotic other," an object of Japan's
colonial gaze.[11] Bert Winther-Tamaki adds that "[Fujishima] may be identified as an agent in the transfer of principles of Orientalism from Europe to
the Japanese framework for the artistic assessment and mediation of colonial Asian culture. As he was an eminent professor of the Tokyo School of
Fine Arts, his opinion also had certain effects on Japan's colonial cultural
policy."[12]

Refraction of European View on "Exotic South" into East Asia

Fujishima developed an affiliation with French painters. Although he
missed the Paris Exposition in 1900, he studied in Europe for four years
after the Russo-Japanese War (1904–05). He first enrolled in the atelier
of Fernand Cormon (1845–1924) in L'École des Beaux-Arts in January in
1906, and remained in the French capital for the next two years. He then
moved to Italy at the end of 1907, to follow Charles Auguste Émile Durand
(who called himself Carolus-Duran; 1837–1917), a renowned painter of
pastoral scenes and the head of L'Académie de France in Rome.[13] After
completing two more years of training there, Fujishima returned to Japan
in January 1910.[14] He did not bring back large works from his European
sojourn. Moreover, extant sketches dating from his Roman period display
minimal associations with contemporary Italian society. Besides a few portraits of professional models, these images were mostly of ancient ruins,
gardens of old villas, and historical sites.

Fujishima praised L'École des Beaux-Arts as the best art school in the
world[15] and criticized the standards of the national art school in Rome as
inferior even to those of the Tokyo School of Fine Arts. This view explained
his decision to study at L'Académie de France even while living in Italy. He
esteemed Italian Renaissance masters such as Raphael and Michelangelo
but considered Italian art to be in decline since the sixteenth century.[16] For
Italian contemporary art he had little respect: "Anyone who travels to Italy
has contempt for [current] Italian art because of its tendency for rough-
ness."[17] Having been schooled in French institutions, Fujishima apparently

adopted certain French biases against Italy. Asai Chū (1856–1907), another painter who traveled to Rome after a sojourn in Paris around 1900, also sentimentalized the ruins of the ancient Roman Empire in several haiku.[18] Both artists thought of Italy as a land with a glorious past but an unimpressive present. The resemblance that Fujishima perceived between Korea and Italy might be read as a justification for Japan's occupation of the former. Not coincidentally, some Japanese artists who had studied in Europe recognized in Taiwan (Japan's colony from 1895 to 1945) reminiscences of Italy. The modern Western (North-western European) idea of the exotic South became "refracted"—transferred from the original and bent in the process—into the Japanese view of its colonies, reinforcing the hegemonic discourse of the Empire.[19]

The exoticized woman-in-kimono appealed not only to Western-style oil painters but also to Japanese-style painters. One of them was Tsuchida Bakusen (1887–1936). Although his medium and formats were traditional Japanese, he likewise admired French art and its language of passion and sexual desire. The manifesto (published in May 1911) of his art group *Ru Masuku* (Le Masque) stated:

> Once Eugène Carrière wrote for an exhibition of Rodin that "La transmission de la pensée par l'art, comme la transmission de la vie, [est une] oeuvre de passion et d'amour". [The transmission of thoughts through art, like the transmission of life, is a work of passion and love.] This is what we want to convey through our works. We also expect that not only our poor works but also our exhibition itself will be an expression of our passion and sexual desire.[20]

This manifesto suggests that eroticism was the core artistic motivation for members of this all-male group. Women naturally became their favorite subject. Paintings of *Ru Masuku* have not been precisely identified, with the exception of Bakusen's *Kami* (Hair, 1911), which was accepted by the fifth Bunten (Monbushō Bijutsu Tenrankai or Fine Arts Exhibition of the Ministry of Education). It shows the left side of the body of a Japanese woman fixing her hair before a mirror—in a typical voyeuristic perspective. Bakusen paints the arms and fingers of the model in pinkish tones to describe her youthful, soft skin. Her armpits are visible through the loose sleeves, though her face is hidden behind the raised arm.

Bakusen's other erotic works, *Shima no On'na* (Island Women, 1912) (see Plate 13) and *Ama* (Woman Divers, 1913), have been analyzed in numerous exhibition catalogs and books as evidence of his interest in French modernism, especially the works of Paul Gauguin. The background of *Shima no On'na* is covered with thick yellowish pigments, approximating the effects of oil painting executed with a palette knife. Bold strokes delineate the female figures, emphasizing their voluptuous hips and substantial breasts. *Shima no On'na* was made after a trip to Hachijō-jima, a small island 178 miles south of Tokyo. In the manner of Gauguin, Bakusen paired erotic bodies with exotic settings. In Japan, interest in the "southern" islands was not unique to Bakusen. Both Wada Sanzō (1883–1967) and Nakamura Tsune (1887–1924), for example, painted Ōshima, the largest among the Izu Islands, which also encompass Hachijō-jima and Miyake-jima. During the Edo period, these islands had been sites of banishment. Japanese painters who assimilated with North-western European eyes for the exotic south found these "southern" islands in Japan as exotic and raw as Gauguin's Tahiti.

Icons of Imperial Japan

After returning from Korea, Fujishima completed several more paintings of Korean women. One of them is now titled *Hanakago* (Flower Basket, 1913) (see Plate 14). It shows a woman donning a white *jeogori* (short jacket) and a red *chima* (skirt) that make up the typical Joseon dress. Depicted frontally and with a flower basket steadied on her head, this figure recalls Carolus-Duran's *Rose Vendor* (1889) (see Plate 15), a painting that was reproduced as the frontispiece of the May 1917 issue of the Japanese fine arts magazine *Bijutsu*. In the same issue appeared Fujishima's own essay on this French master.[21] It is probable that Fujishima knew the French picture before painting *Hanakago*, even though the Japanese publication of the former postdates the latter. Carolus-Duran regularly depicted Italian women from Ciociaria who earned their living by selling flowers in Rome and by modeling for painters. The rose vendor wears a white blouse and a red skirt with a sash. Her basket of flowers repeats this color scheme. Red and white are dominant in Fujishima's *Hanakago* as well. The debts Fujishima owed to Carolus-Duran are hard to miss in this picture. *Hanakago* offers a visual parallel to what its creator regarded as the sensual but lesser cultures of contemporary Italy and Korea. By reconfiguring a European pictorial arrangement in an Asian setting, Fujishima also asserted his status as a disciple and the Japanese equivalent of Carolus-Duran.

Cultural hybridity would remain a defining character of Fujishima's art. In 1924, he painted a profile of a Japanese woman in Chinese costume titled *Tōyō-buri* (In a Manner of the East). On the garment is a pattern of peonies, which are symbols of wealth and honor. The round collar and wide sleeves are references to Chinese women's fashion of the Qing Dynasty (1644–1911). Her face and neck are sensitively modeled, and the luster in the hair and on the surface of the gown is portrayed with superb realism. *Tōyō-buri* represented an artistic breakthrough that went beyond establishing visual parallels between Western and Asian subjects in the real world. Fujishima outlined his sources and intentions thus:

> In the Italian Renaissance artists painted numerous profiles of women. I kept staring at the paintings by Piero della Francesca and Leonardo da Vinci that were hung in the galleries of the art museum in Milan, never bored, because in my mind these paintings triggered a feeling akin to *tōyō teki seishin* [the spirit of the East]. I was especially interested in the brushwork of Piero della Francesca, which is

quite simplified … I really wanted to use a Chinese dress in my painting, and collected as many as fifty or sixty of them … This was not
because I intended to paint a Chinese. I wanted to create an archetypal
tōyō [Eastern] beauty with a Japanese woman as a model … My aim
is to paint something unaffected by Western feeling using exclusively
Western materials. I am not interested in reconstructing the customs
and paraphernalia realistically in accordance with history. We do not
need such exacting research in modern art. I have been insisting for
years on the elimination of the notion of "the East" and "the West."[22]

Tōyō (the East), an ideological construct conceived in counterdistinc-
tion to *seiyō* (the West), gained currency in Japan after its military victory
over China in 1895. It became the unifying concept for *Tōyōshi* (History
of the East), a vast academic discipline encompassing such fields as lin-
guistics, ethnology, geography, and history.[23] A related field of *Tōyō bijutsushi* (History of Eastern Art) came into being as well, its scholarly output
peaking in 1920s and 1930s when Japan actively enlarged its territorial
ambitions. Emphasizing the primacy of Japanese perspectives, studies of
tōyō epitomized *kōkoku shikan* (the Japanese imperial historical view),
which served the goals of nationalism and imperialism.[24] There is no question that Japan had a long-standing relationship to Chinese and Korean art
and culture, but *Tōyō bijutsushi* provided an unprecedented framework for
putting Japan at the center of the region's artistic achievement.

Fujishima used the word "*tōyō*" in the above fraught context. He saw
Japan as having inherited the Chinese tradition and as a modernized
country having also adopted the Western tradition derived from Italy. In
Tōyō-buri, Fujishima did not produce a portrait of a real woman but an
allegory. She is a Japanese dressed as a Chinese and assumes a Renaissance
pose, hence the union of the East and West. On the material level, he
believed that oil painting possessed its own spirit which, according to him,
had grown out of the Latin tradition. By adopting the realistic effects of oil
painting to render sumptuous textiles, hair, and other details, Fujishima
makes palpable the presence of the sitter and draws attention to her Asian
accoutrements. This approach was what he meant by creating "something
unaffected by Western feeling using exclusively Western materials."

After *Tōyō-buri*, Fujishima continued to explore the complex layering
of cultural signifiers by painting profiles of women in Chinese dress. *Hōkei*
(Woman with an Orchid) (see Plate 16) premiered at the first Shōtoku Taishi
Hōsan Bijutsu Tenrankai (Shōtoku Taishi Commemorative Exhibition),
which was held in conjunction with the opening of the Metropolitan Art
Museum in Tokyo in 1926. Compared with *Tōyō-buri*, which has an immediate Eastern flavor due to motifs such as the round fan and the calligraphy panel in the background, the composition of *Hōkei* veers more towards
Renaissance conventions. The woman in *Hōkei* still wears a Chinese dress
but holds an orchid instead of a round fan, and her body is set against a blue
sky. Landscape is a common backdrop in Italian Renaissance portraits by
Piero della Francesca, Leonardo da Vinci, Pisanello, and the like. A woman

holding a flower is also a common motif in Renaissance portraiture, especially in the Northern tradition. In some paintings by the Flemish master Jan van Eyck, for example, the subject holds a blossom as an attribute and possibly to signal devotion. In Fujishima's work, the intended meaning of the orchid is not clear, though traditionally, an orchid is a literati symbol of beauty and noble character in China. The luxurious embroidery on the woman's robe shows patterns of bats, a homophone for good fortune in Chinese. But in the colors in the garment and the shape of the decorated coiffeur, *Hōkei* evokes paintings of the Italian Renaissance, such as *A Portrait of a Young Lady* by Antonio del Pollaiuolo, which is now in Berlin.

In more experimental ways than ever before, Fujishima sought to amalgamate the East and the West in his oil paintings. His art reflected a significant moment in Japanese oil painting when the nation struggled to emerge from the shadow of Western tutelage.

Westernized Eyes Turned to Asian Women

After returning from a stay in Europe from 1921 to 1923, Tsuchida Bakusen was impressed anew by the beauty of Japanese women and the Japanese landscape as if he were a foreigner beholding an exotic spectacle. A new enthusiasm for classical Japanese art also overtook him when he visited the Imperial Household Museum in Kyoto and Nara:

> These works are as magnificent as those with which I was so impressed in France and in Italy … I wonder how such splendid art could be born in this small country of Japan in East Asia … I am pleased to be able to have a fresh interest in looking at Japanese people and landscapes these days as if I were an *étranger*. I am so stunned by the beauty of the houses in the countryside because of their natural and complex structures, by *maiko* hairstyles and by the way *oharame* wear their scarves, that I am stopped in my tracks.[25]

Bakusen marveled at Japanese landscapes, women, and art like a curious foreigner, championing them as great artifacts of world culture. He compared a Japanese handscroll with a Persian miniature, and a Buddhist sculpture by Unkei with a sculpture by Michelangelo. His paintings of Japanese women from this period incorporated Western formal strategies. For *Bugi Rinsen* (A Maiko in a Japanese Garden, 1924) and *Oharame* (Women Peddlers from Ohara, 1927) (see Plate 17), two large works shown at the fourth and the sixth exhibition of the Kokuga Sōsaku Kyōkai (National Creative Painting Association) respectively, Bakusen produced numerous preparatory drawings the same way an academic painter planned his compositions for history paintings in Europe. Painting in large scale was not new to him, but his post-European creations seemed to approach a new level of structural rigor.

In *Bugi Rinsen*, Bakusen pictures the scene of a Kyoto *maiko* (apprentice geisha) sitting in a garden with carefully built-up details. Stones and trees are articulated in simplified geometric forms. The sky and the water share the same greenish-blue color, which unifies the whole composition as they blend with the green lawn and trees. One could identify the influence of modern artists like Cézanne in the geometric composition, as well as traces of Early Renaissance aesthetic. The contrast of the large figure with the small trees and the *maiko*'s round face recall Benozzo Gozzoli and Fra Angelico.[26] In *Oharame*, Bakusen paints dandelions and *yamabuki* (kerria) in round yellow patterns that are disproportionately large. These elements cover the ground and the background, altering the viewer's perception of depth. Such devices also parallel some Early Renaissance paintings and Persian miniatures. The triangular composition of the three figures might be compared with certain altarpieces of the Madonna and Child with saints. The *oharame*'s white scarf is reminiscent of the Virgin Mary's veil. Bakusen's images of women look "Japanese" at first glance, but closer inspection reveals sophisticated quotations of European art.

Bakusen turns to Korean subjects in his famous work *Heishō* (Flat Wooden Bed) of 1933 (see Plate 18), which depicts two Korean *gisaeng* (geisha), identified as such by the bed and the mirror. The color scheme is unusually pale, predominantly white with thin contour lines. At the time, "*Gisaeng* Tourism" was an important source of entertainment for Japanese male travelers, and postcards with photographs of *gisaeng* were widely circulated. Kawamura Minato has pointed out that these postcards always showed the *gisaeng* wearing the *chima* and *jeogori*, and either leaning on something or cocking their heads.[27] On a visit to Korea in 1933, Bakusen no doubt encountered real-life *gisaeng*, but the figures in *Heishō* seemed to be largely an amalgamation of popular imagery and stylization. In a letter, Bakusen acknowledged that he was less interested in Korean models than in Japanese *maiko* because he either could not find any beautiful Korean *gisaeng* or was discouraged by their cheap clothes.[28] Scholars have uncovered evidence of Bakusen looking at ancient Chinese paintings and surmised that the distinctive outline aesthetic used in *Heishō* might have been derived from the Chinese *baimiao* (outline painting) tradition.[29] By emulating this classical and ethereal aesthetic, Bakusen created an image of Korea that differed drastically from his repertoire of vividly colored *maiko* and *oharame*. Bakusen, who had discovered his identity as a painter of Japanese subjects, needed to devise a new expression for the colonized people.[30]

Hayami Gyoshū (1894–1935) is another relevant figure to explore in Japan's art of the Empire. His early affiliations included the private studio of Matsumoto Fūko (1840–1923) and the Sekiyōkai (Red Sun Society, 1914–15). The latter was a group headed by Imamura Shikō (1880–1916) who admired le Salon des Indépendants[31] and sought to vitalize *nanga* (literati painting) using colorful dots. Members wore black mantles with the character for "badness" and made themselves into strange spectacles on the streets of Tokyo.[32] Around 1920, Gyoshū turned to a realistic style using minute brushstrokes, producing small still-lifes that hark back to Chinese paintings of the Song and Yuan Dynasties (tenth to fourteenth century). A number of these paintings had been highly esteemed in Japan since the fifteenth century. When *Tōyō bijutsushi* was established in the early twentieth century, they were added to the list of Japanese "national treasures." Gyoshū's revival of Song-Yuan aesthetics coincided with this development.

In 1930, Gyoshū accompanied the leading nationalist painter, Yokoyama Taikan (1868–1958), to Rome for L'Esposizione d'Arte Giapponese (Japanese Art Exhibition) at IL Palazzo delle Esposizioni. The event was sponsored by Okura Kihachirō of the Okura Financial Group, a private organization, but it anticipated a national policy whereby Japan would formalize a military alliance with Italy in 1937.[33] Mussolini was invited to the opening ceremony, and Emperor Emanuele III came to the exhibition. Around 200 Japanese-style paintings by Teiten (short for Teikoku Bijutsu Tenrankai, or Imperial Art Exhibitions) artists, and members of the Nihon Bijutsu-in (Japan Art Institute) were sent, complete with specially constructed Japanese-style *tokonoma* (display alcoves) for more authentic effects. During this period, such large-scale international exhibitions co-opted Japanese artists for the advancement of nationalist ideologies. Gyoshū, who until that point had been working as an independent citizen, started to get more involved with State art policies.

One in a series of Chōsen Bijutsu Tenrankai (Joseon Art Exhibitions) in Korea was held in 1933. These were official, state-controlled, and juried exhibitions (modeled after the Bunten and the Teiten) to propagate colonial values and hierarchical regulations of the participating Japanese and Korean artists, as well as of their subject matter. Gyoshū was sent along with other leading Japanese artists who were judges. Although not a member of Teikoku Geijutsu-in (the Imperial Academy), he was an important member of the leading *nihonga* group, the Nihon Bijutsu-in, headed by Yokoyama Taikan. The Japanese government intended to unite these independent art groups under its control and thus appointed judges from both. Gyoshū also took this opportunity to tour historical places and sketch Korea's ancient art and landscapes.[34] His impressions of the colony can be summarized in a series centered on women's lives (see Plate 19). All the women are set in vignettes similar to the arrangement of a large illustrated handscroll. This calls to mind Fujishima's statement that, when looking at the scenery of Korea, he felt as though he was examining an ancient handscroll. The females in Gyoshū's series are not classical beauties, however. They represent marginal citizens and the laboring poor, as he wrote:

> When I went to Korea, it was the end of Spring. This season is called Poor Spring in Korea as [people] become most skinny at this time from having depleted their food stocks but not yet received a new harvest. I did not know about such a thing until I went to Korea, but was able to visit there in the season when the most representative Korea could be seen.[35]

Gyoshū's first-hand observations provided materials for these genre pictures. Realism was not always his chief goal, however. For example, he derived the figure of a weaving woman from an eighteenth-century

Korean painting by Kim Hong-do, while he could have relied wholly on his sketches of rural women weaving in the countryside of Gyeongju, the site of the famous Seokguram Grotto, which he also visited.[36] Gyoshū's images of Korean women delivered impressions remote from the everyday experience of urban Japan, and the more exotic these experiences seemed, the more they appealed to Japanese audiences, including the sophisticated family of Prince Chichibu (a younger brother of the Shōwa Emperor) who purchased the series. Gyōshu visualized Korean females as subalterns, poverty-stricken, and still living a traditional country life. These Korean figures suffer the same level of primitivist objectification as the Japanese island women in Bakusen's *Shima no On'na*, only that, for art or for ethnographic curiosity, their adverse circumstances are amplified and exploited.

*　*　*

Since the rise of *Japonisme*, images of exotic women had satisfied European imagination of "primitive" countries. Male Japanese artists who studied in Europe internalized this gaze, at times to emphasize a rediscovered beauty of Japan but also to distinguish Japanese modernity from the backwardness of Korea through various manipulations of cultural and stylistic sources. Where rural backwardness and archaism were inscribed in their paintings, the dominant urban-male position was asserted. Women in these portrayals were more often imagined than real. The male perspective—conflated with modernism, universalism, and colonialism—became a potent symbol for a Japan that was expanding its domain.

Fujishima's archetypal *tōyō* was construed as part of the Italian spirit he admired and tried to resuscitate since its "decline." In his scheme, the liberal uses of Western and Eastern motifs put his art above passive derivation. Bakusen and Gyoshū likewise merged disparate elements, including genre subjects filtered through the lens of popular imagery and classical idioms. Their pictures bore witness to the painters' cosmopolitan taste and artistic maturation. All in all, women in Asian costumes, rather than mere duplicates of Western Orientalist clichés, revealed meanings specific to the modern Japanese experience and reflected their creators' deep investments in their own age, however problematic.

The Gender of Beauty in Architectural and Interior Design Discourse in Modern Japan

Sarah Teasley

How was beauty defined and used in architectural discourse in Japan during the early years of the profession in the late nineteenth and early twentieth centuries? While seemingly straightforward, the question becomes more complicated when we consider that, during this time, which witnessed major changes in the Japanese political, economic, and social landscape following the Meiji Restoration of 1868, "architectural discourse" was anything but uniform. In the early years of the period known as "modern Japan," publications by and for university-trained architects constituted a large part of the landscape of thought and writings on the design and construction of buildings. However, this landscape also included publications for other members of the building trades and publications for women who, while they did not directly participate in the construction economy, were increasingly expected to take charge of the form and furnishings of the home. Similarly, an exploration of the different definitions and uses—or, to put it another way, the presence, absence, and substance—of the concept of beauty in discourse on the design of space in early twentieth-century Japan uncovers formulations of beauty specific to both class and gender of the intended reader and user.

Meiji publications for women on the design, construction, and furnishing of domestic space stressed the importance of imbuing the environment with beauty. These publications exhorted women to keep beautiful homes for the relaxation of their husbands, the edification of their children, and the good of the nation and provided concrete guidelines for the achievement of these goals. By contrast, beauty as a concept—or even a topic for discussion—appeared only rarely in the nascent discursive sphere of professional male architects in the same period. To be sure, some male architects did use such terms as "beauty," "beautiful," "aesthetic," and "artistic" in speeches and written publications for their peers. However, such terms described principles of composition for designing visually pleasing façades rather than an impression to be gained through the subjective experience of occupying a particular space.

Housewives and architects may seem to occupy completely different domains, but the creation of pleasant, comfortable, and functional spaces appropriate for daily life is a central responsibility of both. Furthermore, in early twentieth-century Japan, the architect and the professional housewife were positioned at the apex of their respective industries—that of building for men, and of "being woman" for women. What, then, accounts for the difference in treatments of the concept of beauty in discourse for the two groups during this period in Japan? Where and why did this difference appear, and what can we learn from it about the gendered character of relationships to building in modern Japan?

To answer these questions, this chapter compares the significance of "beauty" in writing for specific groups of men and women engaged in the practice of designing space in the years roughly between 1900 and 1920 in Japan. The chapter proposes factors underlying the differences in discourse for male and female audiences and draws on these distinctions to explain the gendered interventions into the physical environment in modern Japan. It argues that neither architectural beauty itself nor the responsibility to create it were gendered but that the ways in which it was defined and used certainly were, and their gendered character in turn reinforced the roles of the male architect and female housewife. Simply put, while beauty itself was coded as neither masculine nor feminine, the conception and articulation of beauty was. Differing conceptions and suggestions for the application of beauty in design reinforced hegemonic ideas of the relationship of men and women to the practice and products of architecture and of their roles within them. These roles incorporated contemporary European and American concepts of male and female architectural agency but rather than replicating them employed elements from them within local gender roles in designing spaces.

As a way of testing this hypothesis, the chapter begins with "beauty" in professional architectural discourse for and by male architects in the late Meiji period, roughly 1900 to 1912, a moment when Beaux-Arts theory coexisted in the academy with structural rationalism and arguments for the artistic nature of architecture. During this time, architects educated in a system that stressed composition conceived of beauty as the result or sum of rational design principles that could be scientifically calculated and whose judicious application induced visual pleasure for the viewer. Beauty itself was rarely given a gender, but this ostensible neutrality and universality itself marked architectural discourse as a male and elite practice.

After examining the meaning of beauty within the male profession of architecture, the chapter turns to its application in texts that prescribed women's duties to engage in designing, furnishing, and decorating space as part of their work as a housewife or *shufu*. Under examination are the presence and use of beauty as a concept in two types of texts: home economics manuals and interior decoration guides. Unlike texts for male design professionals, i.e., architects, practical and aspirational texts for women listed beauty as an attribute that could be achieved not through the application of classical compositional principles derived from natural form or mathematical ratios but through specific and highly concrete practices of consumption and arrangement. Furthermore, beauty was to be experienced both as visual appreciation and corporeal occupation of a space.

Beauty for the Architect

The modern conception and practice of architecture as a profession in Japan dates to the establishment of a higher-level training program in Western-style architectural design in the 1870s, and to the establishment of a forum for architectural discourse in the Zōka Gakkai (now the Architectural Institute of Japan) and the launching of the association journal *Kenchiku zasshi* (Architectural Journal) in the 1880s. While aesthetic considerations were obviously part of architectural education, beauty as a specific topic did not appear frequently in this journal or other monthly trade magazines such as *Kenchiku sekai* (Architectural World) or *Kenchiku gahō* (The Architectural Graphic) until the 1910s, when some architects began calling for an increased emphasis on artistic expression and the recognition of architecture as a *bijutsu* or "fine art," as opposed to the structural rationalism that had dominated architectural culture in Japan since the 1870s. For example, architect Yamada Eizaburō, writing in 1923, after architects in Japan had encountered Expressionism, argued:

> The joy of the pure beauty of architecture is the same as the pure beauty of music, painting, and poetry, which we feel in a way that is unrelated to its intellectual content. This is fundamentally about affect, but educated people can touch the broad categories of intellectual thought and emotion through its affective appeal. This is fundamentally an exterior pleasure, but it moves our deepest hearts through its exterior characteristics. It is the pleasure of meter, proportion, and form. It arises when we discover that it satisfies the most common rules of innate beauty.[1]

As Yamada's reduction of aesthetic pleasure to "meter, proportion, and form" suggests, many authors in the wave of publication on architectural aesthetics after 1910 argued for the need to treat architecture as a fine art. Still, in most cases, the formulation of beauty remained highly rational and did not allow for subjective interpretation or the Romantic conception of beauty as an encounter with the sublime.

According to most commentators, "kenchikubi" (architectural beauty) was the objective, rational application of universal formal principles that combined to create compositional unity—or in other words, the perfection of proportions in accordance with natural law or mathematical formulas. By this logic, the appropriate use of formal elements would create visual pleasure for the viewer, perceived as "beauty," and which, along with appropriateness of materials and usability, was an essential characteristic of good design. While the architects writing on aesthetics in professional journals and in textbooks for their peers held different opinions on the importance of beauty for architecture, for the most part, they agreed that beauty should be a goal and employed such terms as *bi* (beauty) and *biteki* (beautiful or aesthetic) to refer to the correct composition of a façade, for example, without emphasizing "beauty" as a subjective sensation.[2]

For instance, architect Murooka Sōshichi, writing in *Kenchiku sekai* in 1915, titled his eleven-part treatise on compositional principles "Kenchiku no biteki taikō taii," literally "Outline of the Aesthetic Relations of Architecture," but explained to readers in the first installment that "aesthetic relations of architecture" was a translation of the English phrase "architectural composition."[3] In keeping with the article's title, Murooka begins by discussing beauty as a subjective judgment of the observer but explains that the modern age possesses standards for beauty that can be learned, allowing for a shared understanding and experience of architectural beauty, and then outlines a set of concrete design principles such as *tōitsu* (unity) and *indebijuarité* (individuality) which, if implemented in design practice, will create balanced, visually pleasing work. To illustrate his principles for creating unity, he included two drawings: assemblages of lines, one with a unifying arrangement that created a whole, and one that, lacking overall structure, was simply an image of scattered lines.[4]

In theories like Murooka's, beauty was a formal, visual attribute that required not only the correct application of compositional principles of proportion and contrast based on mathematical relations but also, revealing early twentieth-century architecture's debt to design reformers like William Morris and Christopher Dresser, truthfulness to materials and fitness of use. The anonymous "B. Eng. K. K.," in a three-part explanation of the aesthetic principles for architectural decoration entitled "Sōshokubi" (Decorative Beauty) serialized in *Kenchiku gahō* in five installments from May to December of 1913, listed the *genri* (fundamental principles) of decorative beauty as consisting of three elements: *shinpurishitē* (simplicity or clarity), *torusufurunessu* (truthfulness), and *hittonessu* (fitness), which we might today call "appropriateness." According to K. K.'s model, the architect was responsible for preserving simplicity in his use of decorative elements and for ensuring that decoration was applied in appropriate places and designed appropriately for use. But truthfulness, he explained, applied to materials and construction as well: "Even if we speak of decorative beauty, it is impossible to separate this entirely from structure or materials; both of these must be properly applied."[5] The reference to materials and structure aside, K. K. confined all suggestions for specific design improvements in the multipart treatise to areas like the arrangement of color, the balance of horizontal and vertical lines, repetition and change that applied specifically to a building's façade, and suggested that an architect could create beauty by correctly implementing the principles learned through the study of previously successful buildings. Both the principles and their application stressed visuality, for example, a section on visual trickery that offered readers suggestions like the addition of pillars to a room with a low ceiling in order to improve the viewer's impression of a space or building.

While most architects writing in the journals espoused beauty as a function of rational principles, some did allow for flexibility and ambiguity.

The architect and architectural historian Itō Chūta (1867–1954), in a well-known call for architects to recognize their profession as a fine art, defined beauty, in *Kenchiku zasshi*, as a formless and subjective quality that could not be objectively understood or described. He remained, nonetheless, committed to the notion that the "art of architecture" consisted of "the creation of an artistic combination of the horizontal and the three-dimensional based on the laws of nature."[6] Moving further away from mathematical rationalism, and echoing Schopenhauer's formulation of architectural aesthetics, the literary scholar Wakayanagi Midori assigned compositional principles secondary importance to what he called "tennenryoku" (natural power):

> The pleasure of beauty comes from grasping one idea; when we look at architecture as art, this idea is something natural and basic, and takes gravity, rigidity and cohesion as its true issues. Existing schools of thought considered only regular formal aspects such as proportion and balance, but these are all issues of pure geometry, and, since they concern the essence of space, are not ideas, and cannot be topics for art. It should go without saying that the effect of architecture is not only mathematical but also dynamical … The regularity of the whole of a building or of its parts arises from the necessity of harmonizing the parts and the whole as they are created, and of being appropriate for the goals set for it. This is because it is convenient to understand the whole by looking over the whole, and because a regular form adds beauty by conforming to the rules of space. But these points are not necessarily the duty of architecture, only secondary aspects, even if they are necessary for value.[7]

Wakayanagi's interpretation devalued rational visual composition in favor of "natural power," while Itō argued for the need to recognize subjective beauty. However, by clinging to such ideas as the universal laws of nature, Meiji-period architects never entirely abandoned the pursuit of beauty as a rational, scientific project.

Architect Mitsuhashi Shirō's canonical formulation of this project provides further insight into its general content and goals. In his 2,500-page, three-volume compendium *Wayō kairyō dai kenchikugaku* (Improved Japanese and Western Great Architectural Knowledge), a comprehensive handbook on architecture that quickly became definitive after its first edition was published in 1911, Mitsuhashi titled his chapter on composition "The Artistic Relations and Measures of Architectural Objects."[8] Mitsuhashi explained that the concept of beautiful architecture existed in all cultures but that the study and practice of fundamental principles was necessary to understand it.[9] He outlined the attributes of beautiful composition as consisting of *tōitsu* (Unity), *shugō* (Grouping), *tenka* (Subordinate Parts), *tsubasa* (Appendages), *seisaibu no shugō* (Grouping of Details), and the avoidance of what he called *fuku-taikō* (Double Composition), all written in English as well as Japanese.[10]

Like Murooka, Mitsuhashi identified unity, which he defined as "the clear combination of all parts into a unitary whole," as the key element in any design.[11] In addition, all of the arts including architecture needed what Mitsuhashi termed "grace," or "good form of the parts amalgamated."[12] A building composed of parts that lacked grace would, he noted, not please the eye regardless of the excellence of its grouping. However, before readers could begin to worry about how to achieve this abstract quality, Mitsuhashi elaborated extensive rules for good composition that, he assured readers, would furnish their architecture with the elusive quality, and offered concrete illustrations of these principles. Illustrations included both abstract drawings and images of buildings that either successfully incorporated the principles (Figure 8.1) or else suffered greatly from having ignored them. For example, to elucidate the basic principles of unity he employed a diagram virtually identical to that used by Murooka four years later and gave a similar explanation of the need for a center on which the elements converged. He also provided two photographs of façades whose unlucky arrangement of towers and height of the central tower "greatly damage the beautiful view" (Figure 8.2).

For Mitsuhashi and other Meiji architects, the correct application of compositional principles and decoration were necessary for good architecture but in the end merely the icing on the cake that was a building's structure.[13] This should not be surprising, given that today, Mitsuhashi is

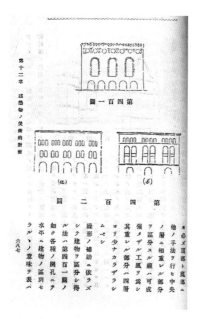

Figure 8.1 Exemplary well-composed façades. Published in Mitsuhashi Shirō, *Wayō kairyō daikenchikugaku* (Tokyo: Ōkura Shoten, 1911), Fig 378.

Figure 8.2 Exemplary façades with bad rhythm. Published in Mitsuhashi Shirō, *Wayō kairyō daikenchikugaku* (Tokyo: Ōkura Shoten, 1911), Figs 423 and 424.

perhaps best known for his research into reinforced concrete construction methods.[14] His forty-seven-page discussion of compositional principles in *Great Architectural Knowledge* comes in the third volume after two volumes on structures and mechanical systems, and follows the 665-page history of world architecture since antiquity that forms the bulk of the third volume. And within building design itself, the usability of space also has to be considered: He wrote, "The deployment of form and choice of color are paramount; in addition, the design should give the client sufficient convenience of use in the plan. The style should be an improved one and must also please the eye...."[15]

Like his theory, Mitsuhashi's built work contributed to and reinforced the state-led project of adapting architectural practices common in Europe and North America for the modernization of the Japanese environment. Take as an example his Nakagyō Post Office in Kyoto, which was designed with fellow Tokyo Imperial University graduate Yoshii Shigenori and built in 1903, during Mitsuhashi's employment as an in-house architect for the Ministry of Communications (see Plate 20).[16] With its trabeated fenestration and red brick banded by white granite, the façade of the two-story neo-Renaissance building was an attempt to realize the principles of regular rhythm, contrast, proportion, and symmetry. Scrolls on the ground floor windows and pediments on the second provide variation, while the standard dimensions of the windows unify the overall composition.

Located on Sanjō, a major thoroughfare in central Kyoto, at the heart of the city's commercial district, the post office's historicist façade and solid appearance embodied the image of a modern yet civilized nation. The simple façade, with plain posts and lintels and without friezes on the pediments, represented the modern functionality of the ministry. The red brick and granite, monumental and solid among central Kyoto's two-story wooden houses and shops, represented the solidity of the state and its parity with European and North American powers at a time when Japan had recently defeated China in the First Sino-Japanese War of 1894–95, and would soon engage Russia in the Russo-Japanese War of 1904–05. Mitsuhashi's use of an eclectic Italianate style, common to Meiji government buildings, bore the stamp of the period's official style. Yoshii and Mitsuhashi had learned well from their mentor Tatsuno Kingo, who adapted the Victorian red-and-white brick construction he observed during his time in London for his numerous civic and corporate buildings and whose own Kyoto branch of the Bank of Japan (1903) was only one block away (see Plate 21).

Even though Mitsuhashi cannot be considered a major innovator, his designs epitomize the mainstream of Meiji architecture—and it is this characteristic, both in his built and theoretical work, that makes him such a useful object for analysis. As many analyses of Meiji architecture have demonstrated, the adoption of Western-style architecture for public and commercial buildings was a political statement about the modernity of the Meiji state.[17] From the establishment of the first school of architecture in the Imperial College of Engineering run by the Department of Public

Works in 1877, architecture students learned contemporary Western principles and methods, first directly from the English architect Josiah Conder and shortly thereafter from British textbooks, then in translations, and in courses led by graduates of the program, from the 1880s on.[18] Schooling was conducted in English, and the structures, materials, and styles taught were those considered suitable in Euro-American settings for public architecture: banks, schools, administrative buildings, train stations, and other public edifices, preferably in solid masonry.

The broad adoption of Western architectural forms and education strengthened the architectural profession's self-identification as part of a universal, masculine, and bourgeois practice, even though the rhetoric of beauty itself addressed neither class nor gender specifically. The elite program at the Imperial College of Engineering was folded into Tokyo Imperial University in 1886, and this program had no direct competitor until the creation of an architecture program at Waseda University in 1910. Graduates worked with their counterparts from the technical schools and with carpenters and master builders trained in an apprenticeship system. However, while architects were only one small subset of the larger group of men who constructed the architectural face of the Meiji state—the ICE/TIU program had a total of 175 graduates between 1879 and 1912—they defined the field through publishing, teaching, and design activities, and positioned their own practice as part of an international community of architects through these activities.

Like their architectural forms and education, the theories of these Meiji architects were connected to the international profession of architecture as a modern, male, and educationally elite practice. Mitsuhashi's decision to bury the section on the aesthetics of architectural composition after two volumes on structures and nearly 700 pages of architectural history suggests that, while he did not deny the primacy of composition in creating good architecture, the actual structure of a building—literally how to build it—had to come first. This reflects the Japanese architectural profession's debt to British architecture, its tradition emerging from civil engineering, which was reflected in the choice of the English architect Josiah Conder as head of the school of architecture.[19] But Mitsuhashi also stressed compositional balance based on the classical orders that he studied in texts by eighteenth-and nineteenth-century British architectural theorists like William Chambers and the father and son Banister Fletcher, whose respective *Civil Architecture* (1759) and *History of Architecture* (1896) he lists as the first two sources in his own 1904 study of the Parthenon.[20]

Mitsuhashi's style and grammar of composition also drew on a Beaux-Arts understanding of design as the analytical addition of parts to create compositional unity, what architectural historian Richard Moore has summarized as "a theory of *dessin*, or design, that reduced depicted objects to geometrical regularity in order to achieve compositional unity."[21] Like Mitsuhashi's early study of the Parthenon and later analyses of world architecture in *Improved Japanese and Western Great Architectural Knowledge*, his programmatically appropriate façades were discrete from the structure and spaces inside and were composed through the application of rational Enlightenment design based on the study of mechanics and classical proportions—as typified by Greek and Roman architecture—rather than through a Romantic ideal of intuitively grasped or sublime beauty. His theories also marked a break from the traditional carpentry measures and techniques that had governed composition in Japanese building prior to the adoption of Western architecture, and continued to influence the form of buildings through their application by carpenters and master builders in the actual building process and transmission to university-trained architects through coursework and articles in *Kenchiku zasshi*.[22]

But at the same time, Mitsuhashi's approach to design reflected French Beaux-Arts principles filtered through the more functionalist approach then popular in the architecture program at Columbia University in New York. Like others in his cohort in the 1890s, he was familiar with the writings of American architects William Robert Ware, founder of the architecture schools at MIT and Columbia, John Beverley Robinson, professor of architecture at Columbia, and John Vredenburg Van Pelt, a New York architect who had trained in Paris.[23] As educators, Ware and Robinson introduced Beaux-Arts eclectic historicism and emphasis on design principles into American architectural education, blending it with more practical content—structures, materials—and on-site experiential learning. Since the actual methods for building in the Western style were of paramount importance to Japanese architects, this hybrid American approach fit well with the Japanese architects' interests. Mitsuhashi, in fact, transposed American principles directly into the Japanese context: Each of his design principles corresponded directly to a chapter title in Robinson's 1899 text *Principles of Architectural Composition*—Unity, Grouping, Subordinate Parts, Appendages, Grouping of Details, and Double Composition—and took some of his illustrations—including the diagram explaining unity also found in Murooka's treatise—directly from Robinson's text.[24]

That said, whether his influences were British, French, or American is less important than the fact that, by tacitly emphasizing the foreign—and therefore "universal"—sense of his design principles, Mitsuhashi makes a further argument for the modernity of his buildings, and of architectural practice. The application of Western aesthetic principles indicated a break with past ideas of style, or at least an ideological resistance to them.[25] By adapting Western professional models and aesthetic discourses to the local context, Japanese architects situated themselves within a transnational cosmopolitan brotherhood, for which masculinity (in addition to class) was a necessary qualification for membership. In this process, beauty did not have to be gendered at all: The very use of supposedly universal aesthetic principles from foreign male architectural culture already performed the same function. Ideals of masculinity and femininity did not appear in the discourse, but it did not need to: The discourse itself was coded as a male domain.[26]

Beauty for the Housewife

While left unsaid, the professional practice of architecture in the late nine-teenth and early twentieth centuries was also gendered as male. This does not mean that women were not privy to information about the design and decoration of spaces, or not assigned responsibility for the aesthetically pleasing performance of both. Rather, in contrast to the architectural pro-fession, which marked these practices as the purview of a select group of men, the ideology of the housewife during this period held that the provi-sion of a beautiful home was the responsibility of all women. Like public buildings, the housewife's beautiful home was meant ultimately to further the national good. Unlike beauty in public architecture, however, beauty in the domestic sphere derived not from the correct application of objective compositional principles but from the furnishing of interior spaces with tasteful, beautiful objects whose combination would offer the occupant an edifying and inspirational polysensory experience.

As in Europe and North America at the time, neither architectural training nor jobs in architectural offices became available to women until educational reforms following World War II.[27] However, this does not mean that women in the early twentieth century were not allowed access to what we might call "architectural information," namely, the specialized knowledge of design, materials, structures, and the construction process necessary to create a built environment. Interior decoration literature for women emerged within the *Kaseigaku* (Home Economics) curriculum for girls' higher schools, an optional extension to compulsory primary educa-tion and the near-exclusive preserve of girls from elite families, until the 1910s.[28] As the target audience for such texts broadened with the expansion of women's education and the growth of the middle class after 1900, the number of home economics manuals and interior decoration guides grew rapidly and began to show crossover in content and greater recognition of the breadth of readers' actual socioeconomic conditions.

In particular, the late 1900s saw a profusion of interior decoration manuals published alongside similar volumes on topics such as cooking, manners, health, sewing, and caring for invalids, in multivolume ency-clopedias of domestic management by major trade publishers. In 1914, the Ministry of Education mandated that all primary schools teach girls Home Economics as well; this coincided with another outpouring of texts from trade publishers, including articles on housing and interior decora-tion magazines like *Shufu no tomo* (The Housewife's Companion) devoted to improving readers' knowledge of and devotion to *ishokujū* (clothing, cooking, and domestic space).

Architectural knowledge within this system taught girls basic struc-tures, materials, design principles, mechanical systems, and interior deco-ration. Housing textbooks focused on the construction and maintenance of the actual building, while interior decoration guidebooks leaned towards the appointment of already finished spaces.[29] Mass-market women's magazines after the mid-1910s also included "reader testimonies" in which devoted readers explained how they had saved the money for a down payment on a new home, as well as descriptions of real and imagined model homes to whose ownership readers might aspire.[30] Some texts were written primarily for use in schools; more often, though, they were written with both girls' school students and women outside the educational system in mind.

The degree to which domestic architecture textbooks, encouraging articles on home-building, and interior design guidebooks addressed the aesthetics of domestic space varied with time, but in nearly all cases, the educators, architects, and social reformers responsible for the texts presented the creation of a beautiful interior as a functional necessity, part of the responsibility of the housewife to create a hygienic, comfortable, and pleasant environment for her family, and interior decoration was the main method by which women were to achieve this.[31] As women's educator Ōe Sumiko explained in her 1916 text *Ōyō kaji seigi* (Detailed Lectures in Practical Housekeeping), "The purpose of decoration is to increase the beauty of the home's general appearance, and to maintain the quality of the home."[32] Decoration need not be luxurious, Ōe said, but should fit with the house itself, provide relaxation and comfort, match the status of the family and preserve its dignity and character. Kondō Shōichi, author of *Shitsunai sōshoku hō* (Principles of Interior Decoration), one volume in a multivolume practical home encyclopedia published by major trade publisher Hakubunkan in 1907, prefaced his specific prescriptions for beautiful interiors with a more general chapter on "the relationship between decoration and the structure of the house." In the preface he cautioned readers to "first carefully survey the structure of the rooms of the house and consider the kind of taste of decoration appropriate for the house, then to take on the decoration afterwards," just as when choosing the pattern for kimono fabric, they would consider the body shape of the wearer—thus avoiding vertical stripes for a tall, thin figure, for example.[33] More generally, Kondō wrote, interior decoration should fit occupants' needs for "educational profit, the comfort of suffering in the battlefield of competition that is being, the conversion of thought and aesthetic enjoyment."[34]

Interior decoration and domestic economy experts like Kondō offered women two ways to learn beautiful decoration: *biiku* (aesthetic education), or the cultivation and refinement of a general aesthetic sensibility through exposure to beauty and for application in all areas of daily life, and specific prescriptive rules for the decoration of domestic interiors. These two were not mutually exclusive. Rather, the refined sensibility produced by aesthetic education would make the creation of beautiful interiors almost automatic, the application of the general principles of beauty of heart and form that the user—the housewife—had learned through moral education, physical education, academic study, and practice. At the same time, time spent in a beautiful environment would function like the experience of beauty through any of the arts to build and hone the interior beauty of all occupants, including the decorator. Either way, while beauty could be achieved through the selection and tasteful combination of aesthetically pleasing objects appropriate for the season, the social status of the occupants, and the use of the room based on existing codes, it was not an objective, universal, and mathematically explainable quality like the "beauty" of architectural composition but a subjective experience.

In the logic of aesthetic education, women were to cultivate taste and sensibility through exposure to artistic, morally enlightening art, ideas, and interiors, and to express it through personal adornment as well as through their interiors. As Kondō reminded readers, "You must not forget to add elements of beauty to your interior decoration. This is not limited only to the decoration of the interior but applies equally to clothing. I believe that is common to nearly all forms of decoration, whether the decoration of the body, of hair, or of boats, but even more essential for the decoration of the interior."[35] It should go without saying that this was because the interior, as a polysensory environment surrounding not only its designer but all occupants of the space, had superior power to suggest and influence the morals of others. Women were responsible for bringing beauty to all areas of daily life, but as the intended mistresses of domestic space, they had particular responsibility to ensure that their own aesthetic and moral sensibilities would enable them to create an appropriate space for the aesthetic and moral education of others, particularly children.

As formulated by late nineteenth-century educators like Shimoda Utako, the head of the Peeresses' School in Tokyo and a major influence on educational theory particularly for girls' education, the purpose of aesthetic education for women was to develop and improve *kokoro no bi* (the beauty of the heart) and *katachi no bi* (the beauty of form) through studies of literature, botany, drawing, and music.[36] Shimoda saw the refinement of the aesthetic sensibility of both men and women as necessary for the national good and achievable through theoretical study and practice. The acquisition and use of interior beauty gained through moral education was more important than that of formal beauty, which was to be gained through physical education and intellectual education.

Early twentieth-century interior decoration texts extended the aesthetic education theory of the previous generation to support the need for women to create beautiful interiors as well—not only for their own edification but also for the aesthetic education of their children. In other words, the point of the beautiful interior was not simply visual pleasure and creature comfort but moral improvement. To this end, interiors had to possess an indefinable, unformed "metaphysical beauty" in addition to their formal visual qualities. Or, as Kondō phrased it,

> In sum, all one needs to do is to take the pure beauty that resides in one's heart and develop and express it in a variety of directions. However, if beauty includes the beauty of external appearance, it also includes interior beauty, which is to say metaphysical beauty, and decoration can only be completed by the combination of both of these. If that spiritual beauty is lacking, then that decoration will not be able to avoid becoming something extremely without taste.[37]

Not only the goal but the means is needed to incorporate "interior beauty." For example, Kondō explained that:

> Decorative beauty does not mean merely decorating a room to be beautiful and gorgeous. Of course, achieving beauty through decoration is one of the necessary conditions, but we cannot forget that decoration is also essential to provide a kind of stimulation— taste that invites aesthetic excitement. Thus, beauty is that which possesses the magical power to take our emotion to the highest sphere, and bring it to the edge of elegance.[38]

This desire for improvement through stimulation of the emotions, Kondō stresses, is innate to human nature. Decoration has power because it "soothes, enlightens, and reconciles the human heart."[39] It synthesizes multiple arts to calm and inspire its inhabitants, generally working on them as only aesthetic objects can—and as the role of women to create for men who experience the spaces. Or, as Kondō opined in 1907:

> When a man who has labored outside with his soul and body comes home at the end of the day and meets the rooms of his domicile, decorated in still elegance and superior beauty, his spirit should immediately be revived. A boy entering a room decorated with things like the portraits of heroes, great, loyal, and valiant men who have left great marks on the history of their nation, or ancient objects related to them will always have a deep impression made on his small, young heart. This can achieve an excellent effect similar to that achieved by reading success stories. Of course, painting, sculpture, and music move the human heart in one way as singular kinds of art, but if you conceive that the ultimate art would be one that brings all of these arts together, it is clearly obvious that the art of interior decoration, which has an even stronger capacity for influence, is the highest form of art.[40]

After Japan's victory in the Russo-Japanese War (1904–05), a time of increased patriotism and new models for masculinity based on military heroes of the war and circulated in newspapers, magazines, and popular novels, including children's literature, women's roles in inspiring such valor and motivation through the enhancement of beauty in domestic space became clear. At the same time, the coding of the private home as an extension of the nation also emerged as part of the housewife ideal.

While metaphysical beauty was the goal, the application of correct principles for interior decoration that imbued a space with formal beauty was still the best way to achieve it. In Kondō's words, "there are consistent principles and methods to decoration, so it is essential that anyone wishing to pour their heart into decoration first grasp these methods."[41] Thus, even authors like Kondō, who stressed the importance of non-formal beauty, provided detailed instructions for the appropriate furnishing of rooms. Kondō's *Shitsunai sōshoku hō* listed combinations appropriate for a variety of seasons and types of rooms, for example, decorations for the study in mid-autumn or the main room in early spring, down to the names of artists whose work was appropriate for particular occasions, and the correct incense for placement on a center table. For example, the *tokonoma* decorative alcove in a Japanese-style room in early spring should combine a hanging scroll by the Tosa School artist Tosa Mitsuoki with a seated sculpture of the god Tamatsushima Meijin, a low red lacquer table, a porcelain incense burner, and a bud vase with a single winter peony. Tellingly, these precise instructions were not illustrated, indicating perhaps that the ideal reader might be sufficiently educated to picture the composition mentally. Indeed, the majority of illustrations indicated not seasonal arrangements but the precise location for generic types of objects in standard rooms and spaces such as *jibukuro*, low shelves adjacent to the *tokonoma* (Figure 8.3).[42] These illustrations retained some of the information and visual language of early modern manuals for the decoration of tea spaces, for example the concern with arrangement and type, while incorporating new perspectival line drawing style (Figure 8.4). In composing interior arrangements, women were also to consider the degree to which an interior met subjective, immeasurable qualities such as *kedakai* (loftiness), *birei* (gorgeous beauty), and *sōdai* (magnificence), in addition to appropriateness.[43]

Pragmatic prescriptions for how to make a room beautiful could also be combined with more general advice on developing a sense of beauty or artistry. A chapter entitled "The Artistic Direction of Houses" in Yamagata Kōhō's 1907 umbrella text *Ishokujū* (Clothing, Food, Housing) begins by outlining the beauty of Japanese architecture and then explains the actual parts of a Japanese house. The tone is similar to that of guides to architectural composition, except that the elements prescribed are not line, form, and color but actual objects like *shōji* paper screens and ceiling boards to purchase and fit into a room, and no illustrations are given.[44]

By the 1910s, however, some women's educators began to teach both decoration and housing information for women more generally in a more practical light. This corresponded to a broader shift towards understanding

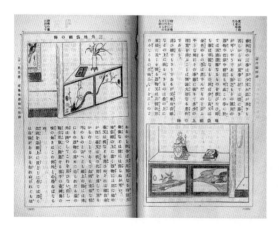

Figure 8.3   Examples of good decorating practice for ornamental shelves (*jibukuro*). Published in Kondō Shōichi, *Shitsunai sōshoku hō* (Tokyo: Hakubunken, 1907), 142–143.

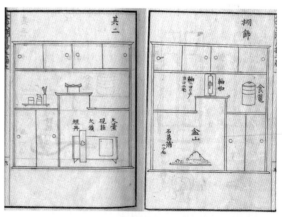

Figure 8.4   Examples of the correct decoration for shelves as part of tea practice. Published in Sogetsu Rōin, *Chashiki kogetsu-shō*, Vol. 5, Part 1 (Tokyo: Shōshodō, 1884 [1851]), 6.

housekeeping as a form of scientific management and towards extending the new knowledge to all women, manifest in the 1914 decision to make domestic education compulsory. In the section on interior decoration in her comprehensive textbook on housing, Ōe, the founder of the Tokyo Kasei Gakuin (Tokyo Academy of Domestic Economy) in 1923, divided her prescriptions into two categories: "decoration by arrangement," by which she meant the selection and placement of objects in a decorative alcove, and "decoration through constructive improvement," or decoration through the selection of structural and cladding materials as an intervention into actual built space.[45] However, compared to the three pages given to arrangement and composition, the section on materials received eighteen pages. The bulk of the 921-page text, too, concentrates on materials, techniques, and conventions for built elements of the home, including walls, windows, sanitary facilities, and heating, suggesting that, unlike Kondō, Ōe was concerned principally with providing women with the information and thus the agency necessary to supervise the construction of a new building rather than to furnish an existing one. Notably, her visual language, too, often borrowed from that of "architecture" proper, down to the use of plans, sections and elevations (Figure 8.5). Again, this was an inroad into a conventionally male area but an area that smacked of late Meiji modernity itself: building and technology rather than the aesthetic life of taste.

To varying degrees, however, interior decoration advice, both in stand-alone guidebooks like Kondō's and as chapters in home economics texts like Ōe's, functioned as an obverse to more practical, scientific domestic economy knowledge. And, while their concrete prescriptions for "good decoration" differ in content from Shimoda and others' more abstract guidelines for the development of an aesthetic sensibility, these texts can also be understood as part of the literature on personal improvement that followed earlier texts on aesthetic education, and were marketed to bourgeois women (and those aspiring to this status) through the 1910s. The reason is that, even in the prescriptive decoration manuals, a beautiful interior was never the end goal in itself but rather the means for achieving a greater goal: an improved environment for the family. A sense of beauty gained through aesthetic education was both necessary to create the interiors and something that could be gained and transmitted through the lived experience of them.

Like architects, educators in the discipline of Home Economics and the housewife herself found models for both in England and America. Shimoda Utako and Ōe Sumiko, for example, studied domestic

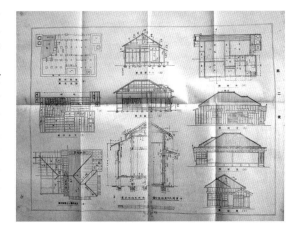

Figure 8.5   Architectural drawings for entrances and other elements of the home. Published in Ōe Sumiko, *Shoron jūkyo*, Vol. 1 of *Ōyo kaji seigi* (Tokyo and Osaka: Hōbunkan, 1916), Chart 2, between pages 622 and 623.

economy in England before returning to teach in Japan, and the mistress of the home as moralizing influence, the "angel of the household," was a common trope in Victorian discourse on gender roles.[46] The Japanese discourse incorporated the Anglo-American assertion that women should use the domestic interior to improve the moral tone of the household but without the claim that it was femininity—women's innate moral superiority or artistic nature—that made women innately more suited to doing so.

Similarly, late Meiji interior decoration experts borrowed the mode of prescribing specific decorative combinations for particular seasons, rooms, and events from an earlier tradition of guides for *shitsurai*, the decoration of tea ceremony spaces written for elite male practitioners beginning in the early modern period.[47] Some texts made the connection clear by employing as models anecdotes about the design of teahouses used by famous tea practitioners: for example, Kondō's mention of Sen no Rikyū's comparison of a cherry tree in the garden outside a teahouse to the mountains at Yoshino, known for their wild cherry blossoms in the springtime, or Yamagata's choice of a rustic-style teahouse as one of the illustrations for his discussion of the aesthetics of Japanese architecture.[48]

Whether the Meiji repositioning of interior aesthetics as a bourgeois pursuit or the later focus on construction materials and techniques introduced as part of the reframing of domestic duties as a scientific, technical practice, the recoding of formerly masculine culture or practices as female bolstered the claim of women's primacy in the domestic sphere even as masculine culture changed over time and crossed class boundaries—or rather posited that gender trumped class, so that formerly elite male culture could be for all women to aspire to if not to practice immediately. While male architects were charged with the informed application of geometry-based aesthetic principles to create a visually appealing façade and envelope for public spaces, female housewives were first to create beautiful domestic spaces to be experienced with all senses from the inside and then to participate in their construction, conscious of the aesthetic of the materials used. Thus, while the degree to which beauty was discussed varied over time and according to genre, the primacy of beauty as a quality with which to endow the home in all genres indicates the connection between femininity and the provision—if not the embodiment—of beauty created as part of the reformulation of gender roles after the Meiji Restoration. As the reappropriation of formerly male practice indicates, beauty in the home was feminine as a practice but not coded as essentially feminine. Women were newly charged with the beautification of the home, but this had to do with their new roles as homemakers, not because of an already existing identification of femininity with interior decoration or beauty. Rather, tying beauty to feminine roles was a way to shift the onus of interior decoration to women. Women themselves were not essentially closer to beauty or morality; rather, a beautiful interior was a central element of the home, and as such, provision of it was a women's responsibility.

Like the writings of male architects, architectural texts for women in the Meiji period were well aware of Western equivalents like Charles Eastlake's *Hints on Household Taste* and perpetuated a gendered division of labor through their choice of content. However, while texts for architects were concerned with defining class-based boundaries for professional identities within building culture, texts for women defined and regulated knowledge to create, disseminate, and reinforce changing new ideals of the housewife as a gender role that transcended class. The treatment of beauty within this process was no exception: Ideals taken from Anglo-American domestic architectural and interior decoration guides for women mixed with aesthetic prescriptions from premodern tea culture texts for men to create a new area of practice and discourse marked as exclusively feminine. While the contents reflected class assumptions and actual application of the texts' prescriptions clearly required belonging to certain classes, the underlying tenets were that gender trumped class, and that all women, regardless of their socioeconomic background, should aspire to become housewives and, as part of the performance of this role, decorate their home.

Conclusion

In the Meiji period, the creation of beautiful space was discussed less frequently in print discourse than were structural or stylistic considerations, but it appeared nonetheless as an important element in the responsibilities of both men and women charged with creating a modern environment through interventions into it as professionals. The actual idea and methods of application of beauty for men and women diverged; however, this had less to do with gendered conceptions of beauty itself and more to do with new gender roles defined by specific practices and spaces.

Unlike texts for male design professionals, i.e., architects, practical and aspirational texts for women engaged professionally in designing, furnishing, and decorating space; in other words, the housewife, or women who were expected to later become housewives, listed beauty as an attribute that could be achieved not through the application of classical compositional principles derived from natural form or mathematical ratios but through specific and highly concrete practices of consumption and arrangement within space—including the arrangement of both objects and the parts of the building itself.

Thus, after the Meiji Restoration, women across social classes were held increasingly responsible for all domestic matters, including those such as the form and furnishing of the home, which were once seen as largely the purview of men. The shift to holding women responsible for the introduction of beauty into the spaces of daily life and offering instruction on how to do this signaled a change in gender roles and a collapsing of class boundaries, or at least the effort to effect a tacit change in them. At the same time, differing concepts of what beauty actually was showed that, while the modern social system asked both (all) women and (some) men to improve the environment of daily life through active intervention into it, the actual ways in which men and women intervened were to remain separate. In other words, while nowhere as overt as the separate streaming of some men into architecture, carpentry, and building trades based on class and all women into marriage, motherhood, household management, and domestic service by virtue of their gender, separate definitions of beauty as a concept in design principles for men and women served to shape and delimit their acts as designers.[49]

Notes

Introduction

1. See Nihon Joshi Daigaku Joshi Kyōiku Kenkyūsho (Japanese Women's University Women's Education Research Center), comp., *Meiji no Joshi Kyōiku (Women's Education of the Meiji Period)* (Tokyo: Kokudosha, 1967), Table 2, 201.
2. The term "good wife, wise mother" was coined by the enlightenment educator Nakamura Masanao (1832–91) and derived from Western and Confucian concepts of womanhood. See Koyama Shizuko, *Ryōsai kenbo to iu kihan* (Tokyo: Keisō Shobō, 1991); Kathleen Uno, "The Origins of 'Good Wife, Wise Mother' in Modern Japan," in *Japanische Frauengeschichte(n),* eds. Erich Pauer and Regine Mathias (Marburg: Forderverein Marburger Japan-Reihe, 1995).
3. "The government stipulated that three kinds of women should be rewarded and praised: first, *jiefu,* women who were widowed before they turned thirty and remained widows past the age of fifty; second, *lienü* or *liefu,* women who died resisting rape, or who committed suicide after being raped, and who committed suicide after being widowed; third, *zhennü,* women whose fiancés died and who then remained virgins until death." This citation comes from Wang Zheng, *Women in the Chinese Enlightenment: Oral and Textual Histories* (Berkeley: University of California Press, 1999), 51. The connection to Han nationalism is described in Louise Edwards, "Chinese Women's Campaigns for Suffrage: Nationalism, Confucianism, and Political Agency," in *Women's Suffrage in Asia,* eds. Edwards and Roces, 62, 69.
4. Edwards, 64–5.
5. Chungmoo Choi, "Nationalism and Construction of Gender in Korea," in *Dangerous Women: Gender and Korean Nationalism,* eds. Elaine H. Kim and Chungmoo Choi (Routledge: New York and London, 1998), 13.
6. See Theodore Jun Yoo, *The Politics of Gender During the Colonial Period: Education, Labor, and Health, 1910–1945* (Berkeley: University of California Press, 2008), 88–93.
7. Martha Banta, *Imaging American Women: Idea and Ideals in Cultural History* (New York: Columbia University Press, 1987), 67.
8. Edwards, 73.
9. For a succinct account of women's rights movements in modern Japan, see Barbara Molony, "Citizenship and Suffrage in Interwar Japan," in *Women's Suffrage in Asia,* eds. Edwards and Roces, 127–51.
10. On women's rights issues, see Yoo, *The Politics of Gender during the Colonial Period,* Chapters 2–4; Ken Wells, "Expanding Their Realm: Women and Public Agency in Colonial Korea," *Women's Suffrage in Asia,* eds Edwards and Roces, 152–60.
11. See Chulwoo Lee, "Modernity, Legality, and Power in Korea under Japanese Rule," in *Colonial Modernity in Korea,* eds. Gi-Wook Shin and Michael Robinson (Cambridge, MA: Harvard University Asia Center, 2001), 47.
12. See Elisabeth Eide, *China's Ibsen: From Ibsen to Ibsenism* (London: Curzon, 1987).
13. See Saburō Satō, "Ibsen's Impact on Novelist Shimazaki Tōson," *Comparative Literature Studies* 33, no. 1, East-West Issue (1996): 75.
14. Ajioka Chiaki, "The Lure of the City," in *Modern Girl: Modernity in Japanese Art 1910–1935,* ed. Jackie Menzies (Sydney: Art Gallery of New South Wales, 1998), 30.

15. Ajioka, 30.

16. See Carol Gluck, *Japan's Modern Myths: Ideology in the Late Meiji Period* (Princeton, NJ: Princeton University Press, 1985), 281–282.

17. See Margit Nagy, "Middle-Class Working Women During the Interwar Years," in *Recreating Japanese Women, 1600–1945,* ed. Gail Lee Bernstein (Berkeley: University of California Press, 1991), 209.

18. Laurel Rasplica Rodd, "Yosano Akiko and the Taishō Debate over the 'New Woman,'" in Bernstein, ed., 176.

19. See Phyllis Hyland Larson, "Yosano Akiko and the Recreation of the Female Self: An Autogynography," *The Journal of the Association of Teachers of Japanese,* Vol. 25, no. 1, Special Issue: Yosano Akiko (1878–1942) (April 1991): 10–26; and Rodd.

20. Rodd, 190.

21. See Yosano Akiko, "Watakushi no teisō kan" (My Views on Chastity), in *Teihon Yosano Akiko no zenshū* (*Teihon Collected Works by Yosano Akiko*), Vol. 14, ed. Kimata Osamu (Tokyo: Kōdansha, 1979), 365–82; for a summary of this article, see Larson, 23–5.

22. See Wang, 51.

23. Wang, 64–6.

24. Wang, 61–3.

25. Marsha Weidner, *Flowering in the Shadows: Women in the History of Chinese and Japanese Painting* (Honolulu: University of Hawai'i Press, 1990); Patricia Fister and Fumiko Yamamoto, *Japanese Women Artists, 1600–1900* (Lawrence: Spencer Museum of Art, University of Kansas, 1988).

26. Articles and books in different languages that explore the links between East Asian women and film are numerous. Two representative examples in English are Catherine Russell, *New Women of the Silent Screen: China, Japan, Hollywood* (Durham, NC: Duke University Press, 2005) and Sheldon H. Lu, *Transnational Chinese Cinema: Identity, Nationhood, Gender* (Honolulu: University of Hawai'i Press, 1997).

27. Joshua S. Mostow, Norman Bryson, and Marybeth Graybill, *Gender and Power in the Japanese Visual Field* (Honolulu: University of Hawai'i Press, 2003); Doris Croissant, et al., *Performing "Nation": Gender Politics in Literature, Theater, and the Visual Arts of Japan and China, 1880–1940* (Leiden: Brill Academic Publishers, 2008).

28. For an overview of the Joseon Art Exhibitions, see Kim Youngna, "Artistic Trends in Korean Painting during the 1930s," in *War, Occupation, and Creativity: Japan and East Asia, 1920–1960,* eds. Marlene J. Mayo, J. Thomas Rimer, and H. Eleanor Kerkham (Honolulu: University of Hawai'i Press, 2001), 121–49. On the modern period in general, see Kim Youngna, *20th Century Korean Art* (London: Laurence King, 2005).

29. Julia Kristeva, *Powers of Horror: An Essay on Abjection* (1980), trans. Leon S. Roudiez (New York: Columbia University Press, 1982), 13.

30. See Philippe Jullian, *The Orientalists: European Painters of Eastern Scenes* (Oxford: Phaidon, 1977); Lynn Thomson, *Women as Portrayed in Orientalist Painting* (Paris: Art-Création-Réalisation, 1994); and Christine Peltre, *Orientalism in Art* (New York: Abbeville Press, 2005).

31. See Ikeda Shinobu, *Nihon kaiga no joseizō—jendā—bijutsu no shiten kara* (The Image of Women in Japanese Painting—Gender—From the Point of View of Art) (Tokyo: Chikuma Shobō, 1998), 167–93.

32. Edward Said, *Orientalism* (1978). See also Benedict Anderson, *Imagined Communities* (London: Verso, 1983) and Eric Hobsbawm and Terrence Ranger, eds., *The Invention of Tradition* (Cambridge: Cambridge University Press, 1983).

Chapter 1

1. Lois W. Banner, *American Beauty* (New York: Knopf, 1983), 255–61.

2. "The Most Beautiful Woman in America," *Chicago Daily Tribune,* July 7, 1907, F4.

3. An article from June 30 stated they had received "over 100,000 pictures of American women, selected by twenty-five of the greatest metropolitan papers of the country, assisted by 1,500 smaller papers," and a feature article on August 11, 1907, reported that nearly 200,000 photographs had been examined by 500 newspapers. See "Why the American Girl is the Most Beautiful in the World," *Chicago Daily*

Tribune, June 30, 1907, F4 and "Simple Rules Revealing the Secrets of Beauty," *Chicago Daily Tribune*, August 11, 1907, G1.

4.   "The Most Beautiful Woman in America," July 7, 1907, F5.

5.   Inoue Shōichi, *Bijin kontesuto hyakunenshi: geigi no jidai kara bishojo made* (One Hundred Years of Beauty Contests: From Geisha to Beautiful Girls) (Tokyo: Shinchosha, 1992), 32–3.

6.   Inoue, 41–2. Patrons of the geisha apparently purchased all of the tickets in an effort to help their favorite beauty win.

7.   Inoue, 48–9.

8.   The contest was heavily promoted in the newspaper throughout the fall, the contest notification and rules being repeatedly published.

9.   "Boshū kisoku" (Application Rules), *Jiji shimpō*, September 15, 1907, reprinted in Ozawa Takeshi, *Koshashin de miru bakumatsu meiji no bijin zukan* (Viewed Through Old Photos: Picture Book of Bakumatsu-Meiji Beauties) (Tokyo: Sekai Bunkasha, 2001).

10.   The *Chicago Daily Tribune* published the following information on the judges: "The jury of award was composed of the most famous authorities on artistic beauty in Japan and included the names of such men as Saburosuke Okada, a painter of the foreign school; Senri Otsaki, a scientific photographer; Takeo Kawai, the foremost actor of the modern school; Koun Takamura, a sculptor; Shogoto Tsubai, professor of anthropology of the Imperial University; Shikwan Nakamura, leading actor of the classical school; Tsurio Mishima, a great physician and one of the advisers of the state department of education; and other noted artists and scientific men." See "Most Beautiful Women of Japan," *Chicago Daily Tribune*, May 17, 1908, F1.

11.   "Most Beautiful Women of Japan," F1.

12.   Presumably the rings were then passed on to the top winner for each district.

13.   The portraits of ten of the top twelve contestants together with the first-prize winner from a number of prefectures are reproduced in Ozawa.

14.   "The Most Beautiful Woman in America," July 7, 1907, F5.

15.   Inoue, 54–5.

16.   For example, Pierre Loti describes the memento box in which his lover, Chrysanthemum, keeps portraits of her friends together with their letters, ca. 1885. Pierre Loti, *Madame Chrysanthemum*, trans. Laura Enslor (New York: Boni and Liveright, 1900), 99.

17.   A *Yomiuri Shimbun* (Yomiuri News) article from May 22, 1889 describes a *miai* meeting via photographs. Suzuki Kōichi, *Nyūsu de ou Meiji nihon hakkutsu* (Discovering Meiji Japan Through the News), Vol. 1 (Tokyo: Kawade Shobō Shinsha, 1994), 166.

18.   Sebastian Dobson, "Reflections of Conflict: Japanese Photographers and the Russo-Japanese War," in *A Much Recorded War: The Russo-Japanese War in History and Imagery*, eds. Frederic A. Sharf, Anne Nishimura Morse, and Sebastian Dobson (Boston: MFA Publications, 2005), 71.

19.   Rebecca Copeland, *Lost Leaves: Women Writers of Meiji Japan* (Honolulu: University of Hawai'i Press, 2000), 221. See pp. 215–25 for further information on this publication. *Bungei kurabu* also held a beauty contest in 1907, calling for photographs of 100 geisha to be published in the magazine, which readers then voted on. See Inoue, 51.

20.   Satō Sakuma Rika, in Ozawa, 218–20.

21.   The book's original English subtitle is *The Belles of Japan*. The 215 women pictured represented the top five contestants from forty-three districts.

22.   Kinoshita Naoyuki, "Portraying the War Dead: Photography as a Medium for Memorial Portraiture," in *Reflecting Truth: Japanese Photography in the Nineteenth Century*, eds. Nicole Rousmaniere and Mikiko Hirayama (Leiden: Brill Publishing and the Sainsbury Institute for the Study of Japanese Arts and Cultures, 2004), 93.

23.   Kinoshita, 94–7.

24.   There were a number of different photographs of Suehiro in circulation, including several versions published in the *Chicago Tribune* and four different images published in *Nihon bijinchō*. It is unclear when any of the photographs were actually taken. While it is certain that Esaki Kiyoshi took the photo initially submitted to the contest, *Nihon bijinchō* does not include any information on any of the photographers.

25. Inoue, 10–1. Note that Marguerite Frey's older sister had also submitted Frey's photograph without her knowledge. Advertisements recruiting for the *Tribune* contest had encouraged people to submit their friends' photographs, so that anyone who wanted to enter could have an appearance of modesty.

26. Inoue, 12–30. Inoue also notes that a common stereotype existed depicting a kind of bifurcated system at work in girls' higher education, those considered to be beauties marrying quickly and dropping out of school prior to graduating, while non-beauties were more serious students who focused their "graduation face" towards finishing school. Furthermore, educational materials of the period used for ethical and moral training denigrated the *bijin*, claiming that they were not good students and were conceited; good students, in contrast, were described as being good-natured and docile non-beauties. See p. 24.

27. Inoue, 12.

28. Their union was announced in the *Jiji shimpō* on October 7, 1908. See also Inoue, 29. One of her grand-daughters later married into the imperial family.

29. For a later example that recalls the 1907 *Jiji shimpō* event, see Jennifer Robertson's discussion of the 1931 Miss Nippon beauty contest in "Japan's First Cyborg? Miss Nippon, Eugenics and Wartime Technologies of Beauty, Body and Blood," in *Body & Society* 7 (January 2001): 1–34, especially 11–24.

30. Aoyogi Yūbi writing in the September 16, 1899 edition of *On'na zasshi* (Ladies' Journal), as cited in Robertson, 35.

31. "Nihon dai ichi bijin no shashin wo boshūsu" (Searching for Photos of Japan's Number One Beauty), *Jiji shimpō*, September 15, 1907, reprinted in Ozawa.

32. "The Most Beautiful Woman in America," *Chicago Daily Tribune*, July 7, 1907, F5.

33. Vera Mackie, *Feminism in Modern Japan: Citizenship, Embodiment and Sexuality* (Cambridge: Cambridge University Press, 2003), 31.

34. Miura Shūsei, *Sensō to Fujin* (War and Women) (Tokyo: Bunmeidō, 1904); Suzuki Akiko, *Gunkoku no Fujin* (Women of Militarism) (Tokyo: Nikkō Yūrindō, 1904); and Hoshioka Shoin, *Gunkoku no Fujin* (Women of Militarism) (Tokyo: Hoshioka Shoin, 1904).

35. Bōbō Gakujin, *Sensō bi to fujin bi* (The Beauty of War and the Beauty of Women) (Tokyo: Keiseisha, 1904).

36. Inoue, 64–6.

37. "Japan Aroused by Beauty War with America," *Chicago Daily Tribune*, November 17, 1907, G3. A later article stated that there were forty-three districts, five women chosen to represent each district, a number that accords with the number of photographs published in *Nihon bijinchō*. See May 17, 1908.

38. See Ogawa, 96. The likely source for this claim is an article in the *Jiji shimpō* on June 21, 1908, that listed the names of the top beauties of six countries, Suehiro's name occurring sixth (last) on this list.

39. "The Most Beautiful Women of Japan," *Chicago Daily Tribune*, May 17, 1908, F1. This page from the *Tribune* also accompanied the June 21 *Jiji shimpō* article cited in the previous footnote.

Chapter 2

1. See Pang Laikwan, *The Distorting Mirror: Visual Modernity in China* (Honolulu: University of Hawai'i Press, 2007), for a short biography of Hang Zhiying; and Ellen Johnston Laing, *Selling Happiness: Calendar Prints and Visual Culture of Early Twentieth-Century Shanghai* (Honolulu: University of Hawai'i Press, 2004).

2. Laing.

3. Wen-hsin Yeh, *Shanghai Splendor: Economic Sentiments and the Making of Modern China, 1843–1949* (Berkeley, Los Angeles, London: University of California Press, 2007), 67, see also n. 59. The term Yeh uses is "classical beauties, fictional or historical."

4. The editors of a recently published anthology of essays on gender in China at about the same period begin with the startling assertion that they are interested in "how masculinity and femininity in China are constructed and performed as *lived experience*, as opposed to represented in artistic works…." It's the word "opposed" that troubles. Pictures are theorized as somehow being irrelevant; they simply don't matter to the lived experience of how gender was performed, understood, and made meaningful. Pictures are bracketed out. But I bring up their notion of representation as being outside the experience of gender performance, not to argue with the editors precisely (to be sure, my brief analysis of the calendar poster perhaps indicates the degree to which I disagree with them). I do so only because

they are echoing the debates of Chinese artists themselves. See the introduction by Jeffrey Wasserstrom and Susan Brownell to *Chinese Femininities/Chinese Masculinities, A Reader* (London, Los Angeles, Berkeley: University of California Press, 2002), 2.

5.   Though there is a story here, one story that the manuals proffer, as we shall see, complements those already told about the uneasy relationship between pictures of women and gender by Joan Judge in her study of exemplary women in late Qing textbooks and journals for girls, Jacqueline Nivard writing on the *Funü zazhi* (Ladies' Journal), and Barbara Mittler in her investigations into Shanghai's early news media. See Judge, "Blended Wish Images: Chinese and Western Exemplary Women at the Turn of the Twentieth Century," in *Beyond Tradition and Modernity: Gender, Genre, and Cosmopolitanism in Late Qing China*, eds. Grace S. Fong, Nanxiu Qian, and Harriet T. Zurndorfer (Leiden, Boston: Brill, 2004), 102–35; Nivard, "Women and the Women's Press: The Case of *The Ladies' Journal (Funü zazhi)*, 1915–1931," *Republican China* 10, no. 1b (November 1984): 37–55; and Mittler, "Defy(N)ing Modernity: Women in Shanghai's Early News-Media (1872–1915)," *Jindai Zhongguo funüshi yanjiu* (Study of Modern Chinese Women's History) , 11 (December 2003): 215–59.

6.   Ralph Cohen, "History and Genre," *New Literary History* 17, no. 2 (Winter 1986): 204.

7.   Jacques Derrida, "The Law of Genre," *Critical Inquiry* 7, no. 1 (Autumn 1980): 64; cit. Cohen, "History and Genre," *New Literary History* 17, no. 2 (Winter 1986): 204, n. 4.

8.   Christopher A. Reed, *Gutenberg in Shanghai: Chinese Print Capitalism, 1876–1937* (Vancouver, Toronto: UBC Press, 2004), 178–9, n. 59, which mentions that, in 1914, Ye Jiuru was one of the joint directors of the Shanghai Booksellers' Guild (Shanghai shuye gongsuo), along with Gong Boyin, assisting the general director, Gao Hanqing.

9.   Wu Peiheng, ed., *Jieziyuan huazhuan: Disiji renwu Chao Xun linben* (Mustard Seed Garden Manual Book Four: Human Figures as Copied by Chao Xun) (Beijing: Renmin Meishu Chubanshe, 1957), preface to Vol. 7.

10.   Dai Kui was a scholar known primarily for his skills as a sculptor, not a painter. According to Li Song, Dai Kui was called repeatedly to serve at the court of Emperor Xiaowu, and despite promises of official high posts, he refused. See *Chinese Sculpture*, eds. Angela Falco Howard et al. (New Haven, CT: Yale University Press; Beijing: Foreign Languages Press, 2006), 467, n. 17.

11.   Refers to Ding Lingguang, the consort of Xiao Yan.

12.   This quotation and all attributed to Ye are from the unpaginated introduction to Volume 13 in the *Sanxitang* set of manuals.

13.   Copies of paintings by Tang Yin (1470–1524) and Fei Danxu (1801–50).

14.   It perhaps goes without saying that the nineteenth- and early twentieth-century imprints of the *Mustard Seed Manual* are not connected to the original first three manuals of the same title published by Li Yu in the late seventeenth and early eighteenth centuries. This does not somehow make them illegitimate subjects of analysis and study, and to be sure, there is nothing in the historical record that suggests that they were viewed in pejorative terms, as fraudulent or best reductively referred to as the "so-called" *Mustard Seed Garden* manuals.

15.   See Wu Hung, "Beyond Stereotypes: The Twelve Beauties in Early Qing Court Art and the *Dream of the Red Chamber*," in *Writing Women in Late Imperial China*, eds. Ellen Widmer and Kang-I Sun Chang (Stanford, CA: Stanford University Press, 1997), 306–65.

16.   See Nivard.

17.   Virtually unknown in painting histories, Wang was relatively well connected in his day. Yang Yi, who would write the *Haishang molin* (Ink Forest of Shanghai) biographies of artists published in 1920, for instance, contributes a preface to the manual. In 1909, Wang joined the Yuanmishan Painting and Calligraphy Association and the Yuyuan Calligraphy and Painting Association (along with famous painters such as Wu Changshuo, Wang Yiting, Qian Huian). The following year he became a member of the Shanghai Calligraphy and Painting Research Group. His edition of the painting manual is perhaps not so well known because it did not circulate broadly, and few are extant today. On Wang, see Zhu Wanzhang, *Wang Kun ketu huagao* (Wang Kun's Drafting Sketches), *Meishu bao* (*China Art Weekly*), 21 (August 19, 2006): 1.

18.   These are *yuan, zhen, li, heng*, often interpreted as the "four cardinal virtues" of the movement of heaven.

19.   One by Qian Huian, one by Gu Luo (1763–after 1837), and two by Pan Zhenyong (1852–1921).

20. Nivard.
21. On Zhou, see Joseph Esherick, *Reform and Revolution in China: The 1911 Revolution in Hunan and Hubei* (Berkeley and Los Angeles: University of California Press, 1976).
22. Attributed to Song Yü, *Shennü fu* (*Wenxuan* 19.9a)
23. This is a subtle point, because it assumes that readers would associate these phrases with popular stories and the poem in which they appeared, instead of taking them literally out of context on their own terms. However, to read the phrase *liuchao jinfen*, for instance, as an expression of the perfected and complete fullness and beauty of women, is to acknowledge the potential for physical beauty to exceed the boundaries it is being given in the manual, an issue to be taken up in the next section.
24. See Stephen Melville and Bill Readings, eds., *Vision and Textuality* (London: Macmillan, 1995), 7.
25. Ye might have consulted a 1915 reprint of the manual by the Shanghai publisher Heji shuju. Collection UCLA Library.
26. John Hay, "The Body Invisible in Chinese Art?" in *Body, Subject & Power in China*, eds. Angela Zito and Tani Barlow (Chicago: The University of Chicago Press, 1994), 42–77.
27. "Personally Viewed by Emperor Qianlong" (*Qianlong yulan zhi bao*); "Precise Authorization Seal of the Hall of Three Rarities" (*Sanxitang jingjianxi*).
28. Craig Clunas, *Pictures and Visuality in Early Modern China* (London: Reaktion Books, 1997), Chap. 5.
29. It is important to note that the imperial collection was not ordered as a "rational" modern museum might have been by artist or chronology but architectonically, by buildings for storage and display within the Forbidden City. See Patricia Berger, *Empire of Emptiness: Buddhist Art and Political Authority in Qing China* (Honolulu: University of Hawai'i Press, 2003), Chap. 3.
30. Melville and Readings, 8.
31. See Wu Hung's discussion of feminine space as Chinese space in *The Double Screen: Medium and Representation in Chinese Painting* (Chicago, IL: University of Chicago Press, 1996), esp. pp. 200–21. On the emotionally pregnant nature of feminine space, see also Lara Caroline Williams Blanchard, "Visualizing Love and Longing in Song Dynasty Paintings of Women," Ph.D. diss. University of Michigan, 2001.
32. Tang Hou, *Tang hua* (Tang Painting), Book 1 of *Huajian* (*Painting Critique*), trans. Osvald Sirén, *Chinese Painting: Leading Masters and Principles* (New York: The Ronald Press Company; London: Lund Humphries, 1956), vol. 1: 169.
33. A certain Wang Qi (1777–1840), whose biography is mentioned by Wang Yun in Chap. 2, 22b of *Yangzhou huayuan lu* (Record of the Painting Gardens of Yangzhou).
34. Wang, Chap. 3, 12b.
35. Li Dou, *Yangzhou huafang lu* (Reminiscences from the Pleasure Boats of Yangzhou) (1799; reproduced. Jiangsu: Guangling Guji Keyinshe, 1984), 45.
36. For a brief biographical sketch of the family, see Ellen Johnston Laing, "Women Painters in Traditional China," in *Flowering in the Shadows: Women in the History of Chinese and Japanese Painting*, ed. Marsha Weidner (Honolulu: University of Hawai'i Press, 1990), 86.
37. For a reprint of the full set of images, see *Wu Youru huabao,* Vol. 2 (Shanghai: Shanghai Shudian Chubanshe, 2002), 1.
38. For an early and preliminary study of this topic, see Claypool, "The Social Body: Beautiful Women Imagery in Late Imperial China" (University of Oregon, M.A. thesis, 1994).
39. *Compendium of New-style Art, Classified Pictures* (Xinpai tuhua fenlei daquan) (Shanghai: Xin Xin Meishushe), 4.
40. Laing, 66.
41. Lu Xun, "Lu Xun zai Zhonghua yishu daxue yanjiang jilu" (Records of Lu Xun's Speech at the Zhonghua Fine Arts Academy) in *Xuexi Lu Xun de meishu sixiang* (Lu Xun's Thoughts on Art) (Beijing: Renmin Meishu Chubanshe, 1979), 2–3, as translated and quoted by Sherman Cochran, "Marketing Medicine and Advertising Dreams in China 1900–1950," in *Becoming Chinese: Passages to Modernity and Beyond 1900–1950*, ed. Wen-hsin Yeh (Berkeley and Los Angeles: University of California Press, 2000), 62.
42. Li Chao, *Shanghai youhua shi* (History of Oil Painting in Shanghai) (Shanghai: Shanghai Renmin Meishu Chubanshe, 1995), 42, passage translated and quoted by Laing, 37, n. 104.

Chapter 3

1. The following explanation appears on the labels attached to all Alan Chan's garments and products: "All designs capture the unique local flavor of modern and nostalgic themes mainly from Hong Kong [*sic*]. This splendid taste of the legendary lifestyle of the orient is made available to you exclusively from Alan Chan Creations."

2. Several publications have recently appeared on the *yuefenpai* genre: Wu Hao, Zhuo Baichang, Huang Ying et.al., *Duhui modeng yuefenpai 1910–1930s* (Modern Metropolitan *yuefenpai*) (Hong Kong: San Lian Shudian, 1994); Zhang Yanfeng, *Lao yuefenpai guanggao hua* (Old Calendar Advertising Posters) (Taipei: Hansheng Zazhishi, 1994); Yi Bin, ed. *Lao Shanghai guanggao* (Old Shanghai Advertisements) (Shanghai: Shanghai Huabao Chubanshi, 1995); Zuo Xuchu, ed., *Lao shangbiao* (Old Trademarks) (Shanghai: Shanghai Huabao Chubanshe, 1999); and Chen Chaonan and Feng Yiyou, *Lao Guanggao* (Old Advertisements) (Shanghai Renmin Meishu Chubanshe: Shanghai, 1998).

3. *Yuefenpai* was related to traditional "New Year prints" produced at the beginning of the new year for auspicious and decorative purposes. According to Pu Ji, the term itself existed before it came into commercial use, referring to a genre of New Year prints with an image in the center and a one- or two-year calendar on the sides. With the introduction of marketing and advertising from the West, traditional *yuefenpai* became an item that major companies would distribute to their clients as a gift at the beginning of the year. *Yuefenpai* would often be given away with the product, as in the case of cigarettes, the customer receiving one poster for a 50-packet carton. See Pu Ji, "Jiefang qian de '*yuefenpai*' nianhua shiliao" (Historical Material on Pre-liberation *yuefenpai* New Year Pictures), *Meishu yanjiu* (Art Research) 2 (1959): 51.

4. Heinrich Otmar Früehauf, "Urban Exoticism in Modern Chinese Literature 1910–1933," Ph.D. diss., University of Chicago, 1990 (Ann Arbor, MI: University Microfilms International, 1994), 294. Leo Ou-fan Lee relates it to a phenomenon that could be considered the Asian version of Orientalism: "It can be argued that exoticism as a phenomenon of urban culture is closely related to a search of modernity and provides a partial solution to the paradox that arises between nationalism and imperialism." Leo Ou-fan Lee, *Shanghai Modern: The Flowering of a New Urban Culture in China 1930–1945* (Cambridge, MA: Harvard University Press, 1999), 203.

5. Often quoted in this respect is the contempt that Lu Xun felt for *yuefenpai*. See Liu Ruli, "Ji Lu Xun xiansheng zai Zhonghua Yi Da de yici jiangyan" (Recollection of a Speech Pronounced by Lu Xun at the Chinese Art University), *Meishu* (Art), 4 (1979): 6–7. For an exhaustive commentary of this speech, see Federico Greselin, "Un discorso di Lu Xun del 1930," *Annali di Ca' Foscari* 20, no. 3 (1981): 171–81.

6. Jing Ying, "Ni dongde zenyang qu zuo, zhan, he zoulu ma" (Do You Know How to Sit, Stand and Walk?), *Jindai Funü* (*The Modern Woman*), 16 (April 1930): 4–5.

7. Concerning the growing representation of women in European *fin-de-siècle* commercial advertising, Rita Felski has remarked how "advertising at this time began to develop increasingly sophisticated marketing techniques, promoting repertoires of identities and lifestyles to which the consumer was encouraged to aspire. Given an extant gender division of labor which identified shopping as women's work, it was women above all who were thus defined in this way through mass-produced images of femininity, even as middle-class women's dependence upon the economic support of men required them to invest far more heavily in modes of fashionable adornment and self-display." Rita Felski, *The Gender of Modernity* (Cambridge, MA and London: Harvard University Press, 1995), 64.

8. Felski, 3.

9. Felski, 14.

10. For the equation made between "New China/New Women" in contemporary Western media, see Grace Thompson Seton, "China's Hope in Her 'New Women,'" *Literary Digest* (November 15, 1924): 39–42; Emma Sarepta Yule, "Miss China," *Scribner's Magazine* LXXI, 1 (January 1922): 66–79; and Lock W. Wei, "Miss Peach Blossom," *Outlook* 154 (January 8, 1930): 50–1, 78.

11. Zhang Yingjin, *The City in Modern Chinese Literature and Film: Configurations of Space, Time and Gender* (Stanford, CA: Stanford University Press, 1996), 189.

12. See Ono Kakuzo, *Chinese Women in A Century of Revolution 1850–1950* (Stanford, CA: Stanford University Press, 1978).

13. P. S. Tseng, "The Chinese Woman Past and Present," in *Symposium on Chinese Culture*, ed. Sophia H. Chen Zhen (Shanghai: China Institute of Pacific Relations, 1931), 292. (Reprint, New York: Paragon Book Reprint Corp., 1969). Miss Tseng further states, "Although all professions are open to women now, they are not able to avail themselves of most of them. This is due to the insufficiency of their education in general and lack of vocational training in particular. Where there is real equality of sexes there is also real competition. Since men are usually better qualified, they easily oust women. A well-known publishing house in Shanghai may be cited as a concrete example. The company opened all its departments to women between 1920 and 1923 and many women were admitted, but gradually most of the women were replaced by men. They were dismissed chiefly through want of intelligence, inefficiency in work, and a general lack of earnestness in profession. The company declared that they did not dismiss them because they were women, but simply because they were poor workers" (290–1).

14. See Stephen Ching-kiu Chan, "The Language of Despair: Ideological Representations of the 'New Woman' by May Fourth Writers," in *Gender Politics in Modern China: Writing and Feminism*, ed. Tani E. Barlow (Durham, NC: Duke University Press, 1993); Zhang Yingjin, 185–231; and Leo-Ou Fan Lee, 194–203.

15. Tani E. Barlow, "Theorizing Woman: *Funü, Guojia, Jiating*" (Chinese Woman, Chinese State, Chinese Family), in *Body, Subject and Power in China*, eds. Angela Zito and Tani Barlow (Chicago, IL: The University of Chicago Press, 1994), 265, 267.

16. Mao Dun [Mao Tun], "First Morning at the Office" (1935), in *Spring Silkworms and Other Stories*, trans. Sidney Shapiro (Beijing: Foreign Language Press, 1956), 263.

17. Zhang Yingjin, 185–231.

18. Zhang Yingjin, 215.

19. "Liu's fiction … bears a certain resemblance to visual materials. This is especially true of Liu's portrayal of heroines, which draws directly from the female figures in the photos and on magazine covers as well as on calendar posters, to say nothing of the movies." Lee, 194.

20. Lee, 209.

21. For the equation established between women and commodities see Hill Gates, "Commodification of Chinese Women," *Signs* 14, no. 4 (Summer 1989): 799–832; and Sue Gronewald, *Beautiful Merchandise: Prostitution in China 1860–1936* (New York: Haworth Press, 1982), 37, 47.

22. James Cahill, "The Flower and the Mirror: Representations of Women in Late Chinese Painting," Lecture 1: "The Real Madam Hotung"; Lecture 2: "Courtesans, Concubines and Willing Women"; Lecture 3: "Women Lorn and Longing." (Papers presented at the Metropolitan Museum, New York, November 11–13, 1994). For more discussion by Cahill see *Pictures for Use and Pleasure: Vernacular Painting in High Qing China* (Berkeley: University of California Press, 2010).

23. Robert J. Maeda, "The Portrait of a Woman of the Late Ming- Early Ch'ing Period: Madame Ho-tung," *Archives of Asian Art* XXVII (1973): 46–51.

24. The authorship of this painting, assigned by Maeda to the seventeenth-century painter Wu Cho, is dismissed by Cahill precisely on the basis of its descriptive modes. Cahill in fact argues that the "real" Madame Hotung—a courtesan raised to the level of wife of a renowned literary man of the time—would never have consented to be represented in a pose explicitly referring to her courtesan's past. Cahill, Lecture 1, 3.

25. Maeda, 48.

26. Anne Birrell, ed. and trans., *New Songs from a Jade Terrace. An Anthology of Early Chinese Love Poetry* (London: George Allen and Unwin, 1982), 19.

27. In reference to the representation of the woman in her luxurious boudoir on the background of a telescopically receding space, Cahill states: "the elaborately detailed interiors … offer experiences to the exploring eyes that are themselves sensual to the point of eroticism. Visual penetration to depth beyond depths is an obvious sensory analogue to sexual penetration." Cahill, Lecture 1, 27.

28. The painting is reproduced in *Sotheby's Auction Catalogue*, November 25, 1991, New York, lot 62.

29. Cahill, Lecture 3, 48.

30. For the fetishistic overtones of the representation of a woman's foot, see Birrell, 13.

31. See Gail Hershatter, *Dangerous Pleasures: Prostitution and Modernity in Twentieth-Century Shanghai* (Berkeley: University of California Press, 1997), 83. Birrell, in her anthology on early Chinese love poetry, remarks how women in love were generally portrayed in luxurious settings: "The court poets

reveal a fascination for the opulent minutiae of feminine fashion. The typical portrait shows woman adorned with fine jewels, costly silk clothes, and elaborate make-up. She indicates her beauty and worth in a very material way through the sheer opulence of her personal décor… What this amounts to is an aesthetic convention of courtly love poetry: woman is adored when adorned." See *New Songs from a Jade Terrace*, 10.

32. The genre of beautiful ladies in the *nianhua* iconographic tradition is often called *shinü*. John Lust defines it broadly as follows: "Beauties. The Dream of Fair Women in China, a category of old art, to appear in the theatre, fiction etc. and as Immortals. There were the slender, ethereal, etc. already in the art of the 4th century BCE, and the observed, modeled on life…. Qing prints have ideal and observed, and the later Shanghai fashion scene. There are two sorts: 1) The mistresses of gentry households 2) Serving girls (on contract, married off when the time came). The prominence of the Beauty related to her place in society. Young women could move into marriage markets, or be recruited for the court for a spectacular career, where a poet could observe fretting young concubines, cooped up in palaces in the spring…." John Lust, *Chinese Popular Prints* (Leiden, New York, Koln: E.J. Brill, 1996), 282–3.

33. Zheng Mantuo was born in Anhui, studied portraiture in Hangzhou, and was eventually employed at the Erwoxuan Photographic Studio in the same city. There he learned the photographic retouching process that would be the base for his "revolutionary" invention, the *cabi dancai* technique, which turned into the very essence of the *yuefenpai* genre and which made the genre extremely popular. In 1914 he moved to Shanghai. He was then "discovered" by Huang Chujiu, a pharmaceutical magnate who understood the potentials of this style and hired him to produce a series of commercial paintings for his company. Zheng Mantuo was also associated with the Shenmei Shudian, a publishing house founded by the painter Gao Jianfu and his brother Gao Shuren of the Lingnan Painting School for an active implementation and distribution of new forms of painting. See Pu Ji, 52; Sherman Cochran, "Marketing Medicine and Advertising Dreams in China 1900–1950," Paper presented at the seminar, Business, Enterprise, and Culture. Princeton University, September 29, 1995, 20–1; and Zhang Yanfen, 88–9.

34. Hershatter, 81.

35. In *Shanghai Modern*, Leo Ou-Fan Lee draws a similar relationship between the figure of the new and modern women with that of the traditional courtesans, via the genre of courtesan literature. "Courtesan literature, in fact, did not fade from modern Chinese publishing; only its public image was displaced by photographs and paintings of modern, and more respectable women. Thus the display of the female body either as a work of art (Western) or as an embodiment of physical health marked the beginning of a new discourse which was made problematic precisely because it was derived from the courtesan journals, in which female bodies indeed carried a market value" (p. 73).

36. In Wu Hao et al., the poster is dated 1931. On stylistic grounds it is comparable with other images by the same author, such as an advertisement of a pharmaceutical company bearing a 1924–25 calendar, and thus I am inclined to attribute this painting to an earlier period, such as the late 1920s.

37. Birrell, 1. She also remarks how the different representation of men and women in poetic conventions are generally marked by the fact that, while the woman remains constantly behind, often by a window—the only outward opening from where to see and be seen—the man, in contrast, "is free to walk down the highways and byways of life" (20).

38. Hershatter, 87. In Cao Yu's play *Richu* (Sunrise), in which the protagonist, Chen Bailu, is a high-class prostitute, most acts are set in a luxurious hotel suite that the author describes as furnished in an eclectic fashion. See Cao Yu, *Sunrise: A Play in Four Acts,* trans. Steven Rendall (Berkeley: University of California Press, 1984), 1.

39. John Hay, "The Body Invisible in Chinese Art?" in *Body, Subject and Power in China*, eds. Angela Zito and Tani Barlow (Chicago, IL: The University of Chicago Press, 1994), 43.

40. The style of the calendar posters was later picked up by the Communist regime, ultimate proof of its popular appeal. Li Mubai, a prominent artist of the successful Zhiying Studio, became an extremely productive author of propaganda posters in the 1950s and early 1960s. See *Shinian lai Shanghai nianhua xuanji* (A Selection of Ten Years of Shanghai *nianhua*) (Shanghai: Shanghai Renmin Meishu Chubanshe, 1959). Another successful *yuefenpai* author, successively "recycled" for propaganda reasons, is Jin Meisheng. See Fan Zhenjia, *Jin Meisheng zuopin xuanji* (Selection of Works by Jin Meisheng) (Shanghai: Shanghai Renmin Meishu Chubanshe, 1985).

41. For this explanation I am indebted to Huang Suning, a Chinese woman artist specializing in folk art and living in New York. Later on, *yuefenpai* would often be executed in a collective manner, artists specializing only in the execution of the face. See Zhang Yanfeng, II, 70, and Wu Hao et al., 11–2. See also Nian Xin, ed. *Shanghai yuefenpai nianhua jifa* (The Technique of Shanghai *yuefenpai* New Year Pictures) (Shanghai: Shanghai Renmin Meishu Chubanshe, 1983).

42. In Wu Hao et al., the poster is attributed to the late 1920s. Again, based on stylistic assumptions in the execution of the woman's body and the style of her dress, I would suggest a later period, such as the early 1930s. See Wu, 54.

43. For more information on Nanyang and its marketing competition with the British-American Tobacco Company, see Sherman Cochran, *Big Business in China. Sino-Foreign Rivalry in the Cigarette Industry, 1890–1930* (Cambridge, MA: Harvard University Press, 1984).

44. Xie Zhiguang was born in Zhejiang and subsequently moved to Shanghai. He studied painting with Zhou Muqiao and scenography with Zhang Luguang. He also took courses at Shanghai's most prominent art school, the Shanghai Fine Arts School. After graduating, he was hired by the advertisement department of the Nanyang Brothers Tobacco Company, of which he eventually became the director. According to Zhang Yanfeng, his studies in scenography influenced the careful staging of his *yuefenpai* scenes and the dramatic sense with which he liked to imbue his figures. He began painting *yuefenpai* in 1922 and continued until the late 1930s. Like Zheng Mantuo he was versed in several themes, including historical and mythological scenes. See Zhang Yanfeng, 93–4, and Pu Ji, 52–3.

45. *Harper's Bazaar* for the years 1928–35, and *Vogue* 1927–35.

46. For a visual documentation of American popular fashion in the 1920s, see Stella Blum, ed., *Everyday Fashions of the Twenties as Pictured in Sears and Other Catalogs* (New York: Dover Publications, 1981).

47. Ding Ling, "A Woman and a Man" (1928), trans. in Ruth Keen and Hal Pollard, *I Myself am a Woman: Selected Writings by Ding Ling*, ed. Tani E., Barlow (Boston, MA: Beacon Press, 1989), 101.

48. Another interesting clue to the possible reading of such images regarding their bodily posture is provided by theories of non-verbal communication. Nancy Henley explains how loose body positions in a woman are generally perceived as "a lack of accepted control over her sexuality." She also describes what are generally understood as invitational gestures specific to women in "quasi-courting" situations: "crossing the legs, exposing the tights, placing a hand on a hip, exhibiting the wrist or palm, protruding the breast, and stroking the thigh or wrist." This set of "feminine" posture functions as "heavier gender identification signals by women in the presence of men." See Henley, *Body Politics. Power, Sex, and Nonverbal Communication* (Englewood Cliffs, NJ: Prentice-Hall, 1977), 91, 140.

49. On the subject of the guides to prostitution, see Hershatter, Part 1 "Classifying and Counting," 34–68.

50. "Upper-class prostitutes (or prostitute-"entertainers") in cities were expected not just to mirror but to be on the cutting edge of…change. Female entertainers were expected to titillate with their modernity. Their flaunting of daring western dress, hairstyle, makeup, cigarettes, and liquors was intended to attract male customers." Gronewald, 58.

51. Lao She, "A Vision," (c.1930s) in *Crescent Moon and Other Stories,* trans. Gladys Yang (Peking: Panda Books, 1985), 90.

52. This advertisement was produced by the professional Zhiying Studio. The studio was founded around 1923 by Hang Zhiying (1901–47), a native of Zhejiang who, at an early age, had been employed in the advertising department of the Commercial Press in Shanghai. Hang made his fortune thanks to his superb technique and the organizational skill with which he managed the studio. Contrary to common practice, he started portraying women only from the neck or shoulders up, a form previously avoided because of associations with bad luck. Profiting from the increasing changes in visual habits brought about by industrialization and new popular media such as movies and photography, Hang started depicting "women with big heads" in a startlingly illusionistic and westernized fashion that became his studio's trademark. Another factor that strongly contributed to his success was the industrial organization of his workshop, where up to eight artists and several assistants would churn out more than eighty paintings a year. Among them, one of the best-known teams was that of Li Mubai (1913–91), who painted the figures, and Jin Xuechen (b.1904), who specialized in landscape and interior settings. In a later period, Hang Zhiying would only supervise the finished product and choose the advertising inscriptions and font types. Zhiying Studio was so successful that it was eventually entrusted with half of the *yuefenpai* production for the British-American Tobacco Company. They can be considered

the last stage of development of the *yuefenpai* genre before its political "reinterpretation" under the Communist regime. As proof of the long-lasting influence of this production, Hang Zhiying's son, Hang Minshi, continued in his father's career, designing auspicious New Year pictures in the Socialist mode and teaching this specific technique of *yuefenpai*—which, after 1949, was subsumed under the general term of *nianhua*—at the Lu Xun Academy in Shenyang. (I owe this information to the artist Huang Suning, who took a course with Hang Minshi in Beijing in the early 1980s). See Zhang Yanfeng, 89–92, and Cochran "Marketing Medicine," 23–6.

53. See below, the "Elegy to Cigarette," 24.

54. This practice, generally employed by smaller companies that could not afford to establish their own designing and printing departments, is confirmed by the existence of posters employing the same image to advertise products of different brands (see, for example, Wu Hao et al., 75, pl. 23, and Zhang Yanfeng, 69, and by many blank posters whose borders and frames are designed to allow space for the company's name and trademark. See Zhang Yanfeng, 117–24.

55. A study on the standard living condition of the working class in Shanghai in 1930 puts cigarettes as a main item among miscellaneous expenses, an average of 185 packets consumed per family annually. Expenditure on cigarettes and wine alone was greater than on sanitation, furniture, or water. Yang Hsi-Meng, *A Study of the Standard of Living of Working Families in Shanghai* (Peiping: Institute of Social Research, 1931), 71.

56. Cochran, *Big Business in China,* 35–8.

57. "The success of these two businesses at adapting to Chinese conditions and Sinifying their operations is perhaps the single most persuasive explanation for the growth of the cigarette market in early twentieth century China; and perhaps the best evidence of their adaptability and Sinification may be found in their advertising…This advertising seems to have been the key to British-American's and Nanyang's commercial success, and, pressed on consumers in intensive campaigns, it attracted enough smokers to make the market for cigarettes in China during the early twentieth century almost as large as the one in the United States." Cochran, *Big Business in China,* 219.

58. Cochran, *Big Business in China,* 47. For the possible sexual references attached to the cigarette, see also Ye Lingfeng, *Weiwan de chanhui lu* (The Unfinished Confession), originally published in 1934. Zhang Yingjin translates the cigarette excerpt in *The City in Modern Chinese Literature and Film,* 219.

Chapter 4

1. Elizabeth Croll, *Changing Identities of Chinese Women: Rhetoric, Experience, and Self-Perception in Twentieth-Century China* (Hong Kong University Press, 1999); Judith Stacey, *Patriarchy and Socialist Revolution in China* (Berkeley: University of California Press, 1983); Christina Gilmartin, *Engendering the Chinese Revolution: Radical Women, Communist Politics, and Mass Movement in the 1920s* (Berkeley: University of California Press, 1995); and Emily Honig and Gail Hershatter, *Personal Voices: Chinese Women in the 1980s* (Stanford, CA: Stanford University Press, 1988).

2. Antonia Finnane, "What should Chinese Women Wear? A National Problem," *Modern China* 22, no. 2 (April 1996): 99–131.

3. Jung Chang, *Wild Swans: Three Daughters of China* (Glasgow: HarperCollins, 1991), 289; Honig and Hershatter, 42.

4. Honig and Hershatter, 11; and Mayfair Yang, *Spaces of Their Own: Women's Public Sphere in Transnational China* (Minneapolis: University of Minnesota Press, 1999), 35–67.

5. Yang; Croll, 151–2; Honig and Hershatter, 11, 41–51; and Harriet Evans, *Woman and Sexuality in China: Female Sexuality and Gender since 1949* (Cambridge: Polity Press, 1997), 82.

6. Beauty here is not treated as an abstract concept. Following Sandra Bartky, whose definition of beauty resonates well with the work of popular writers such as Rita Freedman and Naomi Wolf, I see "feminine beauty" as a culturally constructed quality that is based on a combination of concrete elements, including physical characteristics, adornment, language, movement, gesture, and posture. See Sandra Bartky, *Femininity and Domination: Studies in the Phenomenology of Oppression* (New York: Routledge, 1990), 68, 71–3. To some extent, it may be true that what constitutes beauty is a subjective matter that rests on individual preference. But in analyzing the interest in beauty, I adopt a view that collapses the boundary between the subjective and the objective: When individuals pursue self-adornment or

evaluate their own or others' appearances, the criteria applied are always conditioned by a combination of factors, including their backgrounds and identities and what their cultures or subcultures perceive to be pleasing.

7. Louise Edwards, "Policing the Modern Women in Republican China," *Modern China* 26, no. 2 (April, 2000): 126–7.

8. Ono Kazuko, *Chinese Women in a Century of Revolution, 1850–1950* (Stanford, CA: Stanford University Press, 1989), Chaps. 3 and 4.

9. Qiu Jin, "An Address to Two Hundred Million Fellow Countrywomen," in *Chinese Civilization and Society: A Sourcebook*, ed. Patricia Ebrey (New York: Free Press, 1981 [190?]), 248.

10. Ding Ling, *I Myself Am a Woman: Selected Writings of Ding Ling*, eds. Tani E. Barlow and Gary J. Bjorge (Boston, MA: Beacon Press, 1989), 109.

11. Mao Zedong, *Mao's Road to Power: Revolutionary Writings, 1912–1949*, Vol. 1, Stuart R. Schram ed. (Armonk, NY: M. E. Sharpe, 1992), 353.

12. Zhou Xuqi, *Yijiuyiling dao yijiuerling niandai duhui funü shenghuo fengmao: yi "Funü zazhi" wei fenxi shili* (The Life of Urban Women: "The Ladies' Journal," 1910s–1920s), M.A. thesis, Taiwan Guoli Daxue, 1994; and Tanya McIntyre, "Images of women in popular prints," in *Dress, Sex, and Text in Chinese Culture*, eds. Antonia Finnane and Anne McLaren (Clayton, Australia: Monash Asia Institute, 1999), 74.

13. Zhou, 190–2.

14. Zhou, 190–3.

15. Edwards, 119, 133–4.

16. Edwards, 116.

17. Edwards, 133.

18. See Gilmartin. Also see Ou Xiamin, "Nü xuesheng zhi juewu" (Female Students' Political Consciousness), in *Zhongguo funü yundong lishi ziliao* (Sources of the Women's Rights Movement in China), eds. Zhongguo Quanguo Funü Lianhehui Funü Yundong Lishi Yanjiushi ("Women's Movement" Research Group, the Women's Federation of China) (1926; reprint, Beijing: Renmin Chubanshe, 1986), 548–51; and Luo Qiong, "Changji zai Zhongguo" (Prostitutes in China), in *Zhongguo funü yundong lishi ziliao* (1935; reprint, Beijing: Zhongguo Funü Chubanshe, 1988), 69–74. Also see Luo Suwen, *Nüxing yu jindai Zhongguo shehui* (Women in Modern Chinese Society) (Shanghai: Shanghai Renmin Chubanshe, 1996).

19. "Changsha nüjie lianhehui chengli xuanyan" (The Founding Speech of the Changsha Women's Federation), in *Zhongguo funü yundong lishi ziliao* (1921; reprint, Beijing: Zhongguo Funü Chubanshe, 1986), 8. Also see Xiang Jingyu, "Zhongguo funü xuanchuan yundong de xin jiyuan" (A New Era of the Women's Movement), in *Zhongguo funü yundong lishi ziliao* (1923; reprint, Beijing: Zhongguo Funü Chubanshe, 1986), 275–7. Another useful reference is Nan Yuyue, "Sanbajie yu Zhongguo funü yundong" (March 8 and the Women's Movement in China), in *Zhongguo funü yundong lishi ziliao* (1926; reprint, Beijing: Zhongguo Funü Chubanshe, 1986), 579–83.

20. Xiang; "Zhongguo funü wenti," (The Problems of Chinese Women), in *Zhongguo funü yundong lishi ziliao*, (1927; reprint, Beijing: Zhongguo Funü Chubanshe, 1986), 710–20; Tanfen, "Funü wenti he nanzi" (Women's Problems and Men), in *Cong "yierjiu" yundong kan nüxing de rensheng jiazhi* (1936); reprint, Beijing: Zhongguo Funü Chubanshe, 1988), 312–6.

21. "Zhongguo gongchandang dierci quanguo daibiao dahui guanyu funü wenti de jueyi (??)" (The Second Communist Congress's Resolution on Women's Problems), in *Zhongguo funü yundong lishi ziliao* (1922; reprint, Beijing: Zhongguo Funü Chubanshe, 1986), 29–30; Cai Chang, "Eguo geming yu funü" (The Russian Revolution and Women), in *Zhongguo funü yundong lishi ziliao* (1925; reprint, Beijing: Zhongguo Funü Chubanshe, 1986), 300–5; and Tanfen, 313–6.

22. Ou, 548–81. As part of the revolutionary process, radical women did deliberately reject conventional beauty norms. They sometimes paid dearly for adopting the May Fourth-style appearance. Honig and Hershatter mention that, when Chiang Kai-shek purged the Communist Party in Wuhan, he executed young women with bobbed hair; see *Personal Voices*, 2. Regarding this fact, also refer to Zhang Baojin's recollection in Jing Lingzi, *Shihai gouxuan* (The Mystic Sea of History) (Beijing: Kunlun Chubanshe, 1989), 234. Less dramatically, women who cut their hair in Shanghai in the early 1920s were often ridiculed; see Ding, "Xiang Jingyu tongzhi dui wo de yingxiang" (Comrade Xiang Jingyu's Influence

on Me), in *Ding Ling wenji* (The Works of Ding Ling), Vol. 5 (Changsha: Hunan Renmin Chubanshe, 1984), 194–5. The construction of a new image also entailed physical struggle. Women of various generations—ranging from Ding Ling's mother, Yu Manzhen, to Long Marchers like Wei Gongzi—struggled to be active with their "liberated" bound feet. See Ding, 226–7; also see Guo Chen, *Jinguo liezhuan* (The Heroines in the Long March) (Beijing: Nongcun Duwu Chubanshe, 1986), 144–7.

23. Fang Zhimin zhuan bianxiezu (The Editorial Committee on the Biography of Fang Zhimin), *Fang Zhimin zhuan* (The Biography of Fang Zhimin) (Jiangxi: Jiangxi Renmin Chubanshe, 1982), 95.

24. Fang Zhimin, *Fang Zhimin wenji* (The Works of Fang Zhimin) (Beijing: Renmin Chubanshe, 1984), 166–7.

25. Ye Yonglie, *Jiang Qing zhuan* (Biography of Jiang Qing) (Beijing: Zuojia Chubanshe, 1993), 44–6. Certainly not all revolutionaries had to endure poverty. Their material conditions depended on their connections, professions, and political status and assignment. For instance, the playwright Tian Han, living in Shanghai in the early 1930s, had a much better life (also see Ye, 40).

26. Guo Chen, 55–6.

27. Jing, 53.

28. Jing, 52–3.

29. Gilmartin, 190.

30. Zeng Zhi, *Changzheng nüzhanshi* (Women Fighters of the Long March), Vol. 1 (Changchun: Beifang Funü Ertong Chubanshe, 1986), 326, 356.

31. Quoted in Zeng, 356. The question of whether radicalizing personal appearance helped or hurt the revolution is complex and requires further investigation. In the late 1920s and early 1930s, the Communist Party sometimes found that female cadres' radical appearance, together with their revolutionary behavior, alienated villagers who continued to regard them as women. See "Tonggao" (Public Announcement) no. 18, in *Jiangxi suqu funü yundong shiliao xunbian* (Materials on the Women's Movement in the Jiangxi Soviet Area), eds. Jiangxi sheng funü lianhehui (The Provincial Women's Federation, Jiangxi) and Jiangxi sheng dang'anguan (Jiangxi Provincial Archive) (1934; reprint, Nanchang: Jiangxi Renmin Chubanshe, 1984), 214. But to act as good revolutionaries, women often found it necessary to give up the established symbols of feminine beauty that some still cherished.

32. Li Wenyi, "Yi jingai de Yang Zhihua tongzhi" (My Fond Memories of Yang Zhihua), in *Huiyi Yang Zhihua* (Our Recollections of Yang Zhihua), ed. Shanghai shi fulian fuyun shiliaozu ("Women's Movement" Research Group, the Shanghai Women's Federation) (Hefei: Anhui Renmin Chubanshe, 1983), 53.

33. Yang Mo, *Qingchun zhi ge* (The Song of Youth) (1958; reprint, Beijing: Shiyue Wenyi Chubanshe, 1991), 390.

34. Mao Dun, *Mao Dun zizhuan* (Autobiography of Mao Dun) (1981; reprint, Nanjing: Jiangsu wenyi chubanshe, 1996), 224.

35. Guo Chen, 32–3.

36. See Li Ling, "Fenpei de xifu" (A Party-assigned Wife), in *Zhongguo funü* 370 (1989): 22–3. On the images of fashionable and well-off women in the urban areas in the 1920s and 1930s in recent scholarly literature, see Edwards; Fiannane, 111, 115–20; Luo Suwen; Zhou, "Yijiuyiling dao yijiuerling"; and Leo Ou-fan Lee, *Shanghai Modern: The Flowering of a New Urban Culture in China, 1930–1945* (Cambridge, MA: Harvard University Press, 2000).

37. Wang Xingjuan, *Li Min, He Zizhen he Mao Zedong* (Li Min, He Zizhen, and Mao Zedong) (Beijing: Zhongguo Wenlian Chuban Gongsi, 1993), 5.

38. Hsu Kai-yu, *Chou En-lai: China's Gray Eminence* (New York: Doubleday, 1968), 149.

39. Chang Jung and Jon Halliday, *Mme Sun Yat-sen* (Soong Ching-ling) (Harmondsworth UK: Penguin, 1986), 56–8, 76–8, 92–3, 105–6.

40. Living in Shanghai in the early 1930s, Song won the admiration of Anna Louise Strong and of Edgar and Helen Snow for her appearance. She was described as beautiful, exquisite, and glamorous; Chang and Halliday, 80–1.

41. John K. Fairbank, *Chinabound: A Fifty-Year Memoir* (New York: Harper & Row, 1982), 267–73.

42. Michael Chang, "The good, the bad, and the beautiful: movie actresses and public discourse in Shanghai, 1920s-1930s," in *Cinema and Urban Culture in Shanghai, 1922–1943*, ed. Zhang Yingjing (Stanford, CA: Stanford University Press, 1999), 144.

43. Ni Zhenliang, *Luoru man tianxia—Bai Yang zhuan* (Beautiful Clouds: The Biography of Bai Yang) (Beijing: Zhongguo Wenlian Chubanshe, 1992), 81.

44. Please also refer to Ni.

45. Hung Chang-tai, *War and Popular Culture: Resistance in Modern China, 1937–1945* (Berkeley: University. of California Press, 1994), 77.

46. Hung, 84.

47. Guo Moruo, *Qu Yuan* (The Tragedy of Qu Yuan) (1942; reprint, Beijing: Renmin wenxue chubanshe 1953).

48. Rumor has it that the Party not only used images of beautiful women in popular art and literature but also told attractive Communist women to employ their charm and sexuality to seduce individuals. According to one anti-Communist source—Tang Shaohua, who worked in the movie industry in Shanghai in the 1940s—Bai Yang was twice told to marry a promising young artist whom the CCP wanted to recruit. See Tang Shaohua, *Zhonggong wenyi tongzhan huigu* (My Recollections of the CCP's United Front in Literature and the Arts) (Taipei: Wentan Zazhishe, 1981), 276, 238.

49. Ni.

50. Zheng Chaolin, *Shishi yu huiyi* (History and Historical Memory), Vol. 1 (Hong Kong: Tiandi Tushu Youxian Gongsi, 1997), 287–98.

51. Fang Zhimin zhuan bianxiezu, 95.

52. Deng Yingchao, "Tong qingnian pengyou tantan lianai hunyin wenti" (A Conversation with Young Comrades on Love and Marriage), in *Funü jiefang wenti wenxuan* (Selected Writings on the Problems of Women's Liberation), eds., Deng Yingchao, Cai Chang, and Kang Keqing (1942; reprint, Beijing: Renmin Chubanshe, 1988), 73–5.

53. Rose Terill, *Madame Mao: The White-Boned Demon* (New York: Simon & Schuster, 1992), 140; Zheng, *Shishi yu huiyi*, 285–8; Ding Ling, "Wo suo renshi de Qu Qiubai tongzhi" (My Understanding of Comrade Qu Qiubai), in *Ding Ling wenji* (The Works of Ding Ling), Vol. 5 (Changsha: Hunan Renmin Chubanshe, 1984), 99; and Wang Guanmei "Yongheng de jinian" (My Lasting Memories of Song Qingling), in *Song Qingling jinian ji* (Recollections of Song Qingling) (Hong Kong: Wenhui Bao, 1981), 94.

54. He Zizhen received only a limited education in her native area. Yang Zhihua, once the daughter-in-law of Shen Dingyi, was educated at Shanghai University. Growing up in a wealthy Christian family, Song Qingling was educated in the United States.

55. In the late 1930s and early 1940s, Communist base areas attracted young people, many of whom had received a fair amount of modern education and came from cities. It was also a time when many veteran revolutionaries were enjoying a relatively stable life. These conditions, which allowed revolutionaries to meet a more diverse pool of women and think more about their personal lives, were conducive to displaying attitudes that betrayed revolutionaries' own preference for female beauty.

56. Zhu was Wang Jiaxiang's wife. For information about these women and social life in Yan'an, see Terrill, 134; Lee Hsiao-li, *Good-bye, Yinan*, trans. Dong Qiao (Hong Kong: Wenyi Shushi, 1975), 207; and Shao Yang, *Hongqiang nei de furenmen* (The Wives of the Communist Leaders) (Guizhou: Guizhou Renmin Chubanshe, 1993), 193.

57. Terrill, 151–4; Ye, 171–2.

58. Tie Zhuwei, *Hongjun langmanchu* (The Romances in the Red Army) (Hubei: Hubei Renmin Chubanshe, 1989), 246–7, 250–1; Ye, *Jiang Qing zhuan*, 250.

59. Not all male authorities pursued and married young beauties. Xu Guangdai, one of the key administrators at Resistance University, did not abandon his plain-looking wife, whom he had not seen for years. But he was regarded as a rarity. See Shao, 240–1.

60. Liu Lequn, "Women fufu guanxi weishenme juelie?" (Why do we break up?), *Xin Zhongguo funü* (The Woman of New China), 11 (1955): 6.

61. Terrill, 142–3; Wang Xingjuan, 30.

62. Terrill, 142. Also see Helen Snow and Nym Wales, *The Chinese Communists: Sketches and Autobiographies of the Old Guard* (Westport, CT: Greenwood Press, 1972), 253.

63. Ding, *I Myself Am a Woman*, 319.

64. Helen Young, *Choosing Revolution: Chinese Women on the Long March* (Urbana: University of Illinois Press, 2001), 161.

65. Not all modern young women aspired to a social upward mobility based on relations with powerful males. Some resisted; others yielded only reluctantly. See Tie, 202, 246–7, 250–1; also see Li Ling. But it is also clear that some were quite aggressive in approaching powerful men. See Snow and Wales, 252; and Terrill, 133–8.

66. This section briefly analyzes how women developed some principles of self-adornment in relation to their political identity. It is not meant as an investigation into clothing and fashion or an examination of individual variations in self-adornment.

67. Quoted in Finnane, "What should Chinese Women Wear?" 114.

68. Ding, "Xiang Jingyu tongzhi dui wo de yingxiang," 196.

69. Yan'an Luyi (Lu Xun Arts Academy of Yan'an), "Bai mao nü" (The White-haired Girl), in *Yan'an wenyi congshu* (Art and Literature in Yan'an), Vol. 8: *Gejujuan* (Opera), eds. Ding Yi and Su Yiping (Changsha: Hunan Wenyi Chubanshe, 1987), 382.

70. Ding Ling, *Taiyang zhaozai Sangganhe shang* (The Sun Shines Over the Sanggan River) (1948; reprint, Beijing: Renmin Wenxue Chubanshe, 1955), 301–2.

71. Jing, 154; also see Hu Lanqi, *Hu Lanqi huiyilu* (Hu Lanqi's Memoir) (Chengdu: Sichuan Renmin Chubanshe, 1995), 149–51. The attempts by radical women to beautify their revolutionary appearance raise a couple of interesting questions. First, how can we put this in a comparative perspective? Scholars have noted that women elsewhere sometimes adorn clothing that was supposedly intended to mark a break from conventional femininity; for instance, in the 1970s, women in the West, following the advice of fashion and image experts, adopted power dressing, a strategy aimed at challenging their conventional image as weak but not the conventional notion(s) of female beauty. See Joanne Entwistle, *The Fashioned Body: Fashion, Dress, and Modern Social Theory* (Cambridge: Polity Press, 2000), 187–91. And second, how did revolutionaries, especially women revolutionaries, employ political language to legitimize the pursuit of feminine beauty? On this point, a memoir written by Hu Lanqi, a veteran of the National Revolution, is quite revealing. She mentions that her comrades emphasized the compatibility between Marxism and the pursuit of "material civilization," *Hu Lanqi*, 150–1.

72. Zeng, 314.

73. On conventional practices of self-adornment in rural areas in the first half of the twentieth century, see Luo Suwen, 237–46.

74. Quan Yanchi, *Mao Zedong zouxia shentan* (To Humanize Mao Zedong) (Hong Kong: Nanyue Chubanshe, 1990), 180; Hsu, *Chou En-lai*, 145; Fairbank, *Chinabound*, 265.

75. Snow and Wales, 253.

76. "Yan'an de nüxing" (The Women of Yan'an) (Zhongxi Tushushe, 1946), 5.

77. Quan, 137.

78. Dou Shangchu, "Xuefeng xuexi chubu zongjie" (Preliminary Summing Up of My [problematic attitude toward] Studying in the Rectification Campaign), in *Yan'an zhongyang dangxiao de zhengfeng yundong* (The Rectification Campaign at the Central Party Institute), ed. Yan'an zhongyang dangxiao zhengfeng yundong bianxiezu (The Central Party Institute Study Group), Vol. 1 (1942; reprint, Beijing: Zhongyang dangxiao chubanshe, 1988), 237.

79. Tang, 277–8.

80. Ni, 105.

81. The brief survey in this section is not intended to compare approaches to self-adornment in the revolutionary and post-revolutionary periods.

82. Zhang Ling, "Zhao Yiman" (Zhao Yiman), *Zhongguo qingnian* (Chinese Youth) 3 (1957): 24.

83. Su Yi, "Zhezhong fengqi zhengchang ma" (Is this Trend Normal?), *Zhongguo qingnian* 2 (1957): 40.

84. Evans, 90.

85. Chen Qi, "Luo Liu fufu guanxi polie de yuanyin hezai" (The Causes of Liu's and Luo's Divorce) *Zhongguo funü* 1 (1956): 17–8. Also see Pang Youwen, "Luo Paoyi de xingwei shi boxue jieji sixiang de juti biaoxian" (Luo Paoyi's Behavior is a Manifestation of the Exploitative Class's Ideology), *Zhongguo funü* 1 (1956): 7.

86. Li Yingru, *Yehuo chunfeng dou gucheng* (Revolutionary Struggle in a Historic City) (Beijing: Jiefangjun Wenyi Chubanshe, 1959), 277–90.

87. Gao Anhua, *To the Edge of the Sky: A Story of Love, Betrayal, Suffering, and the Strength of Human Courage* (London: Viking, 2000), 50. Negative characters, too, could be attractive. For instance, in the

movie *The Bold Hero* (*Yingxiong hudan,* 1958), the famous star Wang Xiaotang, who played the heroine in *Revolutionary Struggle in a Historic City* (1963), took on the role of A Lan, an attractive woman spy trying to sabotage the revolution. However, A Lan's attractiveness was coupled with an overt sensuality and "decadent" self-adornment (tight outfit, big earrings, heavy makeup, etc.) that were diametrically opposed to the revolutionary aesthetics of beauty.

88. Su, 40.
89. *The Gate of Heavenly Peace,* 2 videocassettes, prod. and dir. Richard Gordon and Carma Hinton (Brookline, MA: Long Bow Group, in association with Independent Television Service, 1995).
90. Qiu Ti, "Zenyang xuanze fuzhuang de secai" (How can We Match the Colors of our Clothing?), *Zhongguo funü* 4 (1956): 22; and Xia Lianbo, "Baohu lianbu de pifu" (How to Protect our Facial Skin) *Zhongguo funü* 12 (1956): 32.
91. Beijing qing gongye ju fuzhuang yanjiusuo (Institute of Clothes, the Bureau of Light Industry of Beijing), "Jieyue meiguan de qiuyi" (Economical and Beautiful Clothes for the Fall), *Zhongguo funü* 17 (1960): 26. Also see Chen Guitao, "Yitao nüzhuang zhi yong jiuchi bu" (How to Make a Woman's Suit with Nine Square Feet of Fabric) *Zhongguo funü* 12 (1963): 32.
92. Shui Jing, *Teshu de jiaowang* (Special Friendship) (Nanjing: Jiangsu Wenyi Chubanshe, 1992), 117–20.
93. Shui, 117, 68–9.
94. Shui; see pictures in the book.
95. See issues of *Zhongguo qingnian* throughout this period.
96. Liang Heng and Judith Suhapiro, *Son of the Revolution* (New York: Knopf, 1984), 47.
97. For example, see *Zhongguo qingnian,* 6 (1957).
98. For example, see *Zhongguo funü,* 163 (1960).
99. Honig and Hershatter, 244.
100. The questions raised here are beyond the scope of this essay; sources relevant to answering them include Li Xiaojiang's volume, which contains insiders' recollections that emphasize young women's rejection of the practice of pursuing beauty. See Li Xiaojiang, *Funü yanjiu yundong* (Studying Women) (Hong Kong: Oxford University Press, 1997), 1–36, 141–75. See also Wang Zheng, "Call Me 'qingnian' but not 'funü': A Maoist Youth in Retrospect," in *Some of Us: Chinese Women Growing Up in the Mao Era,* eds. Wang Zheng, Zhong Xueping, and Bai Di (New Brunswick, NJ: Rutgers University Press, 2001), 40–9. According to Wang, in fact, not only the Communist attack on bourgeois lifestyle but also the Chinese "feudal tradition" put a concern for appearance in an unfavorable light. But these sources also show that women remained sensitive to their own appearance and to the issue of beauty generally. See Li Xiaojiang, *Funü yanjiu yundong,* 37–60. Wang believes that young women admired good looks but showed disdain for self-beautification. Such observations underscore the importance of exploring in more detail how the complex Communist legacy concerning female appearance shaped women's self-expectations and self-images under the Maoist regime.

Chapter 5

1. Im In-saeng, "Modeonijeum" (Modernism), *Byeolgeongon* (An Unusual World) (Nov. 1930); reprinted in *Hyeondaeseong ui hyeongseong: Seoul e danseuhol eul heohara* (Formation of Modernity: Allow a Dance Hall in Seoul), ed. Kim Jinsong (Seoul: Hyeonsil Munhwa Yeongu, 1999), 57. Kim includes in his book (appendix) the list of important primary sources. My intention here is to introduce the scholarship of the Modern Girl in Korea and to locate the polemical type of womanhood in the international milieu of the era; I will then analyze Na Hye-seok's works of art. Unless otherwise noted, all translations from primary sources are mine.
2. Kim Jinsong, 242–3; Originally "Miseu Koriauyeo, danbalhasiyo" (Miss Korea, Please Have Short Hair), *Donggwang* (East Light) (August 1932), n.p. For China, see Louise Edwards, "Policing the Modern Woman in Republican China," *Modern China* 26, no. 2 (April 2000): 115–47.
3. This anxiety about the female body is discussed in Ju Kyeongmi's article on modern women's jewelry, "Gongye ui hyeongsik gwa gineung" (Form and Function of the Craft), in *Misulsawa sigak munhwa* (Art History and Visual Culture) (2003): 38–59. Also see Jennifer J. Jung-Kim, "Gender and Modernity in Colonial Korea," Ph.D. diss., University of California at Los Angeles, 2005.

4. See Miriam Silverberg, "Modern Girl as Militant," in *Recreating Japanese Women, 1600–1945*, ed. Gail P. Bernstein (Berkeley: University of California Press, 1991), 175–98; "The Café Waitress Serving Modern Japan," in *Mirror of Modernity: Invented Traditions of Modern Japan*, ed. Stephen Vlastos (Berkeley: University of California Press, 1998), 243–61; and Gregory J. Kasza, *The State and the Mass Media in Japan, 1918–1945* (Berkeley: University of California Press, 1988).

5. See Carroll Smith-Rosenberg, *Disorderly Conduct: Visions of Gender in Victoria America* (New York: A.A. Knopf, 1985).

6. Jang Yunshik, "Women in a Confucian Society: The Case of Josun Dynasty Korea (1392–1910)," *Asian and Pacific Quarterly of Cultural and Social Affairs* 14, no. 2 (Summer 1982): 24–42.

7. Kim Youngna, "nolransog ui geundaeseong" (Modernity in Debate: Representing the 'New Woman' and 'Modern Girl), *Misulsawa sigak munhwa* (2003): 8–35; reprinted in *20th Century Korean Art* (London: Laurence King, 2005). The book is the first art history book on Korean modern and contemporary art available in English and introduces major issues in Korean modern and contemporary art. Kim Jinsong, *Hyeondaeseong ui hyeongseong: Seoul e danseuhol eul heohara*. The subtitle of this book derives from an article originally appearing in *Samcheolli* (The Land of Korea) (January 1937). Primary Korean sources and images that I use in this essay were published in Kim Youngna's and Kim Jinsong's books. For the Modern Boy in Korea, see Shin Myeong-jik, *Modeon Boi: Gyeongseong eul geonilda* (The Modern Boy Walks around Seoul) (Seoul: Hyeonsil Munhwa Yeongu, 2003). See also Hong Sun-pyo, "Hanguk geundae misul ui yeoseong pyosang (Representation of Woman in Modern Korean Art: Desexualization and Sexualization of Woman)," *Hanguk geundae misul sahak* (Journal of Korean Modern Art History) (Seoul: Sigonsa, 2002), 63–85.

8. See, for example, Kim Jue-Ree, "Geundaejeok paesyeon ui balgyeon gwa 1930 nyeondae munhakui byeonmo" (The Occurrence of Modern Fashion and the Reformation of Literature in 1930s), *Hanguk hyeondae munhak yeongu* (Journal of Korean Modern Literature) 7 (December 1999): 123–50; and "Geundaejeok sinche damnon ui ilgochal" (Discourse on the Modern Body), *Hanguk hyeondae munhak yeongu* 13 (June 2003): 17–49.

9. J. Menzies, ed., *Modern Boy, Modern Girl: Modernity in Japanese Art, 1910–1935*, exhibition cat. (Sydney: Art Gallery of New South Wales, 1998).

10. For the media construction of the *mobo, moga* in 1920s Japan, see Barbara Hamill Sato, *The New Japanese Woman: Modernity, Media, and Women in Interwar Japan* (Durham, NC: Duke University Press, 2003); and Gregory J. Kasza, *The State and the Mass Media in Japan, 1918–1945* (Berkeley: University of California Press, 1988).

11. Yu Kwangyeol, "Modeon iran mueus'inya" (What is Modern?), *Byeolgeongon* (Dec. 1927); reprinted in Kim Jinsong, 329–30.

12. Yu Kwangyeol; Kim Jinsong, 329.

13. Kim Youngna, 26. The author notes that a variety of commodities sold in Korea in the 1920s were imported from Japan and related to the fashionable lifestyle, including white cosmetic powder, clothing, and foodstuffs.

14. Ulrike Wohr, Barbara Hamill Sato, Suzuki Sadami, eds., *Gender and Modernity: Rereading Japanese Women's Magazines* (Kyoto: International Research Center for Japanese Studies, 1998). Hiratsuka Raichō (1886–1971) and other literary writers founded *Seitō* in 1911. Raichō's manifesto, which was published in *Seitō* 1, no.1 (September 1911), was also reprinted in *La Revue mondiale* (World Review) (November 1923). On Seitō, see Pauline C. Reich and Atsuko Fukuda, "Japan's Literary Feminists: The 'Seitō (Bluestockings)' Group," *Signs: Journal of Woman in Culture and Society*, 2, no. 1 (Autumn 1976): 280–91; and Vera Mackie, *Feminism in Modern Japan: Citizenship, Embodiment and Sexuality* (Cambridge: Cambridge University Press, 2003). See her discussion of the *atarashii on'na* (New Woman) and journals such as *Seitō* and *Fujin Kōron* (Women's Review) established, respectively, in 1911 and 1916. See also Mackie, *Creating Socialist Women in Japan: Gender, Labor and Activism, 1900–1937* (Cambridge: Cambridge University Press, 1997), Chap. 4. Kim Won-ju launched *Cheongdaphoe* (Bluestockings Association) and *Sin Yeoja* (New Woman), as Yung-Hee Kim discusses in "From Subservience to Autonomy: Kim Won-ju's 'Awakening,'" *Korean Studies* 21, no. (1997): 1–30.

15. Kim Jinsong, 82.

16. Government-General of Joseon, *Thriving Joseon: A Survey of Twenty-Five Years' Administration*, October 1935, 1.

17. See Government-General of Joseon; and Hilary Conroy, *The Japanese Seizure of Korea: 1868–1910: A Study of Realism and Idealism in International Relations* (Philadelphia: University of Pennsylvania Press, 1960). Unfortunately, the author depends solely on archives and materials written in Japanese (Japanese Ministry of Foreign Affairs Archives on Library of Congress microfilm), dismissing Korean materials. See also Peter Duus, *The Abacus and the Sword: The Japanese Penetration of Korea, 1895–1910* (Berkeley: University of California Press, 1995).

18. *Tokyo Puck*, October 1, 1919 (cover). The cover of *Tokyo Puck* says "She (Goddess of Peace) had been hungry until her stomach was filled discriminately with such nourishing stuff as the Peace Treaty, the League of Nations, etc. She has now overeaten. Doctors called Japan, England, America, France and other nations seem to be satisfied that the Goddess of Peace is well fed. But will she ever be able to digest what she has taken in?"

19. The issues of cultural nationalism and the resistance movement are examined in Michael Edson Robinson, *Cultural Nationalism in Colonial Korea, 1920–25* (Seattle: University of Washington Press, 1988); and Shin Gi-Wook, *Peasant Protest and Social Change in Colonial Korea* (Seattle: University of Washington Press, 1996). Through collaboration with serial journals, the Korean intelligentsia began a campaign against illiteracy. In a sense, the press circulated a collective memory of humiliation by Japan's annexation of Korea. Therefore, the Korean language, press, schools, meeting places, the Independence Club of 1896, and the like all became the texts in which a cultural nationalism of the colonized was inscribed. See F.A. McKenzie, *Korea's Fight for Freedom* (London and New York, 1920).

20. See Kim Youngna, 20; and Jennifer J. Jung-Kim, 322–7 for the list of women's magazines at that time. See also Kim Keon-su, *Hanguk japjisa yeongu* (The History of Korean Magazines) (Seoul: Hangukhak Yeonguso, 1992).

21. Western lifestyle, interior design, and cooking were frequently discussed in magazines: See Pak Gil-yong, "Saesallim ui bueok eun ireossge hyaeeomyeon" (If I Could do my Kitchen this Way in my New Household!), *Yeoseong* (Woman) (April 1936); "Sinchu ui seoyang yori" (Western Cuisine in the New Year), *Jogwang* (Morning Light) (September 1936).

22. Kim Youngna notes that the image of "wise mother, good wife" was strongly promoted during the 1930s, when Japan was more involved in the war. See Kim Youngna, 20.

23. The term was presumably used after Meiji Japan while intellectuals such as Nakamura Masanao argue how women should act: "Creating Good Mothers," *Meiroku zasshi* (Journal of the Japanese Enlightenment) 33 (March 1875). This source is quoted from Jennifer J. Jung-Kim, 4.

24. Hawsin Department Store, founded by Korean entrepreneur Pak Heung-sik, opened in trendy Jongno Street in Seoul in 1932; he expanded the store in 1937. There were four other Japanese branch department stores in Seoul: Mitsukoshi, Minakai, Chojiya, and Hirata. In Japan, Purantan (*Printemps* in French) opened in 1911. See Takashi Hirano, "Retailing in Urban Japan, 1868–1945," *Urban History* 26 (1999): 373–92.

25. Charles Baudelaire, *The Painter of Modern Life and Other Essays* (London: Phaidon, 1964), 13.

26. O Seok-cheon, "Modeonijeum ui iron" (The Theory of Modernism), *Sinmin* (New People) (June 1931); reprinted in Kim Jinsong, 61.

27. Miriam Silverberg, *Erotic Grotesque Nonsense: The Mass Culture of Japanese Modern Times* (Berkeley: University of California Press, 2007); see also Jennifer J. Jung-Kim, 225. According to Silverberg, the Japanese mass media defined the 1930s as a "time of erotic grotesque nonsense," xv. The author defines the erotic as "energized, colorful vitality." In Korea's case, this ero-gro might be different because it was the colonial subject. See also the discussion of So Rae-seop's *Ero gro nonsense: Geundae jeok jageug ui tansaeng* (Ero Gro Nonsense: The Birth of Modern Sensitivity) (Seoul: Sallim Jisik Chongseo, 2006); and Chae Suk-jin, "Gamgak ui jeguk: EroGro Nonsense" (Sense of the Imperial Japan: Ero Gro Nonsense), *Peminijeum Yeongu* (Feminism Studies) (October 2005): 43–87.

28. Kim Yeong-jin (nom de plume: Geokra Sanin), "Modeon suje" (Notes on the Modern), *Sinmin* (July 1930); reprinted in Kim Jinsong, 330–1.

29. Yeom Sang-seob in *Samdae* (Three Generations) (reprinted, Seoul: Sodam, 1996), 55, 137.

30. After the outbreak of war in 1937, Japanese colonial policy became stricter and a rigid censorship swept over Korea. Koreans were forced to change their names into Japanese. It was called "Changssi gaemyeong" or "identity creation of a new clan."

31. Kim Youngna, 29 (see n. 35). The author argues that the Modern Girl and the flapper were interchangeably used in Korea, although Silverberg discusses the differences between the two terms in "The Modern Girl as Militant."

32. Kenneth A. Yellis, "Prosperity's Child: Some Thoughts on the Flapper," *American Quarterly* 21, no. 1 (Spring 1969), 48; originally Sigmund Freud, *Civilization and Its Discontents* (London, 1949; first published 1930), 50ff. New York produced a cosmopolitan urban culture and took its place as financial capital in spite of the Crash of 1929 and the subsequent Depression. In the interwar period of the 1920s and 1930s, office women and shoppers identified with images of the New Woman in shop windows and advertisements, stimulating the popular imagination. In turn, the demands of the New Woman for products accelerated their production. The Fourteenth Street artists in New York, including Isabel Bishop, Raphael Soyer, Kenneth Haynes Miller, and Reginald March, vividly depicted the commercialized flapper and the New Woman in the interwar period.

33. Yellis, 48.

34. Richard Gilman, *Decadence: The Strange Life of an Epithet* (New York, 1975), 11.

35. "Gyeongseong ap'dwigol" (In the Capital of Seoul), *Hyeseong* (Comet) (November 1931); reprinted in Kim Jinsong, 280–4.

36. Kweon Haeng-ga examines *gisaeng* represented in postcards issued in colonial Korea. See "Iljesidaeui gwangwang yeobseowa gisaeng imiji" (Postcards and Gisaeng Images in Colonial Korea), in *Hanguk geundae misul gwa sigak munhwa* (Korean Modern Art and Visual Culture), ed. Kim Youngna (Seoul: Johyeong Gyoyuk, 2002), 343–66.

37. See George T. Shea, *Leftwing Literature in Japan: A Brief History of the Proletarian Literary Movement* (Tokyo: Hosei University Press, 1964).

38. See Kida Emiko, "Hanil peurolletaria misul undong ui gyoryu (The Exchange of the Korean and Japanese Proletarian Art Movement)," in *Hanguk geundae misul gwa sigak munhwa*, ed. Kim Youngna, 139–64. A comparison of Lee Sang-chun's *Factory Strike*, produced in 1932 in Korea, and Masamu Yanase's *Masses: The Critical Anthology on the Proletariat*, made in 1929 in Japan, reveals compelling similarities. Specifically, the KAPF members distributed writings and prints in Seoul, which had been executed by the NAPF members.

39. Chae Suk-Jin, 46; Silverberg, 29. See Kim Jinsong (p. 316) for the illustrations of this type. For Japan's labor activities, see Vera Mackie, *Creating Socialist Women in Japan: Gender, Labour and Activism, 1900–1937* (Cambridge: Cambridge University Press, 1997). The similar female type in modern China was *funü*, a Mao's girl that the Chinese Communist Party set against a bourgeois *nüxing*. See Tani E. Barlow, "Theorizing Woman," in *Body, Subject and Power*, eds. Angela Zito and Tani Barlow (Chicago, IL: University of Chicago Press, 1994); Tani E. Barlow, "Politics and Protocols of *funü*: (Un)making National Woman," in *Engendering China: Women, Culture, and the State*, eds. Christina Gilmartin et al. (Cambridge, MA: Harvard University Press, 1994); and Shu-mei Shih, "Gender, Race and Semicolonialism: Liu Na-ou's Urban Shanghai Landscape," *Journal of Asian Studies* 55, no. 4 (November 1996): 934–56.

40. Kwon Insook, "'The New Women's Movement' in 1920s Korea: Rethinking the Relationship between Imperialism and Women," *Gender and History* 10, no. 3 (November 1998): 381–405.

41. See George T. Shea, *Leftwing Literature in Japan: A Brief History of the Proletarian Literary Movement* (Tokyo: Hosei University Press, 1964). Kida, 139–64. The author notes that the KAPF was censored more than the Japanese counterpart (p. 142).

42. Na also called herself "Rha, Hye-suk" in English. For a "critical" study of Na's landscape paintings, see Park Carey, "Na Hye-seok ui punggyeonghwa" (Na Hye-seok's Landscape Paintings), *Hanguk geundae misulsahak* (Modern Korean Art History) (2005): 173–206; and Park Carey, "Isip-segi Hanguk hoehwa eseo ui jeontong non" (A Study of Korean Painters' Viewpoints on Tradition in the Twentieth Century), Ph.D. diss., Seoul: Ewha Woman's University, 2006.

43. Kim Yung-hee, "Creating New Paradigms of Womanhood in Modern Korean Literature: Na Hye-Sok [seok]'s 'Kyeong-hui,'" *Korean Studies* 26, no. 1 (2002): 1–60.

44. Na Hye-seok, "Ihon gobaegseo" (Confession of Divorce), *Samcheolli* (August–September 1934); "Doksin yeoja jeongjo ron" (On the Virginity of a Single Woman), *Samcheolli* (October 1935); and "Isang jeok buin" (The Ideal Wife), *Hakjigwang* (Light of Learning) 3 (1914).

45. Na Hye-seok, "Ihon gobaegseo."

46. Compared to her writings, her paintings have been largely neglected due to the paucity of surviving works; Na's paintings and caricatures have mainly been used to elucidate her opinions on women's issues or as illustrations of her biography. Her oeuvre, especially landscape paintings, merit more in-depth examination. Her outspokenness and tragic death have made her a legend. See her biography by Yi Guyeol, *Emi neun seongakja yeotneunira* (Your Mother was a Pioneer: Na Hye-seok's Life) (Seoul: Donghwa Chulpan Gongsa, 1974).

47. Seitō dealt with a special issue on Ibsen's *A Doll's House* in January 1912. The play starring Matsui Sumako (1886–1919) was performed at the dramatic workshop *Bungei Kyōkai* (Association of Literary Arts) led by Tsubouchi Shōyō and Shimamura Hogetsu (1871–1919) in November 1911. Na Hye-seok, "Inhyeong ui jip" (A Doll's House), *Mail sinbo* (Daily Newspaper) (April 3, 1921).

48. Na Hye-seok wrote "Bubugan ui mundap" (Dialog of Wife and Husband), *Sin yeoseong* (New Woman) (November 1923); and "Nora," *Sin Yeoseong* (July 1926).

49. Na's self-portrait can be compared to Yi Jong-wu's *Madame* of 1926, presumably painted in Paris, since the artist was the first Korean artist who studied in Paris.

50. *Na Hye-seokui saengae wa geurim* (Na Hye-seok: Her Life and Art), exh. cat., Seoul: Seoul Art Center, January 15–February 7, 2000. The biographical information here is from this book. See also Yeongu Gonggan, *Sin yeoseong* (Seoul: Hangyeore Sinmun, 2005).

51. Richard Brilliant, *Portraiture* (Cambridge, MA: Harvard University Press, 1991), 26.

52. Roger Scruton, *The Aesthetic Understanding: Essays in the Philosophy of Art and Culture* (London and New York: Methuen, 1983), 11.

53. See Yeongu Gonggan, *Sin Yeoseong* (Seoul: Hangyeore Sinmun, 2005).

54. Robert Lubar, "Unmasking Pablo's Gertrude: Queer Desire and the Subject of Portraiture," *The Art Bulletin* 79, no. 1 (March 1997): 69.

55. See *Na Hye-seok ui saengae wa geurim*, 11.

56. Na Hye-seok, "Sinsaenghwal e deulmyeonseo (Entering a New Life)," *Samcheolli* (February 1935).

Chapter 6

1. Extensive research has been conducted on the Joseon Art Exhibitions. One of the latest pieces of research is a book by Kim Hye-sin, *Hanguk geundae misul yeongu* (Research on Modern Korean Art) (Tokyo: Brüke, 2005).

2. Sim Eun-suk, "Sinyeoseong gwa guyeoseong" (New Women and Traditional Women), *Yeoseong* (Woman) 3 (June 1936): 56.

3. Lee Seong-Hwan, "Hyeonha joseon eseoui jubu roneun yeogyo chulsin i naheunga guyeoja ga naheunga" (Who is Better as a Future Wife, the New Woman or the Traditional Woman?), *Byeolgeongon* (An Unusual World) 3, no. 7 (January 1928): 90–8.

4. *The Story of Chunhyang* was created in the latter part of the Joseon Dynasty (eighteenth century). The author is unknown. It made its first appearance in a *pansori* (a traditional Korean narrative song) and then took root in a fictional novel. The story was published in 1910, when it developed into one of the most widely read Korean classics among the general public. During the 1930s, *The Story of Chunhyang* was popular not only as a novel but also featured in theater productions and movies.

5. Kim Bok-jin (a representative modern Korean sculptor) died in 1940 and was survived by his wife, Heo Hwa-baek.

6. Park Hyang-min, "Geukdan, Insaeng Geukjang ui changnip gongyeon eul bogo" (After Watching the Play by Insaeng Geukjang), *Donga ilbo* (The Donga Daily News) (December 17, 1937).

7. *Mi-in-do is understood to be* "Painting of Beautiful Women"; however, it did not specifically portray a woman. Instead, it was a picture of a young woman clad in clothes representing the fashionable style of the period and served as a form of "pinup girl." Currently, many versions of "Painting of Beautiful Women" from the eighteenth and nineteenth centuries are being circulated.

8. This information about Kim Eun-ho's *Portrait of Chunhyang* comes from Guan Haengga, "Gimeunho ui chunhyangsang ikgi" (The Interpretation of Kim Eun-ho's *Portrait of Chunhyang*), *Hanguk geundae misulsa yeongu* (The History of Modern Korean art) 9 (2001): 191–219.

9. Nam Man-min, "Chunhyang ui jeongjo jaeeummi" (A Look at Chuhyang's Sense of Chastity), *Yeoseong* (October 1936): 38–40.

10. For more information about *Portrait of Unnangja*, see Kim Yisoon, *Hanguk ui moja sang* (Portraits of Mother and Child in Korea) (Seoul: National Museum of Contemporary Art, 2006), 216–29.

11. Gu Jeong-hwa, "Hanguk geundaegi ui yeoseong inmulhwa e natanan yeoseong imiji" (The Female Image in Modern Korean Art), *Hanguk geundae misulsa yeongu* 9 (2001): 138.

12. Lee Gwang-su, "Moseong" (Maternal Love), *Yeoseong* 1, no. 2 (May 1936): 12–3.

13. Lee Gi-yeong, "Widaehan moseong" (Great Maternal Love), *Yeoseong* 5, no. 4 (April 1940): 76–7.

14. See Kim Suk-ja, "Dongnip sinmun e natanan yeoseong gaehwa ui uiji" (Enlightening Efforts for Women in Independent Newspapers), *Hanguksa yeongu* (The Study of Korean History), 54 (September 1986): 59–74; Song In-ja, "Gaehwagi yeoseong gyoyungnon ui uiui wa hangye" (The Meaning and Problems with the Education of Women), *Hanguk gyoyuksahak* (The Hstory of Korean Education) 17 (1995): 127–66; and Shin Yeong-suk, "Daehanjeguk sigi gabujangje wa yeoseong ui yeokhal" (Patriarchism and Women's Role in the Daehan Empire Period), *Yeoseoghak* (The Studies of Women) 11 (1994): 85–110.

15. See Lee Gwang-su, "Moseong jungsim ui janyeo gyoyuk" (Education of Children Based on Maternal Love) *Sinyeoseong* (New Women), (January 1925): 19–20; and Lee Eun-sang, "Joseon ui moseong eun joseon ui moseong" (Maternal Love Represents Women in Joseon), *Sinyeoseong* (May and June 1925): 2–6.

16. See Choi Seok-ju, "Seongtan eul majihaya joseon ui moseong eul saenggakham" (Thinking about Maternal Love of Joseon Women on Christmas Day), *Cheongneon* (The Young) 10, no. 8 (December 1930): 23–6; Ju Yo-seop, "Eomeoni ui sarang" (Maternal Love), *Singajeong* (The New Family) 1 (January 1933): 182–3; and Im Jeong-hyeok, "Janyeo reul gajin cheongsang gwabu ga jaehonham i oreunya, geureunya" (Is it Acceptable for a Widow with Children to Remarry?), *Yeoseong* 1, no. 2 (May 1936): 36–7.

17. For more information about this opinion, see Shin Myoeng-jik, *Modern boi, gyeongseong eul geonilda* (Modern Boy Wandering Around Gyeongseong) (Seoul: Hyeonsil munhwa yeongu, 2003): 75–232.

18. For more articles focusing on maternal love published by women's magazines in the 1930s, see Lee Gim-jeon, "Moyu wa yua" (Breast-feeding and Babies), *Sinyeoseong* 7, no. 6 (June 1933): 86–7; No Ja-yeong, "Munye e natanan moseongae wa Yeongwon ui Byeol" (Maternal Love Described in Literature and Yeongwon ui Byeol), *Singajeong* (March 1934): 74–81; Lee Gwang-su, "Moseong euroseoui yeoja" (Women are Nothing but Maternal Love), *Yeoseong* 2, no. 1 (June 1936): 8; Il Hye, "Widaehan eomeoni anhae ui jonjae" (Great Mothers and Great Wives), *Woori gajeong* (Our Family) (October 1936): 38–40; Hong Jong-in, "Moseongae gunsang" (Maternal Love), *Yeoseong* 2, no. 1 (January 1937): 82–3; Jeon Ae-rok, "Moseongae wa gajeong gyoyuk" (Maternal Love and Family Education), *Yeoseong* 2, no. 4 (April 1937): 70–3; Heo Yoeng-sun, "Moseong gwa moseongae" (Mothers and Maternal Love), *Yeoseong* 3, no. 9 (September 1938): 36–9; Lee Dal-nam, "Jeolmeun eomeoni dokbon" (For Young Mothers), *Yeoseong* 4, no. 1 (January 1939): 71–4; and Min Chon-saeng, "Widaehan moseong eul" (For Great Maternal Love), *Yeoseong* 5, no. 4 (April 1940): 76–8.

19. Starting in the late nineteenth century, this country realized the importance of children. *Seoyugeonmun* (The Record of Europe) and *Dokribsinmun* (Independent Newspaper) by Yu Gil-jun talks about the significance of children as future leaders. Particularly during Japanese colonial rule (1910–45), children were considered saviors of Korea's future. People started to think that children were more like little adults and had their own values. Under these circumstances, Children's Day was designated in 1923.

20. At that time, a radio was a symbol of wealth, owned only by upper-middle-class households.

21. The models for the painting were not actually mother and daughter, but they act these roles in the picture. For more information about the models, see Gu Jeong-hwa, "Hanguk geundaegiui yeoseong inmulhwa e natanan yeoseong imiji" (The Female Image in Modern Korean Art), *Hanguk geundae misulsa yeongu*, no. 9 (2001): 136.

22. At that time it was rare for women and children to wear Western-style shoes. Those shoes indicate an acceptance of Western culture. The Korean *hanbok* coexists in this picture with Western shoes, a symbol of modernization. The combination of the two, however, still makes a relatively conservative image.

23. Hwang Sin-deok, "Joseon eun ireohan eomeoni reul yoguhanda" (Joseon Needs Mothers Like These), *Singajeong* 1 (May 1933): 12–15.

24. Kim Youngna, "Modernity in Debate; Representing the 'New Woman' and 'Modern Girl,'" *20th-Century Korean Art* (London: Laurence King, 2005): 64–87.

25. For more information on the changed social perceptions of women in the colonial era, see Kim Gyeong-il, "Hanguk geundae sahoe ui hyeongseong eseo jeontonggwa geund" (Old Values and New Values in the Process of Korea's Modernization), *Sahoe wa Yeoksa* (Society and History) 54 (1998): 11–42.

26. Sim Hun, "Yakhon saedae ui chueok" (The Memory of Arranged Marriage), *Samcheolli* (The Land of Korea) 12 (1930): 58.

Chapter 7

1. On *Japonisme* in the Euro-American sphere see, for example, Toshio Watanabe, *High Victorian Japonisme* (Bern and New York: P. Lang, 1991); Lionel Lambourne, *Japonisme: Cultural Crossings between Japan and the West* (London: Phaidon, 2005); and Julia Meech and Gabriel P. Weisberg, *Japonisme comes to America: The Japanese Impact on the Graphic Arts, 1876–1925* (New York: H.N. Abrams in association with the Jane Voorhees Zimmerli Art Museum, Rutgers, the State University of New Jersey, 1990).

2. See Mabuchi Akiko, "Butai no ue no Nihon: 1870 nenndai no Pari" (Japan on the Scenes in Paris, in the 1870s), *Nihon Joshi Daigaku kiyô* (Bulletin of Japan Women's University) 12 (2001): 169–88.

3. See Hashimoto Yorimitsu, "Chaya no tenshi: Eikoku seiki-matsu no Operetta Geisha 1896 to sono rekishi-teki haikei" (The Angel in the Tea House: Representations of Victorian Paradise and Playground in *The Geisha*,1896), *Japonisumu Kenkyū* (Studies on Japonisme) 20 (2003): 30–49.

4. Saeki Junko, "Geisha' no Hakken: 'Tasha-ka' sareru Nippon" (Discovery of "Geisha": Japan Gazed as the "Other"), in *Bijutsushi to tasha* (Art History and the 'Other'), eds. Shimamoto Hiroshi and Kasuya Makoto (Kyoto: Kōyōshobō, 2000), 117–52.

5. Fujishima Takeji, "Chōsen Kankō Shokan" (Memory of a Journey to Chōsen), *Bijutsu Shimpō* (Art News) 13, no. 5 (1914): 11–2.

6. Fujishima Takeji, 13.

7. Fujii Keisuke, Saotome Masahiro, Tsunoda Mayumi, Nisiaki Yoshihiro, eds., *Sekino Tadashi Ajia tōsa* (Tadashi Sekino: Explorer of Asia) (Tokyo: Tokyo Daigaku Shuppankai, 2005).

8. Fujishima Takeji, 11.

9. Kuraya Mika, "Künstler auf Koreareise: Das Fremde in Japanischen Blick, 1895 und 1945" (Artists' Journey to Korea: Strangers in Japanese Eyes, from 1895 to 1945), *Comparativ* 3 (1998): 82–97.

10. Fujishima Takeji, 12–3.

11. Kojima Kaoru, "Fujishima no Egaita Josei-zō" (Images of Woman by Fujishima) in *Fujishima Takeji*, ed. Kojima Kaoru (Tokyo: Shinchōsha, 1998), 84–5.

12. Bert Winther-Tamaki, "Oriental Coefficient: The Role of China in the Japanization of Yōga," *Modern Chinese Literature and Culture* 85 (2006): 91.

13. Carolus-Duran had lived in Italy from 1862 to 1865. His tableau, *L'Assassiné, Souvenir de la Campagne Romaine* (The Assassinated, Memory of Roman Countryside) of 1862, was shown at the Salon and purchased by the French government.

14. Tokyo Geijutsu Daigaku Hyakunen-shi Hensan Shitsu (Editorial Office of the Hundred-year History of the Tokyo National University of Fine Arts & Music), ed. *Tokyo Geijutsu Daigaku Hyakunen-shi: Tokyo Bijutsu Gakkō-hen* (Hundred-year History of the Tokyo National University of Fine Arts & Music: Tokyo School of Fine Arts), 2 (Tokyo: Gyōsei, 1992), 317.

15. Fujishima Takeji, "Itari-fū no hekiga" (Wall Paintings in Italian Style), *Yorozu Chōhō* (Yorozu Morning News), (January 24, 1910): 2.

16. Fujishima, "Dekadansu no igi" (The Meaning of "Decadence"), *Bijutsu Shimpō* 10, no. 8 (1911): 7–8.

17. Fujishima, "Taiō kembun sūsoku" (Some Impressions of Europe), *Bijutsu Shimpō* 9, no. 5 (1910): 12.

18. Kojima Kaoru, "*Fujishima Takeji ni okeru 'Seiyō' to 'Tōyō'*" (Fujishima Takeji's "East" and "West"), in *Bijutsushika, Oini Warau: Kōno sensei no tameno Nihon bijutsushi ronshū* (Art Historian, Making Merry: A Collection of Essays on Japanese Art in Honor of Professor Kōno Motoaki), ed. Kōno Motoaki Sensei Taikan Kinen Ronbunshū Henshū Iinkai (Editorial Committee for the Festschrift in Honor of Professor Kōno Motoaki) (Tokyo: Brücke, 2006), 396.

19. See Toshio Watanabe, "Japanese Landscape Painting and Taiwan," in *Refracted Modernity: Visual Culture and Identity in Colonial Taiwan*, ed. Kikuchi Yuko (Honolulu: University of Hawai'i Press, 2007), 74–5.

20. Kyōto Kokuritsu Kindai Bijutsukan (The National Museum of Modern Art, Kyoto), ed. *Kindai Kyoto Gadan to Seiyō: Nihonga no Kishutachi* (Modern Kyoto Painting Circle and Western Culture—Revolutionaries in *nihonga*) (Kyoto: The National Museum of Modern Art, Kyoto, 1999), 124.

21. Fujishima Takeji, "Futsukoku Geien no Ichi Myōjō tarishi Karoryusu Dyuran-shi" (Mr Carolus-Duran who was a Star in French Art), *Bijutsu* (Art) 1, no. 7 (1917): 5–10.

22. Fujishima Takeji, "*Ashiato o Tadorite*" (Tracing Footsteps) in *Geijutsu no Esupuri* (Esprit of Art), ed. Fujishima Takeji (Tokyo: Chūōkōron Bijutsu Shuppansha, 1982).

23. Stefan Tanaka, *Japan's Orient: Rendering Pasts into History*, (Berkeley, Los Angeles, and London: University of California, 1993).

24. Satō Dōshin, "Sekai-kan no Saihen to Rekishi-kan no Saihen" (Reorganizing World Views, Reorganizing Historical Views), in *Ima Nihon no Bijutushigaku wo furikaeru* (The Present, and the Discipline of Art History in Japan), ed. Tōkyō Kokuritsu Bunkazai Kenkyūjo (Tokyo: Tōkyō Kokuritsu Bunkazai Kenkyūjo, 1999), 111–27.

25. Tsuchida Bakusen, "*Kichō-go no Dai-ichi Inshō*" (The First Impression after Coming Back to Japan), *Chūō bijutsu* (Central Art) 9, no. 9 (1923): 140–1.

26. Furuta Ryō, "*Tsuchida Bakusen Shiron: Meishō wo chūshin nisite*" (Tsuchida Bakusen: With a Focus on a *Maiko* Girl), *MUSEUM* 599 (2005): 57–69.

27. Kawamura Minato, *Kîsen: Mono iu hana no bunka-shi* (Cultural History on Gisaeng) (Tokyo: Sakuhinsha, 2001).

28. Tōkyō Kokuritsu Kindai Bijutsukan (The National Museum of Modern Art, Tokyo), ed. *Tsuchida Bakusen-ten* (Tsuchida Bakusen: A Retrospective) (Tokyo: Nihon Keizai Shimbunsha, 1997), 182.

29. Tōkyō Kokuritsu Kindai Bijutsukan, 182.

30. The two *gisaeng* in Bakusen's painting are also shown in submissive poses. As Kim Hyeshin has noted, many Japanese images of *gisaeng*, including that by Bakusen, were products of male and colonial gazes. See Kim Hyeshin, *Kankoku kindai bijutsu kenkyū: Shokuminchiki 'Chōsen Bijutsu Tenrankai ni miru ibunka shihai to bunka hyōshō* (Research on Korean Modern Art: Controls over Korean Culture and its Representation in the Analysis of "Chosen Bijutsu Tenrankai" in the Colonial Period) (Tokyo: Brücke, 2005), 102–10.

31. Kuramoto Taeko, *Hayami Gyoshū no geijutsu* (The Art of Hayami Gyoshū) (Tokyo: Nihon Keizai Shimbunsha, 1992), 102–3.

32. Kuramoto Taeko, 120.

33. Kusanagi Natsuko, "1930-nen kaisai, Nihon Bijutsu-ten ni Kanshite" (On the Art Exhibition of Japanese Art Held in 1930), *Kindai Gasetsu* (Modern Painting Discourse), 11 (2002): 127–40.

34. Tanabe Kōji, "*Chōsen ni okeru Gyoshū-kun*" (Gyoshū in Korea), *Bi no kuni* (Kingdom of Beauty) 11, no.5 (1935): 68–9.

35. Yamatane Museum of Art, ed., *Kaiga no shin seimei: Hayami Gyoshū garon* (A True Spirit of a Painting: Essays on Paintings by Hayami Gyoshū) (Tokyo: Chūōkōron Bijutsu Shuppan, 1996), 18.

36. Katō Shōrin, "*Hayami Sensei no Shasei*" (Sketches by Mr Hayami), in *Hayami Gyoshū*, Vol. 1, ed. Kawakita Michiaki (Tokyo: Gakushū Kenkyūsha), 175–7.

Chapter 8

1. Yamada Eizaburō, "Kenchikubi no honshitsu" (The Essence of Architectural Beauty), *Kenchiku sekai* (Architectural World) 17, no. 4 (1923): 8.

2. Murooka Sōshichi, "Kenchiku no biteki taikō" (Outline of the Aesthetic Relations of Architecture), *Kenchiku sekai* (Architectural World) 2, no. 9 (February 1915): 31–5. The treatise was serialized in *Architectural World* in eleven parts, ending in the April 1916 issue of the journal.

3. Murooka, 31.

4. Murooka, 31.

5. Kogakushi K. K.-sei, "Sōshoku-bi" (Decorative Beauty), Parts 1–5, *Kenchiku gahō* (The Architectural Graphic) 4 (May–December 1913). For each of the three principles, K. K. gives first the Japanese name

in Chinese characters, glossed with a phonetic reading of the English translation, and then the English translation in Roman characters. The principles set out in this series are extremely close to those presented in another article in the same journal two years prior, Fujinami-sei , "Kenchiku-bi gaisetsu" (Outline of Architectural Beauty), *Kenchiku gahō* (The Architectural Graphic) 2, no. 13 (December 1911): 27–9.

6. Itō Chūta and Ichihigashi Kenkichi, "Kenchikujutsu to bijutsu no kankei (Meiji juroku-nen san-gatsu yōka tsujōkai enzetsu)" (The Relationship between Architectural Arts and Fine Art [Speech given at the regular meeting on March 8, 16th Year of the Meiji Era]), *Kenchiku zasshi* (Architectural Journal) 7, no. 75 (March 1893): 86–7. Interestingly, Itō argues for the need for artistic and beautiful architecture for six of the article's seven pages before defining what he means by these terms.

7. Wakayanagi Midori, "Shopenhaueru no kenchikukan" (Schopenhauer's View of Architecture), *Kenchiku sekai* (Architectural World) 10, no. 8 (1916): 69.

8. Mitsuhashi Shirō, "Kenchikubutsu no bijutsuteki taikō" (The Artistic Relations and Measures of Architectural Objects), in *Wayō kairyō daikenchikugaku* (Improved Japanese and Western Great Architectural Knowledge), Vol. 3, 666–713 (Tokyo: Okura Shoten, 1911). For a biography of Mitsuhashi and list and images of major works, see Fujioka Shigeichi, "Seikaiin kōgakushi Mitsuhashi Shirō shi no itami" (The Obituary of Full Member Mitsuhashi Shiro), *Kenchiku zasshi* (Architectural Journal) 30, no. 349 (December 1915): 31–4, iii–iv; and Horiguchi Kankichi, "Mitsuhashi Shirō shi cho dai kenchiku gaku ni tsuite: kenchikushi, kenchiku ishō" (On Mitsuhashi Shiro's *Great Architectural Learning*: Architectural History and Architectural Design). *Gakujutsuron en kōgaishu: Keikaku-kei* (Summaries of Technical Papers of Annual Meeting: Architectural Design) 46 (September 1971): 1075–6 is a summary of the compendium.

9. Mitsuhashi, 666.

10. Mitsuhashi, 667–9.

11. Mitsuhashi, 667.

12. Mitsuhashi, 667.

13. In "Nihon no hyōgen-ha" (Japan's Expressionists), *Shinden ka gokusha ka* (Shrine or Prison?) (Tokyo: Sagami Shobō, 1972), 1–114, Hasegawa Gyō discusses the fissure between technical and art-based practice in the 1910s. For an English-language overview and introduction to the work of Itō and Sano Toshikata (a.k.a. Sano Riki), the main proponent of the technical side, see Jonathan M. Reynolds, "The Formation of a Japanese Architectural Profession," in *The Artist as Professional in Japan*, ed. Melinda Takeuchi (Palo Alto, CA: Stanford University Press, 2004), 180–202.

14. See, for example, Mitsuhashi Shirō, "Tekkin kongyō-do narabi ni sono ōyō" (Reinforced Concrete and its Application), *Kenchiku zasshi* (Architectural Journal) 22, no. 264 (December 1908): 476–90.

15. Mitsuhashi, 667.

16. The Nakagyō Post Office is also famous as the object of a major historic preservation battle in the mid-1970s that ended in the preservation of the façade and construction of a new concrete structure inside.

17. The role of architecture in building the Meiji state has been well researched and well documented. In English, see David Stewart, *The Making of Modern Japanese Architecture* (Tokyo and New York: Kodansha International, 2003), and William Coaldrake, *Architecture and Authority in Japan* (London and New York: Routledge, 1996), Chap. 6.

18. The college was established in 1871; full-time instruction began in 1873, and the full-time architecture program in 1877. English-language sources for early architectural education in Japan include Don Choi, "Domesticated Modern: Hybrid Houses in Meiji Japan, 1870–1900," particularly Chap. 1, "Architectural Education and Residential Architecture in Early Meiji Japan," and Reynolds, "The Formation of a Japanese Architectural Profession," 180–202.

19. The government bureaucrats who founded the school chose to model its architectural training on the British system, which had ties to civil engineering, rather than the French counterpart at the Beaux-Arts, which emphasized drawing (*dessin*, or design) over practical considerations and on-site training. Choi suggests that it was this primary interest in the technical, engineering side of architecture that led to the selection of the British model over the Beaux-Arts model. Choi, 42.

20. Mitsuhashi Shirō, "Parutenon Tempuru" (The Temple of the Parthenon), *Kenchiku zasshi* (Architectural Journal) 18, no. 208 (April 1904): 217.

21. Richard A. Moore, "Academic 'Dessin' Theory in France after the Reorganization of 1863," *The Journal of the Society of Architectural Historians* 36, no. 3 (October 1977): 145.

22. Nakatani Reiji and Nakatani Seminar, *Kinsei kenchiku ronshu* (Pre-modern Architectural Theory) (Kyoto: Acetate, 2004), is a brilliant analysis of the persistence of traditional building and design techniques among Meiji period architectural culture. See also Cherie Wendelken, "The Tectonics of Japanese Style: Architect and Carpenter in the Late Meiji Period," *Art Journal* 55 (1996): 28–37. Reynolds, "The Formation of a Japanese Architectural Profession" also addresses the class split between architect and carpenter. The paradigmatic Meiji approach represented by Mitsuhashi can also be contrasted to that of English design reformers in the late nineteenth century and architects working after the introduction of the International Style in the 1920s. While Mitsuhashi's façade indicated the building's function through the use of a particular style, its form did not depend on structure or materials, the "form follows function" equation central to modernists several decades later.

23. William R. Ware, *Parallel of historical ornament, a selection of ... examples ... arranged ... to present ... a comparative view of their principal features, prepared under the supervision of William R. Ware* (Boston, MA: L. Prang and Company, 1876) and *Modern Perspective: A Treatise upon the Principles and Practice of Plane and Cylindrical Perspective* (Boston, MA: Ticknor, c. 1882). For a biographical sketch of Ware and a discussion of his influence on architectural education in the United States, see J. A. Chewning, "William Robert Ware at MIT and Columbia," *Journal of Architectural Education* 33, no. 2 (November 1979), 25–9, and John Vredenburg Van Pelt, *A Discussion of Composition, Especially as Applied to Architecture* (New York: Macmillan Co., 1902).

24. John Beverly Robinson, *Principles of Architectural Composition: An Attempt to Order and Phrase Ideas which have hitherto been only felt by the Instinctive Taste of Designers* (1899; reprint New York: Van Nostrand, 1908), mentioned in Mitsuhashi, "Kenchikubutsu no bijutsuteki taiko," 709. Mitsuhashi was not alone in deriving his aesthetics of architectural composition from the Beaux-Arts via New York, or in understanding beauty as a product of natural forces. For example, Murooka's treatise also introduced Robinson's principles of architectural composition and borrowed the title of Robinson's book (in translation) for the title of his treatise.

25. For those not well versed in the history of the architectural profession in modern Japan, this complete adherence to Western architecture models could seem odd. By the 1920s, architects had begun to reevaluate the importance of employing vernacular aesthetics within the hybrid architectural framework, and Itō Chūta argued for attention to historical vernacular form from the 1890s. However, the bulk of Meiji architectural culture looked to Western architectural models as modern and appropriate for the new state—which should not be surprising, considering that early architects were trained specifically to build it.

26. In this analysis, I have been inspired by Penny Sparke's argument in *As Long as it's Pink: The Sexual Politics of Taste* (London: Pandora, 1995).

27. For the early years of women's involvement in architectural education and the architectural profession in mid-century Japan, see Matsukawa Junko, "Nihon ni okeru senzen sengō no sōsōki no josei kenchikuka gijutsusha" (The Pioneer Years of Women Architects and Engineers in Prewar and Postwar Japan), *Housing Research Foundation Annual Report* 30 (2003): 251–62.

28. Girls' higher school education was the purview of the elite. In 1899, the Ministry of Education mandated that each prefecture establish and operate at least one girls' higher school; however, no more than three percent of primary school graduates attended in 1912. See Tsunemi Ikuo, *Kateika kyōikushi* (The History of Domestic Economy Education) (Tokyo: Koseikan, 1972), 120–1, 126. By 1926, ten percent of female graduates of primary schools continued to the girls' higher schools (compared to twenty percent of male graduates continuing to middle school). See Jordan Sand, *House and Home in Modern Japan: Architecture, Domestic Space and Bourgeois Culture 1880–1930* (Cambridge, MA: Harvard East Asian Monographs, 2003), for a description and analysis of women's domestic economy education in the late Meiji period.

29. In *House and Home in Modern Japan*, Sand analyzes the rhetoric of prescriptive interior decoration texts, particularly the difference in treatments of "Japanese-" and "Western-" style rooms. See the section "Recoding Interiors," 100–7. This chapter treats some of the same texts but is principally concerned with how the methods for providing beauty they present encode gender roles for the reader within a larger system of gendered spatial creation practices.

30. Because of the growth of suburban single-family housing in the 1910s and '20s, many texts began to include housing law, financing, and site issues, as well as discussions of the relative merits of renting and buying, and advice for the design and management of rental properties. See Sarah Teasley, "Home-builder or Home-maker? Reader Presence in Articles on Home-building in Commercial Women's Magazines in 1920s' Japan," *Journal of Design History* 18, no. 1 (January 2005): 81–97.

31. Among recent analyses, see Sand for an excellent and thorough investigation of the connection between home-building and hygiene texts and the ideology of the home and family circle.

32. Ōe was writing in 1916 but expressed sentiments developed in domestic economy discourse in the Meiji period. Ōe Sumiko, *Shoron Jūkyo* (Assorted Writings and Housing), Vol. 1 of *Ōyo kaji seigi* (Detailed Lectures in Practical Housekeeping) (Tokyo and Osaka: Hōbunkan, 1916), 458.

33. Kondō Shōichi, *Shitsunai sōshoku hō* (Principles of Interior Decoration) (Tokyo: Hakubunkan, 1907), 3–4.

34. Kondō, 1.

35. Kondō, 18.

36. Shimoda Utako, *Katei kyōiku* (Domestic Education), Vol. 12 of *Katei bunko* (The Domestic Library) (Tokyo: Hakubunkan, 1901). Shimoda devoted one chapter of her first home economics textbook to aesthetic education, and the 1890s saw the publication of several texts devoted entirely to arguing the necessity of aesthetic education and proposing ways to achieve it through literature, art, music, architecture, and other arts practices of daily life. See, for example, Watanabe Yoshishige and Nishimura Shōzaburō, *Biiku* (Aesthetic Education) (Tokyo: Fukyūsha, 1893).

37. Kondō, 3.

38. Kondō, 19.

39. Kondō, 2.

40. Kondō, 2–3, 17.

41. Kondō, 3.

42. Kondō, 48.

43. See Kondō, 18–20 for one explanation of aesthetic categories or *bi no bunshi* (elements of beauty). Sand mentions the distribution of different adjectives to Western and Japanese-style interiors. See Sand, 103–4.

44. Yamagata Kōhō ed., *Ishokujū* (Clothing, Food, Housing) (Tokyo: Jitsugyō no Nihonsha, 1907), 5. The emphasis on taste derived partly from Anglo-American domestic manuals like Charles Eastlake's influential 1876 manual *Hints on Household Taste in Furniture, Upholstery, and Other Details* (London: Longmans Green, 1868). It was reinforced in the 1900s by discourse on taste generated by department stores like Mitsukoshi, whose magazine for women was entitled *Shumi* or "Taste," and analyzed in Jinno Yuki, *Shumi no tanjō* (The Birth of Taste) (Tokyo: Keisō Shobō, 1994), and Sand. For department stores, the promotion of taste was part of the campaign to create the image of an informed, educated consumer who would furnish a tasteful home through purchases at the stores.

45. Ōe, 463–85.

46. For an overview of the secondary literature on late nineteenth-century British and American domestic advice manuals, see Deborah Cohen, *Household Gods: The British and their Possessions, 1830–1945* (New Haven, CT: Yale University Press, 2006).

47. For the tea practice as an elite male pastime in the Meiji period, see Christine Guth, *Art, Tea, and Industry: Masuda Takashi and the Mitsui Circle* (Princeton, NJ: Princeton University Press, 1993).

48. Kondō, 15.

49. The examples discussed in this chapter come from major journals, influential textbooks, popular handbooks, and other representative texts, chosen not for their unique viewpoints but for the sheer ubiquity of the opinions and approaches they express. All of my examples come from publications originating in Tokyo, disseminated nationally, including to colonies and overseas Japanese communities, but emerging from and formed by architectural and home economics cultures that developed in Tokyo specifically. As the administrative, educational, and publishing center of the Japanese Empire, Tokyo had an influence on the development of architectural thought throughout Japan but—this great geographical scope notwithstanding—remained a local culture of its own. My conclusions, then, speak at once to the dissemination of gender role ideals through Japan but also to a set of specific and interrelated cultures of designing and dwelling in Tokyo itself.

Glossary

A Ying	阿英	Changsha	長沙
Ama	海女	Chen Yi	陳毅
An Seok-yeong	安夕影 (안석영)	Chen Yun	陳雲
Asai Chū	浅井忠	Chen Zhanghou (Chen Hongshou)	
Ba Jin	巴金	陳章侯 (陳洪綬)	
Baekhwa	白花 (백화)	Chiang Kai-shek	蔣介石
Baek Yun-mun	白潤文 (백윤문)	Chichibu (Prince)	秩父宮
baimiao	白描	*Chihan nōryō*	池畔納涼
Bai Yang	白楊	chima	치마
Ban Jieyu	班婕妤	Choe Rin	崔麟 (최린)
bi	美	Choe Yeong-su	崔永秀 (최영수)
biiku	美育	Chōsen Bijutsu Tenrankai	
bijin	美人	朝鮮美術展覧会	
bijinga	美人画	Chunhyang	春香 (춘향)
Bijin gahō	美人画報	Dai Kui	戴逵
Bijin Kyōshinkai	美人共進会	daizhao	待詔
bijutsu	美術	Deng Yingchao	鄧穎超
birei	美麗	*Dianshizhai huabao*	點石齋畫報
biteki	美的	Dihua	迪化
bugi rinsen	舞妓林泉	Ding Ling	丁玲
Buin	婦人 (부인)	Ding Lingguang	丁令光
Bungaku jidai	文学時代	dingqiu	丁酉
Bungei kurabu	文芸倶楽部	Ding Song	丁悚
bunka seiji	文化政治	Ding Yicheng	丁以誠
Bunten (Monbushō Bijutsu Tenrankai)		*Donggwang*	東光 (동광)
文展 (文部省美術展覧会)		Dong Wanzhen	董琬貞
Byeolgeongon	別乾坤 (별건곤)	Ehuang	娥皇
cabi dancai	擦筆淡彩	Ero-Gro	エログロ (에로그로)
Cai Chang	蔡暢	eroguro nansensu	エログロナンセンス
Cai Heshin	蔡和森	fangjian	房間
Cai Wenji	蔡文姬	Fang Zhimin	方志敏
Cao Yu	曹禺	Fei Danxu	費丹旭
Chae Yong-sin	蔡龍臣 (채용신)	*Feiyingge*	飛影閣
Chanjuan	蟬娟	fu	府
Chao Xun	巢勳	Fujishima Takeji	藤島武二

fuku-taikō	複対衡	Hwang Sin-deok	黃信德 (황신덕)
Funü zazhi	婦女雜誌	hyeonmo yangcheo	賢母良妻 (현모양처)
fūzokuga	風俗画	Imamura Shikō	今村紫紅
Gai Qi	改琦	Im Eung-gu	任應九 (임응구)
Gakushū-in	学習院	Im Hong-eun	任鴻恩 (임홍은)
gaoshi	高士	Im In-saeng	王寅生 (임인생)
Ge Huimin	葛惠敏	indebijuaritē	インデビジュアリテー
genri	原理	Inoue Shōichi	井上章一
geundae	近代 (근대)	ishokujū	衣食住
gidayū	義太夫	Itō Chūta	伊東忠太
gisaeng	妓生 (기생)	Izu (Islands)	伊豆 (諸島)
gongbi	工筆	jeogori	저고리
Gong Peng	龔鵬	*Jeomsim*	點心 (점심)
Gu Bing	顧炳	*Jeongcheong*	靜聽 (정청)
Gu Luo	顧洛	Jeong Do-hwa	鄭道和 (정도화)
Gujin baimei tu	古今百美圖	jibukuro	地袋
Gujin baimei tuyong	古今百美圖詠	*Jiji shimpō*	時事新報
Guo Moruo	郭沫若	Ji Seong-chae	池盛彩 (지성채)
Guomindang	國民黨	Jiangdong Shuju	江東書局
guti	古體	Jiang Qing	江青
Gyeongju	慶州	Jiang Xun	姜壎
Gyeowullal	冬日 (겨울날)	jiefangqu	解放區
Hachijō-jima	八丈島	*Jindai funü*	近代婦女
Haishanghua yinglu	海上畫影錄	Jin Huan	金環
Hakjigwang	學之光 (학지광)	*Jin Ping Mei*	金瓶梅
Hakubunkan	博文館	Jingganshan	井崗山
Hanakago	花籠	Jo Yong-seung	曹龍承 (조용승)
hanbok	韓服 (한복)	jokduri	족두리
Han Eun-jin	韓銀鎮 (한은진)	kaika-e	開化繪
Han Hog-je	韓弘濟 (한홍제)	*Kami*	髮
Hang Zhiying	杭穉英	Kaneda Kenko	金田ケン子
Hatamen	哈德門	Kang Youwei	康有為
Hayami Gyoshū	速水御舟	Kaseigaku	家政学
Heishō	平牀	katachi no bi	形の美
He Zizhen	賀子珍	Kawamura Minato	川村湊
Hinode shimbun	日の出新聞	kedakai	気高い
hittonessu (tekiō)	適應	*Keiko*	稽古
Hōkei	芳蕙	kenchikubi	建築美
Hu Baixiang	胡佰翔	kenchikujutsu	建築術
Hu Die	胡蝶	*Kenchiku gahō*	建築画報
Hu Lanqi	胡蘭畦	*Kenchiku no biteki taikō taii*	
hua guniang	花姑娘	建築の美的対向大意	
Hua Yan	華嵒	*Kenchiku sekai*	建築世界
Huang Jun	黃俊	*Kenchiku zasshi*	建築雜誌
Huihui	嬉嬉 (희희)	Kim (Gim) Bok-jin	金復鎮 (김복진)
Hung Chang-tai	洪長泰	Kim (Gim) Eun-ho	金殷鎬 (김은호)

Kim (Gim) Gi-chang	金基昶 (김기창)
Kim (Gim) Hong-do	金弘道 (김홍도)
Kim (Gim) Jin-song	金鎭宋 (김진송)
Kim (Gim) Lim	金林 (김림)
Kim (Gim) Wu-yeong	金雨英 (김우영)
Kim (Gim) Youngna	金英那 (김영나)
Kinoshita Naoyuki	木下直之
Kōbu Bijutsu Gakkō	工部美術学校
Kohan	湖畔
kōkoku shikan	皇国史観
kokoro no bi	心の美
Kondō Shōichi	近藤正一
Kuroda Seiki	黒田清輝
Lao She	老舍
Lee Gi-yeong	李箕永 (이기영)
Lee Gwang-su	李光洙 (이광수)
Lee Ok-sun	李玉順 (이옥순)
Lee Yong-woo	李龍佑 (이용우)
lei	類
Li Min	李敏
Li Yinqiao	李銀橋
Li Youlan	李又蘭
liangmu	良母
Liang Qichao	梁啟超
Liang you	良友
Lienü zhuan	列女傳
Liu Lequn	劉樂群
Liu Na'ou	劉吶鷗
Liu Shaoqi	劉少奇
Liu Xiang	劉向
Lin Hong	林紅
Lu Guixiu	盧桂秀
Lu Xun	魯迅
Lu Ziwan	陸子萬
Luo Baoyi	羅抱一
maiko	舞妓
Mao Dun	茅盾
Mao Zedong	毛澤東
Mao Zemin	毛澤民
Matsumoto Fūko	松本楓湖
meiren	美人
meiren hua	美人畫
meirenji	美人計
men	門
Meng Yu	孟瑜
miai	見合い
Miao Min	繆敏
mi-in-do	美人圖 (미인도)
Mitsuhashi Shirō	三橋四郎
Miyake-jima	三宅島
Mo	母 (모)
modan gāru	モダンガール
Modan Nihon	モダン日本
modeon geol	모던 걸
moga	モガ
Moja	母子 (모자)
Murooka Sōshichi	室岡惣七
Mu Shiying	穆時英
Na Hye-seok	羅蕙錫 (나혜석)
Naikoku kaiga kyōshinkai	内国絵画共進会
Nakamura Tsune	中村彝
Nam Man-min	南萬民 (남만민)
Namwon, Jeollabuk-do	南原, 全羅北道 (남원, 전라북도)
nanga	南画
nianhua	年畫
Nihon Bijutsu-in	日本美術院
Nihonga	日本画
Nisshin sensō jikki	日清戦争実記
Nogi Maresuke	乃木希典
Nozu Michitsura	野津道貫
nü	女
nüxing	女性
Nüying	女英
obi	帯
Ōe Sumiko	大江スミ子
Ogawa Kazumasa	小川一真
Oharame	大原女
oiran	花魁
Okura Kihachirō	大倉喜八郎
O Seok-cheon	吳石泉 (오석천)
Oshima	大島
Ouyang Yuqian	歐陽予倩
Ōyō kaji seigi	應用家事精義
Pan Jinlian	潘金蓮
pipa	琵琶
Qian Hui'an	錢慧安
Qian Xijun	錢希鈞
Qiao Guanhua	喬冠華
Qinhuai	秦淮
qing	情

qipao	旗袍
Qiu Jin	秋瑾
Qiu Shounian	邱壽年
Qiu Ying	仇英
Qu Qiubai	瞿秋白
Qu Yuan	屈原
Ren Bonian	任伯年
Ren Xiong	任熊
renwu hua	人物畫
Ruan Lingyu	阮玲玉
Ru Masuku	ル・マスク (仮面会)
ryōsai kenbo	良妻賢母
Ryōunkaku	凌雲閣
Samdae	三代 (삼대)
San'ge modeng nüxing	三個摩登女性
Sanxitang	三希堂
Satō Sakuma Rika	佐藤 (佐久間) りか
seisaibu no shugō	精細部の集合
Seitō	青鞜
Seiyō	西洋
Sen no Rikyū	千利休
Seokguram (Grotto)	石窟庵 (석굴암)
shamisen	三味線
Shen Zeming	沈澤民
Shenbao	申報
Sheng Shicai	盛世才
Shidai guniang	時代姑娘
Shimabara	嶋原
Shima no On'na	島の女
Shimoda Utako	下田歌子
shinpuku	信服
shinpurishitē	単純 (シンプルリシテー)
Shinseinen	新青年
shinü	仕女
Shirataki Ikunosuke	白瀧幾之助
Shitsunai sōshoku hō	室内装飾法
shitsurai	室礼
shōji	障子
Shōtoku Taishi Hōsan Bijutsu Tenrankai	
聖徳太子奉賛展覧会	
shufu	主婦
Shufu no tomo	主婦の友
shugō	集合
Shui Jing	水静
sichea	時體兒 (시체아)
Sim Hun	沈熏 (심훈)

Sinmin	新民 (신민)
Sinsegye	新世界 (신세계)
Sin Saimdang buin-do	申師任堂夫人圖 (신사임당 부인도)
Sin Yeoja	新女子 (신여자)
Sin Yeoseong	新女性 (신여성)
Sin Yun-bok	申潤福 (신윤복)
sōdai	壮大
Song Meiling	宋美齡
Song Qingling	宋慶齡
sōshokubi	装飾美
Su Hanchen	蘇漢臣
Suehiro Hiroko	末広ヒロ子
Sunjong (Emperor)	純宗 (순종)
Suzhou	蘇州
Taishō	大正
Tamatsushima Meijin	玉津島名神
Tan Zhenlin	譚震林
Tang Jiaming (Bichun nüshi)	湯嘉名 (碧春女史)
Tang Yifen	湯貽汾
Tang Yin	唐寅
Tatsuno Kingo	辰野金吾
Teikoku Geijutsu-in	帝国芸術院
Teiten (Teikoku Bijutsu Tenrankai)	帝展 (帝国美術院展覧会)
tenka	添加
tennenryoku	天然力
Tian Han	田漢
tidu rusheng	體度如生
tōitsu	統一
tokonoma	床の間
Tōkyō Bijutsu Gakkō	東京美術学校
Tōkyō Kasei Gakuin	東京家政学院
Tōkyō nichi nichi shimbun	東京日日新聞
torusufurunessu (chakushō)	着賞
Tosa Mitsuoki	土佐光起
Tōyō	東洋
Tōyō bijutsushi	東洋美術史
Tōyō-buri	東洋振り
Tōyōshi	東洋史
tōyō teki seishin	東洋的精神
tsubasa	翼
Tsubouchi Shōyō	坪内逍遥
Tsuchida Bakusen	土田麦僊
Tushanwan	土山灣
Unkei	運慶

Wada Sanzō	和田三造	Yi Lixun	伊立勳
wafuku	和服	yōga	洋画
Wakayanagi Midori	若柳翠	Yokoyama Taikan	横山大観
Wang Guangmei	王光美	Yosano Akiko	与謝野晶子
Wang Kun	汪琨	Yoshii Shigenori	吉井茂則
Wang Xiangyan	王香岩	Yoshiwara	吉原
Wang Zhaojun	王昭君	You Xi	游曦
Wayō kairyō dai kenchikugaku 和洋改良大建築学		you yi yu wu guo	有意於吾國
Wei Gongzi	危拱之	yü	慾
wenti	文體	Yu Eok-gyeom	俞億兼 (유억겸)
Wu Jiayou (Youru)	吳嘉猷 (友如)	Yu Jiashen	俞稼神
Wu Daozi	吳道子	Yu Kwang-yeol	柳光烈 (유광열)
Wu Changshuo	吳昌碩	Yu Shu	余叔
Xiang Jingyu	向警予	Yuan Qian	袁倩
Xiang Ying	項英	yuan, zhen, li, heng	元貞利亨
Xia Yan	夏寅	Yuan Shikai	袁世凱
Xie Bingying	謝冰瑩	Yuan Xuefen	袁雪芬
Xier	喜兒	Yue (as in Yue opera)	粵
Xie Zhiguang	謝之光	yuefenpai	月份牌
Xin nüxing	新女性	Yulgok	栗谷 (율곡)
xinpai	新派	zashiki	座敷
Xin Qingnian	新青年	Zeng Xisheng	曾希聖
xinti	新體	Zhang Guangyu	張光宇
Xu Guangping	許廣平	Zhang Qinqiu	張琴秋
Xu Mingqing	徐明清	Zhang Xi	張茜
Yamabuki	山吹	Zhang Yuzhen	張玉貞
Yamada Eizaburō	山田榮三郎	Zhao Yiman	趙一曼
Yamagata Kōhō	山方香峰	Zheng Mantuo	鄭曼陀
Yan'an	延安	zhennü	貞女
Yang Guifei	楊貴妃	*Zhongguo qingnian*	中國青年
Yangliuqing	楊柳青	*Zhonghua ernü*	中華兒女
Yang Mo	楊沫	Zhou Enlai	周恩来
Yang Zhihua	楊之華	Zhou Fang	周昉
Yangzhou	揚州	Zhou Zhenlin	周震鱗
Yecao xianhua	野草閑花	Zhou Zuoren	周作人
Ye Jiuru	葉九如	Zhu Jiangcun	朱疆村
Ye Lingfeng	葉靈風	Zhu Wanzhang	朱萬章
Yeom Sang-seob	廉想涉	Zhu Zhongli	朱仲麗
Yeoseong seonjeonsidae ga omyeon 女性宣傳時代가 오면 (여성선전시대가 오면)		Zōka Gakkai	造家学会

Bibliography

Banner, Lois W. *American Beauty*. New York: Knopf, 1983.

Banta, Martha. *Imaging American Women: Idea and Ideals in Cultural History*. New York: Columbia University Press, 1987.

Barlow, Tani E. and Angela Zito, eds. *Body, Subject, and Power*. Chicago, IL: University of Chicago Press, 1994.

Barlow, Tani E., ed. *Gender Politics in Modern China: Writing and Feminism*. Durham, NC: Duke University Press, 1993.

Bartky, Sandra. *Femininity and Domination: Studies in the Phenomenology of Oppression*. New York: Routledge, 1990.

Baudelaire, Charles. *The Painter of Modern Life and Other Essays*. London: Phaidon, 1964.

Beijing qing gongye ju fuzhuang yanjiusuo (Institute of Clothes, the Bureau of Light Industry of Beijing). "Jieyue meiguan de qiuyi" (Economical and Beautiful Clothes for the Fall). *Zhongguo funü* (Chinese Women) 17 (1960): 26.

Berger, Patricia. *Empire of Emptiness: Buddhist Art and Political Authority in Qing China*. Honolulu: University of Hawai'i Press, 2003.

Birrell, Anne, ed. and trans. *New Songs from a Jade Terrace. An Anthology of Early Chinese Love Poetry*. London: George Allen and Unwin, 1982.

Blanchard, Lara Caroline Williams. "Visualizing Love and Longing in Song Dynasty Paintings of Women." Ph.D. dissertation, University of Michigan, 2001.

Blum, Stella, ed. *Everyday Fashions of the Twenties as Pictured in Sears and Other Catalogs*. New York: Dover Publications, 1981.

Bōbō, Gakujin. *Sensō bi to fujin bi* (The Beauty of War and the Beauty of Women). Tokyo: Keiseisha, 1904.

"Boshū kisoku" (Application Rules). *Jiji shimpō* (Current News) (September 15, 1907). Reprinted in Ozawa Takeshi, *Koshashin de miru bakumatsu meiji no bijin zukan* (Viewed through Old Photos: Picture Book of Bakumatsu-Meiji beauties). Tokyo: Sekai Bunkasha, 2001.

Brilliant, Richard. *Portraiture*. Cambridge, MA: Harvard University Press, 1991.

Cahill, James. "The Flower and the Mirror: Representations of Women in Late Chinese Painting." Lecture 1: "The Real Madam Hotung"; Lecture 2: "Courtesans, Concubines and Willing Women"; Lecture 3: "Women Lorn and Longing." Papers presented at the Metropolitan Museum of Art, New York. November 11–13, 1994.

———. *Pictures for Use and Pleasure: Vernacular Painting in High Qing China*. Berkeley: University of California Press, 2010.

Cai Chang. "Eguo geming yu funü" (The Russian Revolution and Women). In *Zhongguo funü yundong lishi ziliao* (Sources of the Women's Rights Movement in China), edited by Zhongguo Quanguo Funü Lianhehui Funü Yundong Lishi Yanjiushi (Women's Movement Research Group, the Women's Federation of China), 300–5. 1925. Reprint. Beijing: Renmin Chubanshe, 1986.

Cao Yu. *Sunrise: A Play in Four Acts*. Translated by Steven Rendall. Berkeley: University of California Press, 1984.

Chae Suk-jin, "Gamgak ui jeguk: Ero-Gro Nonsense" (Sense of the Imperial Japan: Ero-Gro-Nonsense). *Peminijeum Yeongu* (Feminism Studies) (October 2005): 43–87.

Chang Jung. *Wild Swans: Three Daughters of China*. Glasgow: HarperCollins, 1991.

Chang Jung and Jon Halliday. *Mme Sun Yat-sen* (Soong Ching-ling). Harmondsworth, UK: Penguin, 1986.

Chang, Michael. "The Good, the Bad, and the Beautiful: Movie Actresses and Public Discourse in Shanghai, 1920s–1930s." In *Cinema and Urban Culture in Shanghai, 1922–1943*, edited by Zhang Yingjing, 128–59. Stanford, CA: Stanford University Press, 1999.

"Changsha nüjie lianhehui chengli xuanyan" (The Founding Speech of the Changsha Women's Federation). In *Zhongguo funü yundong lishi ziliao*, edited by Zhongguo Quanguo Funü Lianhehui Funü Yundong Lishi Yanjiushi, 8–10. 1921. Reprint. Beijing: Renmin Chubanshe, 1986.

Chen Chaonan and Feng Yiyou. *Lao guanggao* (Old Advertisements). Shanghai: Shanghai Renmin Meishu Chubanshe, 1998.

Chen Guitao. "Yitao nüzhuang zhi yong jiuchi bu" (How to Make a Woman's Suit with Nine Square Feet of Fabric). *Zhongguo funü* 12 (1963): 32

Chen Qi. "Luo Liu fufu guanxi polie de yuanyin hezai" (The Causes of Liu's and Luo's Divorce). *Zhongguo funü* 1 (1956): 17–8.

Chewning, J. A. "William Robert Ware at MIT and Columbia." *Journal of Architectural Education* 33, no. 2 (November 1979): 25–9.

Chicago Daily Tribune, June 30, 1907–May 17, 1908.

Choi Don. "Domesticated Modern: Hybrid Houses in Meiji Japan, 1870–1900." Ph.D. dissertation, University of California Berkeley, 2003.

Choi Seok-ju. "Seongtan eul majihaya joseon ui moseong eul saeggakham" (Thinking About Maternal Love of Joseon Women on Christmas day). *Cheongneon* (The Young) 10, no. 8 (December 1930): 23–6.

Chou Ju-hsi and Claudia Brown, eds. *Transcending Turmoil: Painting at the Close of China's Empire, 1796–1911*. Phoenix, AZ: Phoenix Art Museum, 1992.

Claypool, Lisa. "The Social Body: Beautiful Women Imagery in Late Imperial China." M.A. thesis, University of Oregon, 1994.

Clunas, Craig. *Pictures and Visuality in Early Modern China*. London: Reaktion Books, 1997.

Coaldrake, William. *Architecture and Authority in Japan*. London and New York: Routledge, 1996.

Cochran, Sherman. *Big Business in China. Sino-Foreign Rivalry in the Cigarette Industry, 1890–1930*. Cambridge, MA: Harvard University Press, 1984.

———. "Marketing Medicine and Advertising Dreams in China 1900–1950." In *Becoming Chinese: Passages to Modernity and Beyond, 1900–1950*, edited by Wen-hsin Yeh, 62–97. Berkeley and Los Angeles: University of California Press, 2000.

Cohen, Deborah. *Household Gods: The British and their Possessions, 1830–1945*. New Haven, CT: Yale University Press, 2006.

Cohen, Ralph. "History and Genre." *New Literary History* 17, no. 2 (Winter 1986): 203–18.

Conroy, Hilary. *The Japanese Seizure of Korea: 1868–1910: A Study of Realism and Idealism in International Relations*. Philadelphia: University of Pennsylvania Press, 1960.

Copeland, Rebecca. *Lost Leaves: Women Writers of Meiji Japan*. Honolulu: University of Hawai'i Press, 2000.

Croll, Elizabeth. *Changing Identities of Chinese Women: Rhetoric, Experience, and Self-Perception in Twentieth-Century China*. Hong Kong: Hong Kong University Press, 1999.

Deng Yingchao. "Tong qingnian pengyou tantan lianai hunyin wenti" (A Conversation with Young Comrades on Love and Marriage). In *Funü jiefang wenti wenxuan* (Selected Writings on the Problems of Women's Liberation), edited by Deng Yingchao, Cai Chang, and Kang Keqing, 73–5. 1942. Reprint. Beijing: Renmin Chubanshe, 1988.

Derrida, Jacques. "The Law of Genre." *Critical Inquiry* 7, no. 1 (Autumn 1980): 55–81.

Ding Ling. *I Myself Am a Woman: Selected Writings of Ding Ling*, edited by Tani E. Barlow and Gary J. Bjorge. Boston, MA: Beacon Press, 1989.

———. *Taiyang zhaozai Sangganhe shang* (The Sun Shines over the Sanggan River). 1948. Reprint. Beijing: Renmin Wenxue Chubanshe, 1955.

———. "Wo suo renshi de Qu Qiubai tongzhi" (My Understanding of Comrade Qu Qiubai) and "Xiang Jingyu tongzhi dui wo de yingxiang" (Comrade Xiang Jingyu's Influence on Me). In *Ding Ling wenji* (The Works of Ding Ling), Vol. 5, 82–112. Changsha: Hunan Renmin Chubanshe, 1984.

Dobson, Sebastian. "Reflections of Conflict: Japanese Photographers and the Russo-Japanese War." In *A Much Recorded War: The Russo-Japanese War in History and Imagery*, edited by Frederic A. Sharf, Anne Nishimura Morse, and Sebastian Dobson, 52–83. Boston, MA: MFA Publications, 2005.

Dou Shangchu. "Xuefeng xuexi chubu zongjie" (Preliminary Summing Up of My [problematic attitude toward] Studying in the Rectification Campaign). In *Yan'an zhongyang dangxiao de zhengfeng yundong* (The Rectification Campaign at the Central Party Institute). Vol. 1, edited by Yan'an zhongyang dangxiao zhengfeng yundong bianxiezu (The Central Party Institute Study Group), 224–37. 1942. Reprint. Beijing: Zhongyang Dangxiao Chubanshe, 1988.

Duus, Peter. *The Abacus and the Sword: The Japanese Penetration of Korea, 1895–1910.* Berkeley: University of California Press, 1995.

Eastlake, Charles L. *Hints on Household Taste in Furniture, Upholstery, and Other Details.* London: Longmans Green, 1868.

Ebrey, Patricia, ed. *Chinese Civilization and Society: A Sourcebook.* New York: Free Press, 1981.

Edwards, Louise. "Policing the Modern Women in Republican China." *Modern China* 26, no. 2 (April 2000): 115–47.

Entwistle, Joanne. *The Fashioned Body: Fashion, Dress, and Modern Social Theory.* Cambridge: Polity Press, 2000.

Esherick, Joseph. *Reform and Revolution in China: The 1911 Revolution in Hunan and Hubei.* Berkeley and Los Angeles: University of California Press, 1976.

Evans, Harriet. *Woman and Sexuality in China: Female Sexuality and Gender since 1949.* Cambridge: Polity Press, 1997.

Fairbank, John K. *Chinabound: A Fifty-Year Memoir.* New York: Harper & Row, 1982.

Fan Zhenjia. *Jin Meisheng zuopin xuanji* (Selection of Works by Jin Meisheng). Shanghai: Shanghai Renmin Meishu Chubanshe, 1985.

Fang Zhimin. *Fang Zhimin wenji* (The Works of Fang Zhimin). Beijing: Renmin Chubanshe, 1984.

Fang Zhimin zhuan bianxiezu (The Editorial Committee on the Biography of Fang Zhimin). *Fang Zhimin zhuan* (The Biography of Fang Zhimin). Jiangxi: Jiangxi Renmin Chubanshe, 1982.

Felski, Rita. *The Gender of Modernity.* Cambridge and London: Harvard University Press, 1995.

Finnane, Antonia. "What should Chinese Women Wear? A National Problem." *Modern China* 22, no. 2 (April 1996): 99–131.

Freud, Sigmund. *Civilization and Its Discontents.* London: Hogarth Press, 1949.

Frühehauf, Heinrich Otmar. "Urban Exoticism in Modern Chinese Literature 1910–1933." Ph.D. dissertation, University of Chicago, 1990. Ann Arbor, MI: University Microfilms International, 1994.

Fujinami-sei. "Kenchiku-bi gaisetsu" (Outline of Architectural Beauty). *Kenchiku Gahō* (The Architectural Graphic) 2, no. 13 (December 1911): 27–9.

Fujioka Shigeichi. Seiin kōgakushi Mitsuhashi Shirō shi no fu (The Obituary of Full Member Mitsuhashi Shiro). *Kenchiku zasshi* (Architectural Journal) 30, no. 349 (12): 31–4, iii–iv.

Gao Anhua. *To the Edge of the Sky: A Story of Love, Betrayal, Suffering, and the Strength of Human Courage.* London: Viking, 2000.

Gates, Hill. "Commodification of Chinese Women." *Signs* 14, no. 4 (Summer 1989): 799–832.

Gilman, Richard. *Decadence: The Strange Life of an Epithet.* New York: Farrar, Straus, and Girou, 1975.

Gilmartin, Christina. *Engendering the Chinese Revolution: Radical Women, Communist Politics, and Mass Movement in the 1920s.* Berkeley: University of California Press, 1995.

Gordon, Richard and Carma Hinton. (Producer and director). *The Gate of Heavenly Peace.* Brookline, MA: Long Bow Group, in association with Independent Television Service, 1995. 2 video cassettes.

Government-General of Joseon. *Thriving Joseon: A Survey of Twenty-Five Years' Administration.* October 1935.

Greselin, Federico. "Un discorso di Lu Xun del 1930" (A Discussion of Lu Xun, 1930). *Annali di Ca' Foscari* XX, no. 3 (1981): 171–81.

Gronewald, Sue. *Beautiful Merchandise: Prostitution in China 1860–1936.* New York: Haworth Press, 198.

Gu Bing. *Gushi huapu* (Master Gu's Painting Manual). 1603. Reprint. Shanghai: Heji Shuju, 1915.

Gu Jeong-hwa. "Hanguk geundaegiui yeoseong inmulhwa e natanan yeoseong imiji" (The Female Image in Modern Korean Art). *Hanguk geundae misulsa yeongu* (The History of Modern Korean Art) 9 (2001): 105–41.

Guo Chen. *Jinguo liezhuan* (The Heroines in the Long March). Beijing: Nongcun Duwu Chubanshe, 1986.

Guo Moruo. *Qu Yuan* (The Tragedy of Qu Yuan). 1942. Reprint. Beijing: Renmin Wenxue Chubanshe, 1953.

Guth, Christine. *Art, Tea, and Industry: Masuda Takashi and the Mitsui Circle*. Princeton, NJ: Princeton University Press, 1993.

Hasegawa Gyō. **"Nihon no hyōgen-ha"** (Japan's Expressionists), *Shinden ka gokusha ka* (Shrine or Prison?) Tokyo: Sagami Shobō, 1972, 1–114.

Hay, John. "The Body Invisible in Chinese Art?" In *Body, Subject & Power in China*, edited by Angela Zito and Tani Barlow, 42–77. Chicago, IL: The University of Chicago Press, 1994.

Henley, Nancy. *Body Politics. Power, Sex, and Nonverbal Communication*. Englewood Cliffs, NJ: Prentice-Hall, 1977.

Heo Yoeng-sun. "Moseong gwa moseongae" (Mothers and Maternal Love). *Yeoseong* (Woman) 3, no. 9 (September 1938): 36–9.

Hershatter, Gail. *Dangerous Pleasures: Prostitution and Modernity in Twentieth-Century Shanghai*. Berkeley: University of California Press, 1997.

Hiratsuka Raichō. "Manifesto." *Seitō* 1, no. 1 (September 1911). Reprinted in *La Revue mondiale* (November 1923).

Honig, Emily and Gail Hershatter. *Personal Voices: Chinese Women in the 1980s*. Stanford, CA: Stanford University Press, 1988.

Hong Jong-in. "Moseongae gunsang" (Maternal Love). *Yeoseong* 2, no. 1 (January 1937): 82–3.

Hong Sun-pyo, "Hanguk geundae misul ui yeoseong pyosang" (Representation of Woman in Modern Korean Art: Desexualization and Sexualization of Woman). *Hanguk geundae misul sahak* (Journal of Korean Modern Art History) (Seoul: Sigonsa, 2002), 63–85.

Horiguchi Kankichi. "Mitsuhashi Shirō shi cho Dai kenchiku gaku ni tsuite: Kenchikushi, Kenchiku ishō" (On Mitsuhashi Shiro's *Great Architectural Learning*: Architectural History and Architectural Design). *Gakujutsuron en kōgaishu: Keikaku-kei* (Summaries of Technical Papers of Annual Meetings: Architectural Design) 46 (September 1971): 1075–6.

Hoshioka Shoin. *Gunkoku no Fujin* (Women of Militarism). Tokyo: Hoshioka Shoin, 1904.

Howard, Angela Falco et al. *Chinese Sculpture*. New Haven, CT: Yale University Press; Beijing: Foreign Languages Press, 2006.

Hsu Kai-yu. *Chou En-lai: China's Gray Eminence*. New York: Doubleday, 1968.

Hu Lanqi. *Hu Lanqi huiyilu* (Hu Lanqi's Memoir). Chengdu: Sichuan Renmin Chubanshe, 1995.

Hu Peiheng, ed. *Jieziyuan huazhuan: Disiji renwu Chao Xun linben* (Mustard Seed Garden Manual, Book Four: Human Figures as Copied by Chao Xun). Beijing: Renmin Meishu Chubanshe, 1957.

Hung Chang-tai. *War and Popular Culture: Resistance in Modern China, 1937–1945*. Berkeley: University of California Press, 1994.

Hwang Sin-deok. "Joseon eun ireohan eomeoni reul yoguhanda" (Joseon Needs Mothers like These). *Singajeong* (The New Family) 1 (May 1933): 12–5.

Il Hye. "Widaehan eomeoni anhae ui jonjae" (Great Mothers and Great Wives). *Woori gajeong* (Our Family) (October 1936): 38–40.

Im Jeong-hyeok. "Janyeo reul gajin cheongsang gwabu ga jaehonham i oreunya, geureunya" (Is it Acceptable for a Widow with Children to Remarry?). *Yeoseong* 1, no. 2 (May 1936): 36–7.

Inoue Shōichi. *Bijin kontesuto hyakunenshi: geigi no jidai kara bishojo made* (One Hundred Years of Beauty Contests: From Geisha to Beautiful Girls). Tokyo: Shinchosha, 1992.

Itō Chūta and Ichihigashi Kenkichi. "Kenchikujutsu to bijutsu no kankei (Meiji juroku-nen san-gatsu yōka tsujōkai enzetsu)" (The Relationship between Architectural Arts and Fine Art) (Speech Given at the Regular Meeting on March 8, 16th Year of the Meiji Era). *Kenchiku zasshi* (Architectural Journal) 7, no. 75 (March 1893): 80–7.

Jang Yunshik. "Women in a Confucian Society: The Case of Josun Dynasty Korea (1392–1910)." *Asian and Pacific Quarterly of Cultural and Social Affairs* 14, no. 2 (Summer 1982): 24–42. Reprinted in *Traditional Thought and Practices in Korea*, edited by Eui-Young Yu and Earl H. Phillips. Los Angeles: Center for Korean-American and Korean Studies, University of California, Los Angeles, 1988.

Jeon Ae-rok. "Moseongae wa gajeong gyoyuk" (Maternal Love and Family Education). *Yeonseong* 2, no. 4 (April 1937): 70–3.

Jing Ying. "Ni dongde zenyang qu zuo, zhan, he zoulu ma?" (Do You Know How to Sit, Stand and Walk?). *Jindai Funü* (The Modern Woman) 16 (April 1930): 4–5.

Jing Lingzi. *Shihai gouxuan* (The Mystic Sea of History). Beijing: Kunlun Chubanshe, 1989.

Jinno Yuki. *Shumi no tanjō* (The Birth of Taste). Tokyo: Keisō Shobō, 1994.

Ju Kyeongmi. "Gongye ui hyeongsik gwa gineung" (Form and Function of the Craft). *Misulsawa sigak munhwa* (Art History and Visual Culture) (2003): 38–59.

Ju Yo-seop. "Eomeoni ui sarang" (Maternal Love). *Singajeong* 1 (January 1933): 182–3.

Judge, Joan. "Blended Wish Images: Chinese and Western Exemplary Women at the Turn of the Twentieth Century." In *Beyond Tradition and Modernity: Gender, Genre, and Cosmopolitanism in Late Qing China*, edited by Grace S. Fong, Nanxiu Qian, and Harriet T. Zurndorfer, 102–35. Leiden, Boston: Brill, 2004.

———. "Meng Mu Meets the Modern: Female Exemplars in Early Twentieth-Century Textbooks for Girls and Women." *Jindai Zhongguo funüshi yanjiu* (Study of Modern Chinese Women's History) 8 (June 2000): 129–77.

Jung-Kim, Jennifer J. "Gender and Modernity in Colonial Korea." Ph.D dissertation, University of California, Los Angeles, 2005.

Kasza, Gregory J. *The State and the Mass Media in Japan, 1918–1945*. Berkeley: University of California Press, 1988.

Kim Gyeong-il. "Hanguk geundae sahoe ui hyeongseong eseo jeontonggwa geund" (Old Values and New Values in the Process of Korea's Modernization). *Sahoe wa Yeoksa* (Society and History) 54 (1998): 11–42.

Kim Hye-sin. *Hanguk geundae misul yeongu* (Research on Modern Korean Art). Tokyo: Brüke, 2005.

Kim, Jinsong, ed. *Hyeondaeseong ui hyeongseong: Seoul e danseuhol eul heohara* (Formation of Modernity: Allow a Dance Hall in Seoul). Seoul: Hyeonsil Munhwa Yeongu, 1999.

Kim Jue-Ree. "Geundaejeok *paesyeon* ui balgyeon gwa 1930 nyeondae munhakui byeonmo" (The Occurrence of Modern Fashion and the Reformation of Literature in the 1930s). *Hanguk hyeondae munhak yeongu* (Journal of Korean Modern Literature) 7 (December 1999): 123–50.

———. "Geundaejeok sinche damnon ui ilgochal" (Discourse on the Modern Body). *Hanguk hyeondae munhak yeongu* (Journal of Korean Modern Literature) 13 (June 2003): 17–49.

Kim Keon-su. *Hanguk Japjisa yeon'gu* (The History of Korean Magazines). Seoul: Hangukahk yeonguso, 1992.

Kim Suk-ja. "Dongnip sinmun e natanan yeoseong gaehwa ui uiji" (Enlightening Efforts for Women in Independent Newspapers). *Hanguksa yeongu* (The Study of Korean History) 54 (September 1986): 59–74.

Kim Yisoon. *Hanguk ui moja sang* (Portraits of Mother and Child in Korea). Seoul: National Museum of Contemporary Art, 2006, 216–29.

Kim Youngna, ed. *Hanguk geundae misul gwa sigak munhwa* (Korean Modern Art and Visual Culture). Seoul: Johyeong Gyoyuk, 2002.

Kim Youngna. "Nolransog ui geundaeseong" (Modernity in Debate: Representing the "New Woman" and "Modern Girl"). *Misulsawa sigak munhwa* (2003): 8–35. Reprinted in *20th Century Korean Art*, London: Laurence King, 2005.

———. "Artistic Trends in Korean Painting during the 1930s." In *War, Occupation, and Creativity: Japan and East Asia, 1920–1960*, edited by Marlene J. Mayo, J. Thomas Rimer, and H. Eleanor Kerkham, 121–49. Honolulu: University of Hawai'i Press, 2001.

Kim Yung-hee. "Creating New Paradigms of Womanhood in Modern Korean Literature: Na Hye-Sok[seok]'s 'Kyeong-hui.'" *Korean Studies* 26, no. 1 (2002): 1–60.

Kinoshita Naoyuki. "Portraying the War Dead: Photography as a Medium for Memorial Portraiture." In *Reflecting Truth: Japanese Photography in the Nineteenth Century*, edited by Nicole Rousmaniere and Mikiko Hirayama, 86–97. Leiden: Brill Publishing and the Sainsbury Institute for the Study of Japanese Arts and Cultures, 2004.

Kogakushi K. K-sei. "Sōshoku-bi" (Decorative Beauty). Parts 1–5. *Kenchiku Gahō* (The Architectural Graphic) 4 (May–December 1913).

Kondō Shōichi. *Shitsunai sōshoku hō* (Principles of Interior Decoration). Tokyo: Hakubunkan, 1907.

Kwon Insook. "'The New Women's Movement' in 1920s Korea: Rethinking the Relationship between Imperialism and Women." *Gender and History* 10, no. 3 (November 1998): 381–405.

Laing, Ellen Johnston. *Selling Happiness: Calendar Prints and Visual Culture of Early Twentieth-Century Shanghai*. Honolulu: University of Hawai'i Press, 2004.

Lao She. "A Vision." In *Crescent Moon and Other Stories*. Translated by Gladys Yang. Beijing: Panda Books, 1985.

Lee Dal-nam. "Jeolmeun eomeoni dokbon" (For Young Mothers). *Yeoseong* 4, no. 1 (January 1939): 71–4.

Lee Eun-sang. "Joseon ui moseong eun joseon ui moseong" (Maternal Love Represents Women in Joseon). *Sinyeoseong* 2, no. 5 (May and June 1925): 2–6.

Lee Gi-yeong. "Widaehan moseong" (Great Maternal Love). *Yeoseong* 5, no. 4 (April 1940): 76–7.

Lee Gim-jeon. "Moyu wa yua" (Breast-feeding and Babies). *Sinyeoseong* 7, no. 6 (June 1933): 86–7.

Lee Gwang-su. "Moseong" (Maternal love). *Yeoseong* 1, no. 2 (May 1936): 12–3.

———. "Moseong euroseoui yeoja" (Women are Nothing but Maternal Love). *Yeoseong* 1, no. 3 (June 1936): 8.

———. "Moseong jungsim ui janyeo gyoyuk" (Education of Children Based on Maternal Love). *Sinyeoseong* (January 1925): 19–20.

Lee Hsiao-li. *Good-bye, Yinan*. Translated by Dong Qiao. Hong Kong: Wenyi Shushi, 1975.

Lee, Leo Ou-fan. *Shanghai Modern: The Flowering of a New Urban Culture in China, 1930–1945*. Cambridge, MA: Harvard University Press, 2000.

Li Chao. *Shanghai youhua shi* (History of Oil Painting in Shanghai). Shanghai: Shanghai Renmin Meishu Chubanshe, 1995.

Li Dou. *Yangzhou huafang lu* (Reminiscences from the Pleasure Boats of Yangzhou). 1799. Reprint. Jiangsu: Guangling Guji Yeyinshe, 1984.

Li Ling. "Fenpei de xifu" (A Party-assigned Wife). In *Zhongguo funü yundong lishi ziliao*, edited by Zhongguo quanguo funü lianhehui funü yundong lishi yanjiushi. Vol. 370, 8–27. Beijing: Zhongguo Funü Chubanshe, 1989.

Li Wenyi. "Yi jingai de Yang Zhihua tongzhi" (My Fond Memories of Yang Zhihua). In *Huiyi Yang zhihua* (Our Recollections of Yang Zhihua), edited by Shanghai shi fulian fuyun shiliaozu (Women's Movement Research Group, the Shanghai Women's Federation), 53–62. Hefei: Anhui Renmin Chubanshe, 1983.

Li Xiaojiang. *Funü yanjiu yundong* (Studying Women). Hong Kong: Oxford University Press, 1997.

Li Yingru. *Yehuo chunfeng dou gucheng* (Revolutionary Struggle in a Historic City). Beijing: Jiefangjun Wenyi Chubanshe, 1959.

Liang Heng and Judith Shapiro. *Son of the Revolution*. New York: Knopf, 1984.

Liu Lequn. "Women fufu guanxi weishenme juelie?" (Why Do We Break Up?). *Xin Zhongguo funü* (The Women of New China) 11 (1955): 6.

Liu Ruli. "Ji Lu Xun xiansheng zai Zhonghua Yi Da de yici jiangyan" (Recollection of a Speech Pronounced by Lu Xun at the Chinese Art University). *Meishu* (Art) 4 (1979): 6–7.

Loti, Pierre. *Madame Chrysanthemum*. Translated by Laura Enslor. New York: Boni and Liveright, 1900.

Lubar, Robert. "Unmasking Pablo's Gertrude: Queer Desire and the Subject of Portraiture." *The Art Bulletin* 79, no. 1 (March 1997): 56–84.

Luo Qiong. "Changji zai Zhongguo" (Prostitutes in China). In *Zhongguo funü yundong lishi ziliao*, edited by Zhongguo quanguo funü lianhehui funü yundong lishi yanjiushi, 69–74. 1935. Reprint. Beijing: Zhongguo Funü Chubanshe, 1988.

Luo Suwen. *Nüxing yu jindai Zhongguo shehui* (Women in Modern Chinese Society). Shanghai: Shanghai Renmin Chubanshe, 1996.

Lust, John. *Chinese Popular Prints*. Leiden, New York, Koln: E. J. Brill, 1996.

Mackie, Vera. *Creating Socialist Women in Japan: Gender, Labour and Activism, 1900–1937*. Cambridge: Cambridge University Press, 1997.

———. *Feminism in Modern Japan: Citizenship, Embodiment and Sexuality*. Cambridge: Cambridge University Press, 2003.

Maeda, Robert J. "The Portrait of a Woman of the Late Ming–Early Ch'ing Period: Madame Ho-tung." *Archives of Asian Art* XXVII (1973): 46–51.

Mao Dun. *Mao Dun zizhuan* (Autobiography of Mao Dun). 1981. Reprint. Nanjing: Jiangsu Wenyi Chubanshe, 1996.

Mao Zedong. *Mao's Road to Power: Revolutionary Writings, 1912–1949*. Vol. 1. Edited by Stuart R. Schram. Armonk, NY: M. E. Sharpe, 1992.

Matsukawa Junko. "Nihon ni okeru senzen sengō no sōsōki no josei kenchikuka gijutsusha" (The Pioneer Years of Women Architects and Engineers in Prewar and Postwar Japan). *Housing Research Foundation Annual Report* 30 (2003): 251–62.

McIntyre, Tanya. "Images of women in popular prints." In *Dress, Sex, and Text in Chinese Culture,* edited by Antonia Finnane and Anne McLaren, 58–80. Clayton, Australia: Monash Asia Institute, 1999.

McKenzie, F.A. *Korea's Fight for Freedom.* London and New York: Fleming H. Revell, 1920.

Melville, Stephen and Bill Readings, eds. *Vision and Textuality.* London: Macmillan, 1995.

Menzies, J., ed. *Modern Boy, Modern Girl: Modernity in Japanese Art, 1910–1935.* Sydney: Art Gallery of New South Wales, 1998.

"Miseu Koriauyeo, danbalhasiyo" (Miss Korea, Please Have Short Hair). *Donggwang* (East Light) (April 1932): n.p.

Mitsuhashi Shirō. "Parutenon Tempuru" (The Temple of the Parthenon). *Kenchiku zasshi* (Architectural Journal) 18, no. 208 (April 1904): 217–27.

———. "Tekkin kongyō-do narabi ni sono ōyō" (Reinforced Concrete and its Application). *Kenchiku zasshi* (Architectural Journal) 22, no. 264 (December 1908): 476–90.

———. *Wayō kairyō daikenchikugaku* (Improved Japanese and Western Great Architectural Knowledge). 3 Vols. Tokyo: Okura Shoten, 1911.

Mittler, Barbara. "Defy(N)ing Modernity: Women in Shanghai's Early News-Media (1872–1915)." *Jindai Zhongguo funüshi yanjiu* 11 (December 2003): 215–59.

Miura Shūsei. *Sensō to Fujin* (War and Women). Tokyo: Bunmeidō, 1904.

Moore, Richard A. "Academic 'Dessin' Theory in France after the Reorganization of 1863." *The Journal of the Society of Architectural Historians* 36, no. 3 (Oct. 1977): 145–74.

Murooka Sōshichi. "Kenchiku no biteki taikō" (Outline of the Aesthetic Relations of Architecture). *Kenchiku sekai* (Architectural World) 2, no. 9 (February 1915): 31–5.

Na Hye-seok. "Doksin yeoja jeongjo ron" (On the Virginity of a Single Woman). *Samcheolli* (The Land of Korea) (October 1935).

———. "Inhyeong ui jip" (A Doll's House). *Mail sinbo* (Daily Newspaper) (April 3, 1921).

———. "Ihon gobaegseo" (Confession of Divorce). *Samcheolli* (The Land of Korea) (August–September 1934).

———. "Isang jeok buin" (The Ideal Wife). *Hakjigwang* (Light of Learning) 3 (1914).

———. "Bubugan ui mundap" (Dialogue of Wife and Husband). *Sin yeoseong* (The New Woman) (November 1923).

———. "Sinsaenghwal e deulmyeonseo" (Entering a New Life). *Samcheolli* (The Land of Korea) (February 1935).

Na Hye-seokui saengae wa geurim (Na Hye-seok: Her Life and Art), exh. cat., Seoul: Seoul Art Center, January 15–February 7, 2000.

Nakatani Reiji and Nakatani Seminar. *Kinsei kenchiku ronshu* (Pre-modern Architectural Theory). Kyoto: Acetate, 2004.

Nam Man-min. "Chunhyang ui jeongjo jaeeummi" (A Look at Chuhyang's Sense of Chastity). *Yeoseong* 1, no. 6 (October 1936): 38–40.

Nan Yuyue. "Sanbajie yu Zhongguo funü yundong" (March 8 and the Women's Movement in China). In *Zhongguo funü yundong lishi ziliao,* edited by Zhongguo quanguo funü lianhehui funü yundong lishi yanjiushi, 579–83. 1926. Reprint. Beijing: Renmin Chubanshe, 1986.

Nian Xin, ed. *Shanghai Yuefenpai Nianhua Jifa* (The Technique of Shanghai *yuefenpai* New Year Pictures). Shanghai: Shanghai Renmin Meishu Chubanshe, 1983.

Ni Zhenliang. *Luoru man tianxia—Bai Yang zhuan* (Beautiful Clouds: The Biography of Bai Yang). Beijing: Zhongguo Wenlian Chubanshe, 1992.

Nivard, Jacqueline. "Women and the Women's Press: The Case of *The Ladies' Journal (Funü zazhi),* 1915–1931." *Republican China* 10, no. 1b (November 1984): 37–55.

No Ja-yeong. "Munye e natanan moseongae wa Yeongwon ui Byeol" (Maternal Love Described in Literature and Yeongwon ui Byeol). *Singajeong* (March 1934): 74–81.

Ōe Sumiko. *Shoron Jūkyo* (Assorted Writings and Housing). Vol. 1 of *Ōyo kaji seigi* (Detailed Lectures in Practical Housekeeping). Tokyo and Osaka: Hōbunkan, 1916.

Ono Kazuko. *Chinese Women in a Century of Revolution, 1850–1950*. Stanford, CA: Stanford University Press, 1989.

——. "Nü xuesheng yingyou zhi juewu" (Female Students' Political Consciousness). In *Zhongguo funü yundong lishi ziliao*, edited by Zhongguo Quanguo Funü Lianhehui Funü Yundong Lishi Yanjiushi, 548–51. 1926. Reprint. Beijing: Renmin Chubanshe, 1986.

Ozawa Takeshi. *Koshashin de miru bakumatsu meiji no bijin zukan* (Viewed Through Old Photos: Picture Book of Bakumatsu-Meiji Beauties). Tokyo: Sekai Bunkasha, 2001.

Pak Gil-yong, "Saesallim ui bueok eun ireossge hyaeeomyeon" (If I Could Do my Kitchen this Way in My New Household!). *Yeoseong* (Woman) (April 1936).

——. "Sinchu ui seoyang yori" (Western Cuisine in the New Year). *Jogwang* (Morning Light) (September 1936).

Pang, Laikwan. *The Distorting Mirror: Visual Modernity in China*. Honolulu: University of Hawaiʻi Press, 2007.

Pang Youwen. "Luo Paoyi de xingwei shi boxue jieji sixiang de juti biaoxian" (Luo Paoyi's Behavior is a Manifestation of the Exploitative Class's Ideology). *Zhongguo funü* 1 (1956): 7.

Park Carey, "Na Hye-seok ui punggyeonghwa" (Na Hye-seok's Landscape Paintings). *Hanguk geundae misulsahak* (Modern Korean Art History) (2005): 173–206.

——. "Isip-segi hanguk hoehwaeseo'ui jeontong ron" (A Study of Korean Painters' Viewpoints on Tradition in the Twentieth Century). PhD dissertation, Seoul, Ewha Womans University, 2006.

Pu Ji. "Jiefan qian de 'yuefenpai' nianhua shiliao" (Historical Material on Pre-liberation *yuefenpai* New Year Pictures). *Meishu yanjiu* (Art Research) 2 (1959): 51.

Quan Yanchi. *Mao Zedong zouxia shentan* (To Humanize Mao Zedong). Hong Kong: Nanyue Chubanshe, 1990.

Reed, Christopher A. *Gutenberg in Shanghai: Chinese Print Capitalism, 1876–1937*. Vancouver, Toronto: UBC Press, 2004.

Reynolds, Jonathan M. "The Formation of a Japanese Architectural Profession." In *The Artist as Professional in Japan*, edited by Melinda Takeuchi, 180–202. Palo Alto, CA: Stanford University Press, 2004.

Robertson, Jennifer. "Japan's First Cyborg? Miss Nippon, Eugenics and Wartime Technologies of Beauty, Body and Blood." *Body & Society* 7 (January 2001): 1–34.

Robinson, John Beverly. *Principles of Architectural Composition: An Attempt to Order and Phrase Ideas which have hitherto been only felt by the Instinctive Taste of Designers*. New York: The Architectural Record, 1899. Reprint. New York: Van Nostrand, 1908.

Robinson, Michael Edson. *Cultural Nationalism in Colonial Korea, 1920–25*. Seattle: University of Washington Press, 1988.

Sand, Jordan. *House and Home in Modern Japan: Architecture, Domestic Space and Bourgeois Culture 1880–1930*. Cambridge, MA: Harvard East Asian Monographs, 2003.

Sato, Barbara Hamill. *The New Japanese Woman: Modernity, Media, and Women in Interwar Japan*. Durham, NC: Duke University Press, 2003.

Scruton, Roger. *The Aesthetic Understanding: Essays in the Philosophy of Art and Culture*. London and New York: Methuen, 1983.

Seton, Grace Thompson. "China's Hope in her 'New Women.'" *Literary Digest* (November 15, 1924): 39–42.

Shao Yang. *Hongqiang nei de furenmen* (The Wives of the Communist Leaders). Guizhou: Guizhou Renmin Chubanshe, 1993.

Shea, George T. *Leftwing Literature in Japan: A Brief History of the Proletarian Literary Movement*. Tokyo: Hosei University Press, 1964.

Shih, Shu-mei. "Gender, Race and Semicolonialism: Liu Na-ou's Urban Shanghai Landscape." In *The Lure of the Modern: Writing Modernism in Semicolonial China, 1917–1937*. Berkeley: University of California Press, 2001. First published in *Journal of Asian Studies* 55, no. 4 (November 1996): 934–56.

Shimoda Utako. *Katei kyōiku* (Domestic Education). Tokyo: Hakubunkan, 1901.

Shin Gi-Wook. *Peasant Protest and Social Change in Colonial Korea*. Seattle: University of Washington Press, 1996.

Shin Myeong-jik, *Modeon Boi: Gyeongseong eul geonilda* (The Modern Boy Walks around Seoul). Seoul: Hyeonsil Munhwa Yeongu, 2003.

Shui Jing. *Teshu de jiaowang* (Special Friendship). Nanjing: Jiangsu Wenyi Chubanshe, 1992.

Silverberg, Miriam. *Erotic Grotesque Nonsense: The Mass Culture of Japanese Modern Times*. Berkeley: University of California Press, 2007.

———. "Modern Girl as Militant." In *Recreating Japanese Women, 1600–1945*, edited by Gail P. Bernstein, 239–66. Berkeley: University of California Press, 1991.

———. "The Café Waitress Serving Modern Japan." In *Mirror of Modernity: Invented Traditions of Modern Japan*, edited by Stephen Vlastos, 243–61. Berkeley: University of California Press, 1998.

Sim Eun-suk. "Sinyeoseong gwa guyeoseong" (New Women and Traditional Women). *Yeoseong* 3 (June 1936): 56.

Sim Hun. "Yakhon saedae ui chueok" (The Memory of Arranged Marriage). *Samcheolli* 12 (1930): 58.

Sirén, Osvald. *Chinese Painting: Leading Masters and Principles*. New York: The Ronald Press Company; London: Lund Humphries, 1956.

Smith-Rosenberg, Carroll. *Disorderly Conduct: Visions of Gender in Victoria America*. New York: A. A. Knopf, 1985.

Snow, Helen and Nym Wales. *The Chinese Communists: Sketches and Autobiographies of the Old Guard*. Westport, CT: Greenwood Press, 1972.

So Rae-seop. *Ero gro nonsense: Geundae jeok jageug ui tansaeng* (Ero Gro Nonsense: The Birth of Modern Sensitivity). Seoul: Sallim Jisik Chongseo, 2006.

Song In-ja. "Gaehwagi yeoseong gyoyungnon ui uiui wa hangye" (The Meaning and Problems with the Education of Women). *Hanguk gyoyuksahak* (The History of Korean Education) 17 (1995): 127–66.

Sotheby's Auction Catalogue. November 25, 1991, New York.

Sparke, Penny. *As Long as it's Pink: The Sexual Politics of Taste*. London: Pandora, 1995.

Stacey, Judith. *Patriarchy and Socialist Revolution in China*. Berkeley: University of California Press, 1983.

Stewart, David. *The Making of Modern Japanese Architecture*. Tokyo and New York: Kodansha International, 2003.

Su Yi. "Zhezhong fengqi zhengchang ma" (Is this Trend Normal?). *Zhongguo qingnian* (Chinese Youth) 2 (1957): 40.

Suzuki Akiko. *Gunkoku no Fujin* (Women of Militarism). Tokyo: Nikkō Yūrindō, 1904.

Suzuki Kōichi. *Nyūsu de ou Meiji nihon hakkutsu* (Discovering Meiji Japan through the News). Vol. 1. Tokyo: Kawade shobô shinsha, 1994.

Takashi Hirano. "Retailing in Urban Japan, 1868–1945." *Urban History* 26 (1999): 373–92.

Tanfen. "Funü wenti he nanzi" (Women's Problems and Men). In *Cong 'yierjiu' yundong kan nüxing de rensheng jiazhi* (Women's Life Values in the Context of the December Ninth Movement). Zhongguo quanguo funü lianhehui funü yundong lishi yanjiushi (Women's Movement Research Group, the Women's Federation of China), 312–16. 1936. Reprint. Beijing: Renmin Chubanshe, 1986.

Tang Shaohua. *Zhonggong wenyi tongzhan huigu* (My Recollections of the CCP's United Front in Literature and the Arts). Taipei: Wentan Zazhishe, 1981.

Teasley, Sarah. "Home-builder or Home-maker? Reader Presence in Articles on Home-building in Commercial Women's Magazines in 1920s' Japan." *Journal of Design History* 18, no. 1 (January 2005): 81–97.

Terill, Rose. *Madame Mao: The White-Boned Demon*. New York: Simon & Schuster, 1992.

Tie Zhuwei. *Hongjun langmanchu* (The Romances in the Red Army). Hubei: Hubei Renmin Chubanshe, 1989.

"Tonggao" (Public Announcement) no. 18. In *Jiangxi suqu funü yundong shiliao xunbian* (Materials on the Women's Movement in the Jiangxi Soviet Area), edited by Jiangxi Sheng Funü Lianhehui (The Provincial Women's Federation, Jiangxi) and Jiangxi Sheng Dang'anguan (Jiangxi Provincial Archive), 213–16. 1934. Reprint. Nanchang: Jiangxi Renmin Chubanshe, 1984.

Tseng, P. S. "The Chinese Woman Past and Present." In *Symposium in Chinese Culture*, edited by Sophia H. Chen Zhen. Shanghai: China Institute of Pacific Relations, 292. 1931. Reprint. New York: Paragon Book Reprint Corp., 1969.

Tsunemi Ikuo. *Kateika kyōikushi* (The History of Domestic Economy Education). Tokyo: Koseikan, 1972.

Van Pelt, John Vredenburg. *A Discussion of Composition, Especially as Applied to Architecture*. New York: Macmillan Company, 1902.

Wakayanagi Midori. "Shopenhaueru no kenchikukan" (Schopenhauer's View of Architecture). *Kenchiku sekai* (Architectural World) 10, no. 8 (1916): 64–69.

Wang Guanmei. "Yongheng de jinian" (My Lasting Memories of Song Qingling). In *Song Qingling jinian ji* (Recollections of Song Qingling), 94–6. Hong Kong: Wenhui Bao, 1981.

Wang Xingjuan. *Li Min, He Zizhen he Mao Zedong* (Li Min, He Zizhen, and Mao Zedong). Beijing: Zhongguo Wenlian Chuban Gongsi, 1993.

Wang Zheng. "Call me 'qingnian' but not 'funü': A Maoist Youth in Retrospect." In *Some of Us: Chinese Women Growing Up in the Mao Era*, edited by Wang Zheng, Zhong Xueping, and Bai Di, 40–9. New Brunswick, NJ: Rutgers University Press, 2001.

Ware, William R. *Modern Perspective: A Treatise upon the Principles and Practice of Plane and Cylindrical Perspective*. Boston, MA: Ticknor, c.1882.

———. *Parallel of Historical Ornament, A Selection of Examples Arranged to Present a Comparative View of their Principal Features, Prepared under the Supervision of William R. Ware*. Boston, MA: L. Prang and Company, 1876.

Wasserstrom, Jeffrey and Susan Brownell, eds. *Chinese Femininities/Chinese Masculinities, A Reader*. London, Los Angeles, Berkeley: University of California Press, 2002.

Watanabe Yoshishige and Nishimura Shōzaburō. *Biiku* (Aesthetic Education). Tokyo: Fukyūsha, 1893.

Wei, Lock W. "Miss Peach Blossom." *Outlook* 154 (January 8, 1930): 50–1.

Wendelken, Cherie. "The Tectonics of Japanese Style: Architect and Carpenter in the Late Meiji Period." *Art Journal* 55 (1996): 28–37.

Wohr, Ulrike, Barbara Hamill Sato, and Suzuki Sadami, eds. *Gender and Modernity: Rereading Japanese Women's Magazines*. Kyoto: International Research Center for Japanese Studies, 1998.

Wu Hao, Zhuo Baichang, Huang Ying et al. *Duhui Modeng Yuefenpai 1910–1930s* (Modern Metropolitan *yuefenpai*). Hong Kong: San Lian Shudian, 1994.

Wu Hung. "Beyond Stereotypes: The Twelve Beauties in Early Qing Court Art and the *Dream of the Red Chamber*. In *Writing Women in Late Imperial China*, edited by Ellen Widmer and Kang-I Sun Chang, 306–65. Stanford, CA: Stanford University Press, 1997.

———. *The Double Screen: Medium and Representation in Chinese Painting*. Chicago, IL: University of Chicago Press, 1996.

Wu Youru. *Wu Youru huabao* (Wu Youru Painting Treasures). Shanghai: Shanghai Shudian Chubanshe, 2002.

Xia Lianbo. "Baohu lianbu de pifu" (How to Protect our Facial Skin). *Zhongguo funü* 12 (1956): 32.

Xiang Jingyu. "Zhongguo funü xuanchuan yundong de xin jiyuan" (A New Era of the Women's Movement). In *Zhongguo funü yundong lishi ziliao*, edited by Zhongguo Quanguo Funü Lianhehui Funü Yundong Lishi Yanjiushi, 275–77. 1923. Reprint. Beijing: Renmin Chubanshe, 1986.

———. "Zhongguo funü wenti" (The Problems of Chinese Women). In *Zhongguo funü yundong lishi ziliao*, edited by Zhongguo Quanguo Funü Lianhehui Funü Yundong Lishi Yanjiushi, 710–20. 1927. Reprint. Beijing: Renmin Chubanshe, 1986.

Yamada Eizaburō. "Kenchikubi no honshitsu" (The Essence of Architectural Beauty). *Kenchiku sekai* (Architecture World) 17, no. 4 (1923): 6–9.

Yamagata Kōhō, ed. *Ishokujū* (Clothing, Food, Housing). Tokyo: Jitsugyō no Nihonsha, 1907.

Yan'an Luyi (Lu Xun Arts Academy of Yan'an). "Bai mao nü" (The White-haired Girl). In *Yan'an wenyi congshu* (Art and Literature in Yan'an). Vol. 8 of *Gejujuan* (Opera). Edited by Ding Yi and Su Yiping. Changsha: Hunan Wenyi Chubanshe, 1987.

Yang Hsi-Meng. *A Study of the Standard of Living of Working Families in Shanghai*. Peiping: Institute of Social Research, 1931.

Yang Mo. *Qingchun zhi ge* (The Song of Youth). 1958. Reprint. Beijing: Shiyue Wenyi Chubanshe, 1991.

Ye Lingfeng. *Weiwan de chanhui lu* (The Unfinished Confession). Shanghai: Jindai Shudian, 1936.

Ye Yonglie. *Jiang Qing zhuan* (Biography of Jiang Qing). Beijing: Zuojia Chubanshe, 1993.

Yeh, Wen-hsin. *Shanghai Splendor: Economic Sentiments and the Making of Modern China, 1843–1949*. Berkeley, Los Angeles, London: University of California Press, 2007.

Yellis, Kenneth A. "Prosperity's Child: Some Thoughts on the Flapper." *American Quarterly* 21, no. 1 (Spring 1969), 44–64.

Yeom Sang-seob. *Samdae* (Three Generations). Reprint. Seoul: Sodam, 1996.

Yeongu Gonggan. *Sin yeoseong* (New Woman). Seoul: Hangyeore Sinmun, 2005.

Yi Bin, ed. *Lao Shanghai guangao* (Old Shanghai Advertisements). Shanghai: Shanghai Huabao Chubanshi, 1995.

Yi Guyeol. *Emineun seongakja yeosneunira* (Your Mother Was a Pioneer: Na Hye-seok's Life). Seoul: Donghwa chulpan gongsa, 1974.

Yong, Mayfair. *Spaces of Their Own: Women's Public Sphere in Transnational China*. Minneapolis: University of Minnesota Press, 1999.

Young, Helen. *Choosing Revolution: Chinese Women on the Long March*. Urbana: University of Illinois Press, 2001.

Yule, Emma Sarepta. "Miss China." *Scribner's Magazine* LXXI, no. 1 (January 1922): 66–79.

Yun Seongsang. "Namseongui mujeongjo hanguijang" (Against Male Promiscuity). *Samcheolli* (October 1930).

Zeng Zhi. *Changzheng nüzhanshi* (Women Fighters of the Long March). Vol. 1. Changchun: Beifang Funü Ertong Chubanshe, 1986.

Zhang Ling. "Zhao Yiman." *Zhongguo qingnian* (Chinese Youth) 3 (1957): 23–6.

Zhang Yanfeng. *Lao Yuefenpai Guanggao Hua* (Old Calendar Advertising Posters). Taipei: Hansheng Zazhishi, 1994.

Zhang Yingjin. *The City in Modern Chinese Literature and Film: Configurations of Space, Time and Gender*. Stanford, CA: Stanford University Press, 1996.

Zhang, Zhen. "Urban Dreamscape, Phantom Sisters, and the Identity of an Emergent Art Cinema." In *The Urban Generation: Chinese Cinema and Society at the Turn of the Twenty-first Century*, edited by Zhang Zhen, 344–88. Durham and London: Duke University Press, 2007.

Zheng Chaolin. *Shishi yu huiyi* (History and Historical Memory). Vol. 1. Hong Kong: Tiandi Tushu Youxian Gongsi, 1997.

"Zhongguo gongchandang dierci quanguo daibiao dahui" (The Second Communist Congress's Resolution on Women's Problems). In *Zhongguo funü yundong lishi ziliao*, edited by Zhongguo Quanguo Funü Lianhehui Funü Yundong Lishi Yanjiushi, 29–30. 1922. Reprint. Beijing: Renmin Chubanshe, 1986.

Zhou Xuqi. "Yijiuyiling dao yijiuerling niandai duhui funü shenghuo fengmao: yi "Funü zazhi" wei fenxi shili" (The Life of Urban Women: "The Ladies' Journal," 1910s–1920s). M.A. thesis, Taiwan Guoli Daxue, 1994.

Zhu Wanzhang. "Wang Kun ketu huagao" (Wang Kun's Drafting Sketches). *Meishu bao* (China Art Weekly) 21 (August 19, 2006): 1.

Zhuwei. *Hongjun langmanchu* (The Romances in the Red Army). Hubei: Hubei Renmin Chubanshe, 1989.

Zuo Xuchu, ed. *Lao shangbiao* (Old Trademarks). Shanghai: Shanghai Huabao Chubanshe, 1999.

Index